When the Framework Fractures

The Complete Diagnostic Companion to *Built to Father*

A full analysis of all 247 failure permutations across the SHEPHERD framework

Doug Androsky

Published by Douglas Androsky
ISBN 979-8-9955281-2-8
First Edition
Fathering the Fatherless™, Built to Father™, and The SHEPHERD Framework™ are trademarks. All rights reserved.
Printed in the United States of America

When the Framework Fractures is part of the *Built to Father* Series.

Built to Father Trilogy

Book One

Built to Father

The SHEPHERD Framework for Fathers

Book Two

When the Framework Fractures

The Complete Diagnostic Companion to Built to Father

Book Three

Built to Father: The Study Guide

The Companion Workbook to Built to Father

This book is the diagnostic companion to *Built to Father*. It is designed to be used alongside that volume — not in place of it.

Built to Father introduces the SHEPHERD framework: eight interconnected pillars of fatherhood that define what it means to father with intention. Chapter 12 of that book examines what happens when pillars fail in combination. *When the Framework Fractures* extends that chapter into a complete reference — mapping all 247 failure combinations so that any man can locate his specific situation and understand what it is costing his family.

If you are using this book without having read *Built to Father*, the Self-Diagnostic on page 3 and the Symptom Index on page 387 will orient you. The framework is explained in How to Use This Book. You do not need to have read Book One to use this volume. But you will want to.

The third book in the series — *Built to Father: The Study Guide* — is the application workbook for *Built to Father*. Thirteen structured sessions, pillar by pillar, built for solo work, for a man and his wife, or for a small group. Where this book names what is broken, the Study Guide is the instrument for doing something about it.

Built to Father and the Built to Father: The Study Guide are available wherever books are sold.

Contents

Use the Self-Diagnostic on page 3 if you are unsure which pillars are fractured in your home. Use the Symptom Index on page 387 to find your scenario by what you are observing.

How to Use This Book

Built to Father presents the SHEPHERD framework as eight interconnected pillars of fatherhood. Chapter 12 of that book addresses what happens when pillars fail in combination — examining the most structurally significant scenarios across pairs, trios, near-total, and total collapse.

This companion volume does what a chapter cannot: it documents every permutation. With eight pillars, there are 247 distinct failure combinations — from two failing simultaneously to seven failing while one remains. This book maps all of them.

This is not a book to be read front to back. It is a diagnostic reference. A man who recognizes which pillars are under strain in his own life can locate the relevant scenario, read the analysis, and understand what he is carrying, what it is costing, and what his children are absorbing in the meantime.

The scenarios are organized by the number of pillars failing, from two through seven, concluding with total collapse. Within each section, scenarios follow the natural combinatorial order of the SHEPHERD acronym.

The Eight Pillars

S — Spiritual Leader

H1 — Husband Who Loves Sacrificially

E1 — Encourager & Nurturer

P — Protector & Provider

H2 — Heart of Integrity

E2 — Example Who Inspires Potential

R — Reprover & Wise Mentor

D — Discipliner

In each scenario, **Fractured Pillars** identifies what has broken down. **Solid Pillars** identifies what is still functioning — though as you will see, solid does not mean unaffected. **What Happens to the Family** names the specific cost to the wife, the children, and the generation that comes after — whether the father intends it or not.

A note on language: where this book references a wife, read it as your co-parent, your former spouse, or the mother of your children — whatever that relationship currently is. The relational cost of a fractured pillar does not disappear because the marriage did.

A note on the math: 247 is the number of non-empty proper subsets of eight items up through seven items failing (leaving one remaining). The 247th scenario — all eight pillars failing — is total collapse and is addressed in the final section.

Self-Diagnostic

You do not need to know the SHEPHERD framework to use this book. You need to know what is true in your home.

Read each statement below. Answer honestly — not as the father you intend to be, but as the father your wife and children are currently experiencing. Check every statement that is true right now.

- **S — Spiritual Leader**

  My wife carries the spiritual weight of our home. I am not leading us toward God — I am either absent from that role entirely, or I show up for it only when it is convenient.

  If this is true → S is fractured.

- **H1 — Husband Who Loves Sacrificially**

  My wife does not feel pursued. Our marriage runs on routine. I am providing for her, but I am not investing in her — the covenant is maintained, not cultivated.

  If this is true → H1 is fractured.

- **E1 — Encourager & Nurturer**

  I do not regularly speak identity and purpose into my children. I correct them. I provide for them. But I am not naming who they are and what God placed in them before the world gets there first.

  If this is true → E1 is fractured.

- **P — Protector & Provider**

  My family does not feel covered. Whether the gap is financial, emotional, or physical — my wife and children are not confident that I am standing between them and what threatens them.

  If this is true → P is fractured.

- **H2 — Heart of Integrity**

  There is a gap between the man my family sees in public and the man they live with. My private habits, my private conduct, or my private character do not match the commitments I make out loud.

  If this is true → H2 is fractured.

- **E2 — Example Who Inspires Potential**

  I am not living toward my own God-given design. My children do not have a picture of what a man fully alive to his purpose looks like — because I have not shown them one.

  If this is true → E2 is fractured.

- **R — Reprover & Wise Mentor**

  I am not the voice my children and wife turn to when they need someone to tell them the true thing. I avoid hard conversations, stay surface-level, or only speak correction without wisdom behind it.

  If this is true → R is fractured.

- ■ **D — Discipliner**

  The lines in my home are not being held. Standards I once enforced I have quietly stopped enforcing — and my wife is absorbing what I have put down.

  If this is true → D is fractured.

Once you have identified your fractured pillars, turn to Find Your Scenario on the next page to locate your combination and its page number directly. If you are still unsure which pillars a specific symptom points to, turn to the Symptom Index at the back of this book.

Find Your Scenario

Locate your fractured pillars below, then turn to the page listed.

TWO PILLARS FAILING

S + H1 · p.9

S + E1 · p.10

S + P · p.11

S + H2 · p.12

S + E2 · p.13

S + R · p.14

S + D · p.15

H1 + E1 · p.17

H1 + P · p.18

H1 + H2 · p.19

H1 + E2 · p.20

H1 + R · p.21

H1 + D · p.22

E1 + P · p.23

E1 + H2 · p.24

E1 + E2 · p.25

E1 + R · p.26

E1 + D · p.27

P + H2 · p.29

P + E2 · p.30

P + R · p.31

P + D · p.32

H2 + E2 · p.33

H2 + R · p.34

H2 + D · p.35

E2 + R · p.36

E2 + D · p.37

R + D · p.38

THREE PILLARS FAILING

S + H1 + E1 · p.40

S + H1 + P · p.42

S + H1 + H2 · p.43

S + H1 + E2 · p.44

S + H1 + R · p.46

S + H1 + D · p.47

S + E1 + P · p.48

S + E1 + H2 · p.50

S + E1 + E2 · p.51

S + E1 + R · p.52

S + E1 + D · p.53

S + P + H2 · p.55

S + P + E2 · p.56

S + P + R · p.57

S + P + D · p.58

S + H2 + E2 · p.60

S + H2 + R · p.61

S + H2 + D · p.62

S + E2 + R · p.64

S + E2 + D · p.65

S + R + D · p.66

H1 + E1 + P · p.68

H1 + E1 + H2 · p.69

H1 + E1 + E2 · p.70

H1 + E1 + R · p.72

H1 + E1 + D · p.73

H1 + P + H2 · p.74

H1 + P + E2 · p.76

H1 + P + R · p.77

H1 + P + D · p.78

H1 + H2 + E2 · p.79

H1 + H2 + R · p.81

H1 + H2 + D · p.82

H1 + E2 + R · p.83

H1 + E2 + D · p.85

H1 + R + D · p.86

E1 + P + H2 · p.87

E1 + P + E2 · p.89

E1 + P + R · p.90

E1 + P + D · p.91

E1 + H2 + E2 · p.93

E1 + H2 + R · p.94

E1 + H2 + D · p.95

E1 + E2 + R · p.97

E1 + E2 + D · p.98

E1 + R + D · p.99

P + H2 + E2 · p.101

P + H2 + R · p.102

P + H2 + D · p.103

P + E2 + R · p.105

P + E2 + D · p.106

P + R + D · p.107

H2 + E2 + R · p.109
H2 + R + D · p.111

H2 + E2 + D · p.110
E2 + R + D · p.113

FOUR PILLARS FAILING

S + H1 + E1 + P · p.115
S + H1 + E1 + E2 · p.118
S + H1 + E1 + D · p.122
S + H1 + P + E2 · p.125
S + H1 + P + D · p.128
S + H1 + H2 + R · p.132
S + H1 + E2 + R · p.135
S + H1 + R + D · p.138
S + E1 + P + E2 · p.142
S + E1 + P + D · p.145
S + E1 + H2 + R · p.148
S + E1 + E2 + R · p.151
S + E1 + R + D · p.155
S + P + H2 + R · p.158
S + P + E2 + R · p.161
S + P + R + D · p.165
S + H2 + E2 + D · p.168
S + E2 + R + D · p.171
H1 + E1 + P + E2 · p.175
H1 + E1 + P + D · p.178
H1 + E1 + H2 + R · p.181
H1 + E1 + E2 + R · p.185
H1 + E1 + R + D · p.188
H1 + P + H2 + R · p.191
H1 + P + E2 + R · p.195
H1 + P + R + D · p.198
H1 + H2 + E2 + D · p.201
H1 + E2 + R + D · p.205
E1 + P + H2 + R · p.208
E1 + P + E2 + R · p.211
E1 + P + R + D · p.215
E1 + H2 + E2 + D · p.218
E1 + E2 + R + D · p.221
P + H2 + E2 + D · p.225
P + E2 + R + D · p.228

S + H1 + E1 + H2 · p.117
S + H1 + E1 + R · p.120
S + H1 + P + H2 · p.123
S + H1 + P + R · p.127
S + H1 + H2 + E2 · p.130
S + H1 + H2 + D · p.133
S + H1 + E2 + D · p.137
S + E1 + P + H2 · p.140
S + E1 + P + R · p.143
S + E1 + H2 + E2 · p.146
S + E1 + H2 + D · p.150
S + E1 + E2 + D · p.153
S + P + H2 + E2 · p.156
S + P + H2 + D · p.160
S + P + E2 + D · p.163
S + H2 + E2 + R · p.166
S + H2 + R + D · p.170
H1 + E1 + P + H2 · p.173
H1 + E1 + P + R · p.176
H1 + E1 + H2 + E2 · p.180
H1 + E1 + H2 + D · p.183
H1 + E1 + E2 + D · p.186
H1 + P + H2 + E2 · p.190
H1 + P + H2 + D · p.193
H1 + P + E2 + D · p.196
H1 + H2 + E2 + R · p.200
H1 + H2 + R + D · p.203
E1 + P + H2 + E2 · p.206
E1 + P + H2 + D · p.210
E1 + P + E2 + D · p.213
E1 + H2 + E2 + R · p.216
E1 + H2 + R + D · p.220
P + H2 + E2 + R · p.223
P + H2 + R + D · p.226
H2 + E2 + R + D · p.230

FIVE PILLARS FAILING

S + H1 + E1 + P + H2 · p.232
S + H1 + E1 + P + R · p.236
S + H1 + E1 + H2 + E2 · p.239
S + H1 + E1 + H2 + D · p.243
S + H1 + E1 + E2 + D · p.247
S + H1 + P + H2 + E2 · p.251
S + H1 + P + H2 + D · p.254
S + H1 + P + E2 + D · p.258
S + H1 + H2 + E2 + R · p.262
S + H1 + H2 + R + D · p.266
S + E1 + P + H2 + E2 · p.270
S + E1 + P + H2 + D · p.273

S + H1 + E1 + P + E2 · p.234
S + H1 + E1 + P + D · p.238
S + H1 + E1 + H2 + R · p.241
S + H1 + E1 + E2 + R · p.245
S + H1 + E1 + R + D · p.249
S + H1 + P + H2 + R · p.253
S + H1 + P + E2 + R · p.256
S + H1 + P + R + D · p.260
S + H1 + H2 + E2 + D · p.264
S + H1 + E2 + R + D · p.268
S + E1 + P + H2 + R · p.272
S + E1 + P + E2 + R · p.275

S + E1 + P + E2 + D · p.277
S + E1 + H2 + E2 + R · p.281
S + E1 + H2 + R + D · p.285
S + P + H2 + E2 + R · p.289
S + P + H2 + R + D · p.293
S + H2 + E2 + R + D · p.297
H1 + E1 + P + H2 + R · p.301
H1 + E1 + P + E2 + R · p.305
H1 + E1 + P + R + D · p.308
H1 + E1 + H2 + E2 + D · p.312
H1 + E1 + E2 + R + D · p.316
H1 + P + H2 + E2 + D · p.320
H1 + P + E2 + R + D · p.324
E1 + P + H2 + E2 + R · p.328
E1 + P + H2 + R + D · p.332
E1 + H2 + E2 + R + D · p.336

S + E1 + P + R + D · p.279
S + E1 + H2 + E2 + D · p.283
S + E1 + E2 + R + D · p.287
S + P + H2 + E2 + D · p.291
S + P + E2 + R + D · p.295
H1 + E1 + P + H2 + E2 · p.299
H1 + E1 + P + H2 + D · p.303
H1 + E1 + P + E2 + D · p.306
H1 + E1 + H2 + E2 + R · p.310
H1 + E1 + H2 + R + D · p.314
H1 + P + H2 + E2 + R · p.318
H1 + P + H2 + R + D · p.322
H1 + H2 + E2 + R + D · p.326
E1 + P + H2 + E2 + D · p.330
E1 + P + E2 + R + D · p.334
P + H2 + E2 + R + D · p.338

SIX PILLARS FAILING

S + H1 + E1 + P + H2 + E2 · p.340
S + H1 + E1 + P + H2 + D · p.343
S + H1 + E1 + P + E2 + D · p.346
S + H1 + E1 + H2 + E2 + R · p.349
S + H1 + E1 + H2 + R + D · p.352
S + H1 + P + H2 + E2 + R · p.355
S + H1 + P + H2 + R + D · p.358
S + H1 + H2 + E2 + R + D · p.361
S + E1 + P + H2 + E2 + D · p.364
S + E1 + P + E2 + R + D · p.367
S + P + H2 + E2 + R + D · p.370
H1 + E1 + P + H2 + E2 + D · p.373
H1 + E1 + P + E2 + R + D · p.376
H1 + P + H2 + E2 + R + D · p.379

S + H1 + E1 + P + H2 + R · p.342
S + H1 + E1 + P + E2 + R · p.345
S + H1 + E1 + P + R + D · p.348
S + H1 + E1 + H2 + E2 + D · p.351
S + H1 + E1 + E2 + R + D · p.354
S + H1 + P + H2 + E2 + D · p.357
S + H1 + P + E2 + R + D · p.360
S + E1 + P + H2 + E2 + R · p.363
S + E1 + P + H2 + R + D · p.366
S + E1 + H2 + E2 + R + D · p.369
H1 + E1 + P + H2 + E2 + R · p.372
H1 + E1 + P + H2 + R + D · p.375
H1 + E1 + H2 + E2 + R + D · p.378
E1 + P + H2 + E2 + R + D · p.381

SEVEN PILLARS FAILING

S + H1 + E1 + P + H2 + E2 + R · p.383
S + H1 + E1 + P + H2 + R + D · p.386
S + H1 + E1 + H2 + E2 + R + D · p.389
S + E1 + P + H2 + E2 + R + D · p.391

S + H1 + E1 + P + H2 + E2 + D · p.385
S + H1 + E1 + P + E2 + R + D · p.387
S + H1 + P + H2 + E2 + R + D · p.390
H1 + E1 + P + H2 + E2 + R + D · p.393

TOTAL COLLAPSE

S + H1 + E1 + P + H2 + E2 + R + D · p.395

Two Pillars Failing

28 scenarios

When two pillars fail simultaneously, the home loses two structural commitments at once. The load they were carrying transfers to whatever remains — to the other six pillars, to the wife, to the children, to the space between what was promised and what is being delivered. These are the earliest compound failures, and they are the most common. Most men reading this will recognize at least one pairing in this section.

Scenario 1

Fractured Pillars: S (Spiritual Leader) + H1 (Husband Who Loves Sacrificially)

Solid Pillars: E1 (Encourager & Nurturer) + P (Protector & Provider) + H2 (Heart of Integrity) + E2 (Example Who Inspires Potential) + R (Reprover & Wise Mentor) + D (Discipliner)

What Happens to the Family:

Six of his eight pillars are holding, but the two that are down are placing undue pressure on everything still standing. His wife carries the spiritual weight of the home alone — praying over children her husband will not lead to the altar, covering in faith a family designed to move under his authority. His wife is not being pursued — she is being maintained; the covenant runs on autopilot, and she carries the relational weight of the marriage alone, managing rather than being led. His children grow up with a picture of God as ceremonially present and practically irrelevant — faith is what their mother did, not what their father modeled. His children are absorbing a picture of marriage as coexistence — two people occupying the same house — and they will bring that picture into their own relationships before they understand where it came from. He provides for the family materially but has stopped investing in the marriage — provision without pursuit leaves his wife feeling like a dependent, not a covenant partner. What his children are building their picture of manhood from is a man who provides, corrects, and leads in most things — but who has never shown them what a marriage pursued with intention looks like, or what a life surrendered to something greater than himself looks like. They will carry both gaps into adulthood without knowing where they came from.

Scenario 2

Fractured Pillars: S (Spiritual Leader) + E1 (Encourager & Nurturer)

Solid Pillars: H1 (Husband Who Loves Sacrificially) + P (Protector & Provider) + H2 (Heart of Integrity) + E2 (Example Who Inspires Potential) + R (Reprover & Wise Mentor) + D (Discipliner)

What Happens to the Family:

Six pillars remain — but the two that are down are not simply absent; they are transferring their load to what is still standing. His wife carries the spiritual weight of the home alone — praying over children her husband will not lead to the altar, covering in faith a family designed to move under his authority. His wife speaks into a silence — there is no voice in the home naming what she carries, affirming who she is, or calling out what God placed in her. His children grow up with a picture of God as ceremonially present and practically irrelevant — faith is what their mother did, not what their father modeled. No one is speaking the child's design into existence before the world gets there first; their sense of self is built entirely from external mirrors — peer approval, performance, whatever fills the silence. He provides presence without direction — the children can see their father in the room but cannot find God in his example. A child who is never named by their father and never sees faith lived out — only performed — will reach adulthood searching for identity in one hand and transcendence in the other, and rarely find either in the right place.

Scenario 3

Fractured Pillars: S (Spiritual Leader) + P (Protector & Provider)

Solid Pillars: H1 (Husband Who Loves Sacrificially) + E1 (Encourager & Nurturer) + H2 (Heart of Integrity) + E2 (Example Who Inspires Potential) + R (Reprover & Wise Mentor) + D (Discipliner)

What Happens to the Family:

Six of his eight pillars are holding. The two that are not holding are costing more than their absence — they are redistributing weight across everything that remains. His wife carries the spiritual weight of the home alone — praying over children her husband will not lead to the altar, covering in faith a family designed to move under his authority. His wife is unprotected — whether the failure is material, emotional, or spiritual; she has learned that the perimeter is unmanned and she cannot rely on him to stand between her and what threatens the home. His children grow up with a picture of God as ceremonially present and practically irrelevant — faith is what their mother did, not what their father modeled. His children are growing up inside a home with an unlocked door — exposed to whatever fills the vacuum the father has left, and no one standing watch. He provides presence without direction — the children can see their father in the room but cannot find God in his example. A home without spiritual covering or physical security is a home that teaches its children to brace for impact. They will become adults who are competent but cannot rest — always scanning, never settled.

Scenario 4

Fractured Pillars: S (Spiritual Leader) + H2 (Heart of Integrity)

Solid Pillars: H1 (Husband Who Loves Sacrificially) + E1 (Encourager & Nurturer) + P (Protector & Provider) + E2 (Example Who Inspires Potential) + R (Reprover & Wise Mentor) + D (Discipliner)

What Happens to the Family:

Two pillars have failed. The other six carry what eight were designed to share — and the home begins to feel the difference. His wife carries the spiritual weight of the home alone — praying over children her husband will not lead to the altar, covering in faith a family designed to move under his authority. His wife is married to two men — the one the world sees and the one she lives with; she has learned that the gap between his public commitments and his private behavior is real, and she carries that knowledge alone. His children grow up with a picture of God as ceremonially present and practically irrelevant — faith is what their mother did, not what their father modeled. His children will find the gap — they always do — and when they do, they will not merely lose respect for their father; they will lose their capacity to trust authority, and sometimes God, for years. He provides presence without direction — the children can see their father in the room but cannot find God in his example. When the only version of God a child sees is one who shows up on Sunday and disappears in private, they grow up with a faith they cannot trust and an authority they cannot believe in. The damage is quiet and it takes years to name.

Scenario 5

Fractured Pillars: S (Spiritual Leader) + E2 (Example Who Inspires Potential)

Solid Pillars: H1 (Husband Who Loves Sacrificially) + E1 (Encourager & Nurturer) + P (Protector & Provider) + H2 (Heart of Integrity) + R (Reprover & Wise Mentor) + D (Discipliner)

What Happens to the Family:

Six of his eight pillars are still standing, but the two that are down are working against the six that remain. His wife carries the spiritual weight of the home alone — praying over children her husband will not lead to the altar, covering in faith a family designed to move under his authority. His wife sees a man going through the motions of his own life — never fully alive to his design, never modeling what it looks like to pursue the thing God placed in him. His children grow up with a picture of God as ceremonially present and practically irrelevant — faith is what their mother did, not what their father modeled. His children have no picture of what a man who carries his God-given design actually looks like in daily life; the father's own unlived potential becomes the ceiling the children cannot see past. He provides presence without direction — the children can see their father in the room but cannot find God in his example. They will reach adulthood with good instincts and no compass — capable of building, but unsure what they are building toward or whose image they are supposed to bear.

Scenario 6

Fractured Pillars: S (Spiritual Leader) + R (Reprover & Wise Mentor)

Solid Pillars: H1 (Husband Who Loves Sacrificially) + E1 (Encourager & Nurturer) + P (Protector & Provider) + H2 (Heart of Integrity) + E2 (Example Who Inspires Potential) + D (Discipliner)

What Happens to the Family:

Two of the eight pillars are failing. The rest are holding — but they were not built to carry this alone. His wife carries the spiritual weight of the home alone — praying over children her husband will not lead to the altar, covering in faith a family designed to move under his authority. His wife has no one in the home willing to tell her the true thing — not in cruelty, but in love; she navigates without the steady voice of a man who knows her and speaks honestly into her life. His children grow up with a picture of God as ceremonially present and practically irrelevant — faith is what their mother did, not what their father modeled. His children are drifting without calibration — no trusted voice that both knows them and tells them the true thing about where they are heading before the consequences arrive. He provides presence without direction — the children can see their father in the room but cannot find God in his example. A child who grows up without spiritual grounding and without a voice willing to tell them the true thing will reach adulthood holding two voids: they cannot find God, and they cannot trust the voices that claim to speak for Him.

Scenario 7

Fractured Pillars: S (Spiritual Leader) + D (Discipliner)

Solid Pillars: H1 (Husband Who Loves Sacrificially) + E1 (Encourager & Nurturer) + P (Protector & Provider) + H2 (Heart of Integrity) + E2 (Example Who Inspires Potential) + R (Reprover & Wise Mentor)

What Happens to the Family:

Six pillars are holding. The two that are not holding are costing the family more than their absence suggests. His wife carries the spiritual weight of the home alone — praying over children her husband will not lead to the altar, covering in faith a family designed to move under his authority. His wife is holding the lines alone — whatever the father has stopped enforcing, she absorbs, until the weight of being the only authority in the home begins to cost her something she cannot recover. His children grow up with a picture of God as ceremonially present and practically irrelevant — faith is what their mother did, not what their father modeled. His children are growing up in a home with no held line — not because no one cares, but because the person designed to hold it has stopped; and what a mother holds alone is never quite the same as what a father and mother hold together. He provides presence without direction — the children can see their father in the room but cannot find God in his example. His encouragement and example point his children toward purpose, but without spiritual grounding or held lines, that purpose has no foundation and no structure to grow inside. They will feel seen and still be lost.

Scenario 8

Fractured Pillars: H1 (Husband Who Loves Sacrificially) + E1 (Encourager & Nurturer)

Solid Pillars: S (Spiritual Leader) + P (Protector & Provider) + H2 (Heart of Integrity) + E2 (Example Who Inspires Potential) + R (Reprover & Wise Mentor) + D (Discipliner)

What Happens to the Family:

Six of his eight pillars are functioning. The two that have failed are already redistributing their weight to what remains. His wife is not being pursued — she is being maintained; the covenant runs on autopilot, and she carries the relational weight of the marriage alone, managing rather than being led. His wife speaks into a silence — there is no voice in the home naming what she carries, affirming who she is, or calling out what God placed in her. His children are absorbing a picture of marriage as coexistence — two people occupying the same house — and they will bring that picture into their own relationships before they understand where it came from. No one is speaking the child's design into existence before the world gets there first; their sense of self is built entirely from external mirrors — peer approval, performance, whatever fills the silence. He provides for the home materially but has stopped investing in either the marriage or the people inside it — provision without pursuit, correction without naming, leaves his family feeling managed rather than known. Adults who were never named by their father and never saw a marriage worth pursuing tend to spend their lives either achieving to fill the silence or repeating the coexistence — and they rarely trace it back to the right source.

Fractured Pillars: H1 (Husband Who Loves Sacrificially) + P (Protector & Provider)

Solid Pillars: S (Spiritual Leader) + E1 (Encourager & Nurturer) + H2 (Heart of Integrity) + E2 (Example Who Inspires Potential) + R (Reprover & Wise Mentor) + D (Discipliner)

What Happens to the Family:

Six remain standing. Two have failed — and what failed does not simply disappear. It transfers. His wife is not being pursued — she is being maintained; the covenant runs on autopilot, and she carries the relational weight of the marriage alone, managing rather than being led. His wife is unprotected — whether the failure is material, emotional, or spiritual; she has learned that the perimeter is unmanned and she cannot rely on him to stand between her and what threatens the home. His children are absorbing a picture of marriage as coexistence — two people occupying the same house — and they will bring that picture into their own relationships before they understand where it came from. His children are growing up inside a home with an unlocked door — exposed to whatever fills the vacuum the father has left, and no one standing watch. He provides for the family materially but has stopped investing in the marriage — provision without pursuit leaves his wife feeling like a dependent, not a covenant partner. Children who grew up unprotected and watched their parents' marriage run on autopilot either over-protect everything in their adult lives or give up on pursuit entirely — and they will not know which one they are doing.

Fractured Pillars: H1 (Husband Who Loves Sacrificially) + H2 (Heart of Integrity)

Solid Pillars: S (Spiritual Leader) + E1 (Encourager & Nurturer) + P (Protector & Provider) + E2 (Example Who Inspires Potential) + R (Reprover & Wise Mentor) + D (Discipliner)

What Happens to the Family:

Two pillars down. Six still holding — and carrying more than they were designed to carry. His wife is not being pursued — she is being maintained; the covenant runs on autopilot, and she carries the relational weight of the marriage alone, managing rather than being led. His wife is married to two men — the one the world sees and the one she lives with; she has learned that the gap between his public commitments and his private behavior is real, and she carries that knowledge alone. His children are absorbing a picture of marriage as coexistence — two people occupying the same house — and they will bring that picture into their own relationships before they understand where it came from. His children will find the gap — they always do — and when they do, they will not merely lose respect for their father; they will lose their capacity to trust authority, and sometimes God, for years. He leads spiritually in appearance but not in private — the vertical commitment he performs on Sunday is contradicted by the man his family sees Monday through Saturday. The fracture integrity creates is not loud — it is quiet and cumulative; the children do not announce the day they stopped believing him. They simply stop, and by then the marriage his children are modeling their own after is already the one they watched: maintained, not cultivated.

Scenario 11

Fractured Pillars: H1 (Husband Who Loves Sacrificially) + E2 (Example Who Inspires Potential)

Solid Pillars: S (Spiritual Leader) + E1 (Encourager & Nurturer) + P (Protector & Provider) + H2 (Heart of Integrity) + R (Reprover & Wise Mentor) + D (Discipliner)

What Happens to the Family:

Six of his eight pillars are holding, but the two that are down have not disappeared quietly. They have handed their weight to what is left. His wife is not being pursued — she is being maintained; the covenant runs on autopilot, and she carries the relational weight of the marriage alone, managing rather than being led. His wife sees a man going through the motions of his own life — never fully alive to his design, never modeling what it looks like to pursue the thing God placed in him. His children are absorbing a picture of marriage as coexistence — two people occupying the same house — and they will bring that picture into their own relationships before they understand where it came from. His children have no picture of what a man who carries his God-given design actually looks like in daily life;

the father's own unlived potential becomes the ceiling the children cannot see past. He speaks into his children but has nothing to point them toward — encouragement without example produces children who feel seen but have no picture of what they are being built for. Children without a model of inspired potential and a picture of pursued marriage tend to either settle far beneath what they carry or chase greatness that has no roots in covenant — and they will not know which one they are doing.

Scenario 12

Fractured Pillars: H1 (Husband Who Loves Sacrificially) + R (Reprover & Wise Mentor)

Solid Pillars: S (Spiritual Leader) + E1 (Encourager & Nurturer) + P (Protector & Provider) + H2 (Heart of Integrity) + E2 (Example Who Inspires Potential) + D (Discipliner)

What Happens to the Family:

Two pillars have failed, and the remaining six feel every ounce of it. His wife is not being pursued — she is being maintained; the covenant runs on autopilot, and she carries the relational weight of the marriage alone, managing rather than being led. His wife has no one in the home willing to tell her the true thing — not in cruelty, but in love; she navigates without the steady voice of a man who knows her and speaks honestly into her life. His children are absorbing a picture of marriage as coexistence — two people occupying the same house — and they will bring that picture into their own relationships before they understand where it came from. His children are drifting without calibration — no trusted voice that both knows them and tells them the true thing about where they are heading before the consequences arrive. He provides for the family materially but has stopped investing in the marriage — provision without pursuit leaves his wife feeling like a dependent, not a covenant partner. Adults who were never reproved by someone who also knew and pursued them either resist all correction as attack or accept it as the only language of care they understand — neither of which is wisdom, and both of which are expensive.

Scenario 13

Fractured Pillars: H1 (Husband Who Loves Sacrificially) + D (Discipliner)

Solid Pillars: S (Spiritual Leader) + E1 (Encourager & Nurturer) + P (Protector & Provider) + H2 (Heart of Integrity) + E2 (Example Who Inspires Potential) + R (Reprover & Wise Mentor)

What Happens to the Family:

Six of his eight pillars are functioning. The gap left by the other two is already showing. His wife is not being pursued — she is being maintained; the covenant runs on autopilot, and she carries the relational weight of the marriage alone, managing rather than being led. His wife is holding the lines alone — whatever the father has stopped enforcing, she absorbs, until the weight of being the only authority in the home begins to cost her something she cannot recover. His children are absorbing a picture of marriage as coexistence — two people occupying the same house — and they will bring that picture into their own relationships before they understand where it came from. His children are growing up in a home with no held line — not because no one cares, but because the person designed to hold it has stopped; and what a mother holds alone is never quite the same as what a father and mother hold together. He provides for the family materially but has stopped investing in the marriage — provision without pursuit leaves his wife feeling like a dependent, not a covenant partner. The daughters will accept less than they deserve in relationships and not know why; the sons will drift toward the same emotional distance their father modeled, and provision without pursuit will feel to them like love.

Scenario 14

Fractured Pillars: E1 (Encourager & Nurturer) + P (Protector & Provider)

Solid Pillars: S (Spiritual Leader) + H1 (Husband Who Loves Sacrificially) + H2 (Heart of Integrity) + E2 (Example Who Inspires Potential) + R (Reprover & Wise Mentor) + D (Discipliner)

What Happens to the Family:

Six pillars remain. The two that are missing are not simply gone — they are pressing down on everything still standing. His wife speaks into a silence — there is no voice in the home naming what she carries, affirming who she is, or calling out what God placed in her. His wife is unprotected — whether the failure is material, emotional, or spiritual; she has learned that the perimeter is unmanned and she cannot rely on him to stand between her and what threatens the home. No one is speaking the child's design into existence before the world gets there first; their sense of self is built entirely from external mirrors — peer approval, performance, whatever fills the silence. His children are growing up inside a home with an unlocked door — exposed to whatever fills the vacuum the father has left, and no one standing watch. He corrects his children but never names them — reproof without encouragement produces a child who knows what they did wrong and has no idea who they are. Adults who were never named and never felt fully covered either spend their lives achieving to fill the silence or cannot recognize when they are safe — and they rarely trace either back to the right source.

Scenario 15

Fractured Pillars: E1 (Encourager & Nurturer) + H2 (Heart of Integrity)

Solid Pillars: S (Spiritual Leader) + H1 (Husband Who Loves Sacrificially) + P (Protector & Provider) + E2 (Example Who Inspires Potential) + R (Reprover & Wise Mentor) + D (Discipliner)

What Happens to the Family:

Two pillars failing does not produce two isolated problems. It produces a redistribution — and the six pillars still holding are carrying it. His wife speaks into a silence — there is no voice in the home naming what she carries, affirming who she is, or calling out what God placed in her. His wife is married to two men — the one the world sees and the one she lives with; she has learned that the gap between his public commitments and his private behavior is real, and she carries that knowledge alone. No one is speaking the child's design into existence before the world gets there first; their sense of self is built entirely from external mirrors — peer approval, performance, whatever fills the silence. His children will find the gap — they always do — and when they do, they will not merely lose respect for their father; they will lose their capacity to trust authority, and sometimes God, for years. He leads spiritually in appearance but not in private — the vertical commitment he performs on Sunday is contradicted by the man his family sees Monday through Saturday. A child who is never named by their father and eventually finds the gap in his character does not simply lose respect — they lose the ability to receive encouragement from authority at all, because the voice that should have built them turned out to be split.

Scenario 16

Fractured Pillars: E1 (Encourager & Nurturer) + E2 (Example Who Inspires Potential)

Solid Pillars: S (Spiritual Leader) + H1 (Husband Who Loves Sacrificially) + P (Protector & Provider) + H2 (Heart of Integrity) + R (Reprover & Wise Mentor) + D (Discipliner)

What Happens to the Family:

Six of his eight pillars are holding, but the two that have failed are shaping the home as much as the six that remain. His wife speaks into a silence — there is no voice in the home naming what she carries, affirming who she is, or calling out what God placed in her. His wife sees a man going through the motions of his own life — never fully alive to his design, never modeling what it looks like to pursue the thing God placed in him. No one is speaking the child's design into existence before the world gets there first; their sense of self is built entirely from external mirrors — peer approval, performance, whatever fills the silence. His children have no picture of what a man who carries his God-given design actually looks like in daily life; the father's own unlived potential becomes the ceiling the children cannot see past. He corrects his children but never names them — reproof without encouragement produces a child who knows what they did wrong and has no idea who they are. A child who is never named and has no picture of what a man fully alive to his purpose looks like will reach adulthood not knowing who they are or what they are for — and they will search for both in places that cannot give them those things.

Scenario 17

Fractured Pillars: E1 (Encourager & Nurturer) + R (Reprover & Wise Mentor)

Solid Pillars: S (Spiritual Leader) + H1 (Husband Who Loves Sacrificially) + P (Protector & Provider) + H2 (Heart of Integrity) + E2 (Example Who Inspires Potential) + D (Discipliner)

What Happens to the Family:

Two pillars are down. The remaining six are doing the work of eight. His wife speaks into a silence — there is no voice in the home naming what she carries, affirming who she is, or calling out what God placed in her. His wife has no one in the home willing to tell her the true thing — not in cruelty, but in love; she navigates without the steady voice of a man who knows her and speaks honestly into her life. No one is speaking the child's design into existence before the world gets there first; their sense of self is built entirely from external mirrors — peer approval, performance, whatever fills the silence. His children are drifting without calibration — no trusted voice that both knows them and tells them the true thing about where they are heading before the consequences arrive. He disciplines his children but offers neither naming nor wisdom with it — correction without encouragement or mentorship teaches a child what the line is, but not who they are or why the line matters. Adults who were never named by their father spend their lives either achieving to fill the silence or collapsing when achievement fails to do it — and they rarely trace it back to the right source.

Scenario 18

Fractured Pillars: E1 (Encourager & Nurturer) + D (Discipliner)

Solid Pillars: S (Spiritual Leader) + H1 (Husband Who Loves Sacrificially) + P (Protector & Provider) + H2 (Heart of Integrity) + E2 (Example Who Inspires Potential) + R (Reprover & Wise Mentor)

What Happens to the Family:

Six pillars are still functioning. The two that are not holding are already costing the home more than their absence alone accounts for. His wife speaks into a silence —

there is no voice in the home naming what she carries, affirming who she is, or calling out what God placed in her. His wife is holding the lines alone — whatever the father has stopped enforcing, she absorbs, until the weight of being the only authority in the home begins to cost her something she cannot recover. No one is speaking the child's design into existence before the world gets there first; their sense of self is built entirely from external mirrors — peer approval, performance, whatever fills the silence. His children are growing up in a home with no held line — not because no one cares, but because the person designed to hold it has stopped; and what a mother holds alone is never quite the same as what a father and mother hold together. He corrects his children but never names them — reproof without encouragement produces a child who knows what they did wrong and has no idea who they are. A child who is never named and lives in a home without held lines grows up doubting both who they are and whether standards mean anything — a combination that tends to produce adults who are either self-destructive or incapable of holding anything in place.

Scenario 19

Fractured Pillars: P (Protector & Provider) + H2 (Heart of Integrity)

Solid Pillars: S (Spiritual Leader) + H1 (Husband Who Loves Sacrificially) + E1 (Encourager & Nurturer) + E2 (Example Who Inspires Potential) + R (Reprover & Wise Mentor) + D (Discipliner)

What Happens to the Family:

Six of his eight pillars are holding. What the two that are failing are costing is different from what it looks like from the outside. His wife is unprotected — whether the failure is material, emotional, or spiritual; she has learned that the perimeter is unmanned and she cannot rely on him to stand between her and what threatens the home. His wife is married to two men — the one the world sees and the one she lives with; she has learned that the gap between his public commitments and his private behavior is real, and she carries that knowledge alone. His children are growing up inside a home with an unlocked door — exposed to whatever fills the vacuum the father has left, and no one standing watch. His children will find the gap — they always do — and when they do, they will not merely lose respect for their father; they will lose their capacity to trust authority, and sometimes God, for years. He leads spiritually in appearance but not in private — the vertical commitment he performs on Sunday is contradicted by the man his family sees Monday through Saturday. Children who grew up unprotected either over-protect everything in their adult lives, unable to rest, or cannot recognize danger until it has already done its work — and if they also found the gap in their father's integrity, they will not know who to trust when it matters most.

Scenario 20

Fractured Pillars: P (Protector & Provider) + E2 (Example Who Inspires Potential)

Solid Pillars: S (Spiritual Leader) + H1 (Husband Who Loves Sacrificially) + E1 (Encourager & Nurturer) + H2 (Heart of Integrity) + R (Reprover & Wise Mentor) + D (Discipliner)

What Happens to the Family:

Two of his eight pillars have failed. The other six remain — and they are beginning to feel the weight of what is missing. His wife is unprotected — whether the failure is material, emotional, or spiritual; she has learned that the perimeter is unmanned and she cannot rely on him to stand between her and what threatens the home. His wife sees a man going through the motions of his own life — never fully alive to his design, never modeling what it looks like to pursue the thing God placed in him. His children are growing up inside a home with an unlocked door — exposed to whatever fills the vacuum the father has left, and no one standing watch. His children have no picture of what a man who carries his God-given design actually looks like in daily life; the father's own unlived potential becomes the ceiling the children cannot see past. He speaks into his children but has nothing to point them toward — encouragement without example produces children who feel seen but have no picture of what they are being built for. Children who grew up unprotected either over-protect everything in their adult lives, unable to rest, or cannot recognize danger until it has already done its work.

Scenario 21

Fractured Pillars: P (Protector & Provider) + R (Reprover & Wise Mentor)

Solid Pillars: S (Spiritual Leader) + H1 (Husband Who Loves Sacrificially) + E1 (Encourager & Nurturer) + H2 (Heart of Integrity) + E2 (Example Who Inspires Potential) + D (Discipliner)

What Happens to the Family:

Six pillars holding. Two failing. And in a framework built for eight, two failures do not stay contained. His wife is unprotected — whether the failure is material, emotional, or spiritual; she has learned that the perimeter is unmanned and she cannot rely on him to stand between her and what threatens the home. His wife has no one in the home willing to tell her the true thing — not in cruelty, but in love; she navigates without the steady voice of a man who knows her and speaks honestly into her life. His children are growing up inside a home with an unlocked door — exposed to whatever fills the vacuum the father has left, and no one standing watch. His children are drifting without calibration — no trusted voice that both knows them and tells them the true thing about where they are heading before the consequences arrive. He disciplines his children but offers no wisdom with it — correction without mentorship teaches a child what the line is but not why it matters or who they become by holding it. Children who grew up unprotected either over-protect everything in their adult lives, unable to rest, or cannot recognize danger until it has already done its work.

Fractured Pillars: P (Protector & Provider) + D (Discipliner)

Solid Pillars: S (Spiritual Leader) + H1 (Husband Who Loves Sacrificially) + E1 (Encourager & Nurturer) + H2 (Heart of Integrity) + E2 (Example Who Inspires Potential) + R (Reprover & Wise Mentor)

What Happens to the Family:

Six of his eight pillars are functioning, but the two that are down are doing something the other six cannot compensate for. His wife is unprotected — whether the failure is material, emotional, or spiritual; she has learned that the perimeter is unmanned and she cannot rely on him to stand between her and what threatens the home. His wife is holding the lines alone — whatever the father has stopped enforcing, she absorbs, until the weight of being the only authority in the home begins to cost her something she cannot recover. His children are growing up inside a home with an unlocked door — exposed to whatever fills the vacuum the father has left, and no one standing watch. His children are growing up in a home with no held line — not because no one cares, but because the person designed to hold it has stopped; and what a mother holds alone is never quite the same as what a father and mother hold together. He tries to hold lines in the home but has stopped providing the covering that makes discipline feel like love rather than control — children without protection experience correction as threat. Children who grew up unprotected either over-protect everything in their adult lives, unable to rest, or cannot recognize danger until it has already done its work.

Scenario 23

Fractured Pillars: H2 (Heart of Integrity) + E2 (Example Who Inspires Potential)

Solid Pillars: S (Spiritual Leader) + H1 (Husband Who Loves Sacrificially) + E1 (Encourager & Nurturer) + P (Protector & Provider) + R (Reprover & Wise Mentor) + D (Discipliner)

What Happens to the Family:

Two pillars have failed. The remaining six carry the load — and the family feels the redistribution, even if they cannot name it. His wife is married to two men — the one the world sees and the one she lives with; she has learned that the gap between his public commitments and his private behavior is real, and she carries that knowledge alone. His wife sees a man going through the motions of his own life — never fully alive to his design, never modeling what it looks like to pursue the thing God placed in him. His children will find the gap — they always do — and when they do, they will not merely lose respect for their father; they will lose their capacity to trust authority, and sometimes God, for years. His children have no picture of what a man who carries his God-given design actually looks like in daily life; the father's own unlived potential becomes the ceiling the children cannot see past. He leads spiritually in appearance but not in private — the vertical commitment he performs on

Sunday is contradicted by the man his family sees Monday through Saturday, and a life not fully lived becomes the only picture of purpose his children have. The fracture integrity creates is not loud — it is quiet and cumulative; the children do not announce the day they stopped believing him. They simply stop, and he rarely sees it coming.

Scenario 24

Fractured Pillars: H2 (Heart of Integrity) + R (Reprover & Wise Mentor)

Solid Pillars: S (Spiritual Leader) + H1 (Husband Who Loves Sacrificially) + E1 (Encourager & Nurturer) + P (Protector & Provider) + E2 (Example Who Inspires Potential) + D (Discipliner)

What Happens to the Family:

Six pillars are holding. Two are not — and the home does not experience those as neutral absences. His wife is married to two men — the one the world sees and the one she lives with; she has learned that the gap between his public commitments and his private behavior is real, and she carries that knowledge alone. His wife has no one in the home willing to tell her the true thing — not in cruelty, but in love; she navigates without the steady voice of a man who knows her and speaks honestly into her life. His children will find the gap — they always do — and when they do, they will not merely lose respect for their father; they will lose their capacity to trust authority, and sometimes God, for years. His children are drifting without calibration — no trusted voice that both knows them and tells them the true thing about where they are heading before the consequences arrive. He leads spiritually in appearance but not in private — the vertical commitment he performs on Sunday is contradicted by the man his family sees Monday through Saturday. The fracture integrity creates is not loud — it is quiet and cumulative; the children do not announce the day they stopped believing him. They simply stop, and he rarely sees it coming.

Scenario 25

Fractured Pillars: H2 (Heart of Integrity) + D (Discipliner)

Solid Pillars: S (Spiritual Leader) + H1 (Husband Who Loves Sacrificially) + E1 (Encourager & Nurturer) + P (Protector & Provider) + E2 (Example Who Inspires Potential) + R (Reprover & Wise Mentor)

What Happens to the Family:

Six of his eight pillars remain. The two that have failed are not simply missing. They are pressing on everything that remains. His wife is married to two men — the one the world sees and the one she lives with; she has learned that the gap between his public commitments and his private behavior is real, and she carries that knowledge alone. His wife is holding the lines alone — whatever the father has stopped enforcing, she absorbs, until the weight of being the only authority in the home begins to cost her something she cannot recover. His children will find the gap — they always do — and when they do, they will not merely lose respect for their father; they will lose their capacity to trust authority, and sometimes God, for years. His children are growing up in a home with no held line — not because no one cares, but because the person designed to hold it has stopped; and what a mother holds alone is never quite the same as what a father and mother hold together. He leads spiritually in appearance but not in private — the vertical commitment he performs on Sunday is contradicted by the man his family sees Monday through Saturday. The fracture integrity creates is not loud — it is quiet and cumulative; the children do not announce the day they stopped believing him. They simply stop, and the lines they no longer hold were already gone before they noticed.

Scenario 26

Fractured Pillars: E2 (Example Who Inspires Potential) + R (Reprover & Wise Mentor)

Solid Pillars: S (Spiritual Leader) + H1 (Husband Who Loves Sacrificially) + E1 (Encourager & Nurturer) + P (Protector & Provider) + H2 (Heart of Integrity) + D (Discipliner)

What Happens to the Family:

Two pillars are failing. Six are not. But two failures in a framework of eight do not stay in their lane. His wife sees a man going through the motions of his own life — never fully alive to his design, never modeling what it looks like to pursue the thing God placed in him. His wife has no one in the home willing to tell her the true thing — not in cruelty, but in love; she navigates without the steady voice of a man who knows her and speaks honestly into her life. His children have no picture of what a man who carries his

God-given design actually looks like in daily life; the father's own unlived potential becomes the ceiling the children cannot see past. His children are drifting without calibration — no trusted voice that both knows them and tells them the true thing about where they are heading before the consequences arrive. He disciplines his children but offers no wisdom with it — correction without mentorship teaches a child what the line is but not why it matters or who they become by holding it. Children without a model of inspired potential tend to either settle far beneath what they carry or chase a version of greatness that has no roots — and they will not know which one they are doing.

Scenario 27

Fractured Pillars: E2 (Example Who Inspires Potential) + D (Discipliner)

Solid Pillars: S (Spiritual Leader) + H1 (Husband Who Loves Sacrificially) + E1 (Encourager & Nurturer) + P (Protector & Provider) + H2 (Heart of Integrity) + R (Reprover & Wise Mentor)

What Happens to the Family:

Six of his eight pillars are holding, and the two that are not holding are already shaping what his family experiences every day. His wife sees a man going through the motions of his own life — never fully alive to his design, never modeling what it looks like to pursue the thing God placed in him. His wife is holding the lines alone — whatever the father has stopped enforcing, she absorbs, until the weight of being the only authority in the home begins to cost her something she cannot recover. His children have no picture of what a man who carries his God-given design actually looks like in daily life; the father's own unlived potential becomes the ceiling the children cannot see past. His children are growing up in a home with no held line — not because no one cares, but because the person designed to hold it has stopped; and what a mother holds alone is never quite the same as what a father and mother hold together. He speaks into his children but has nothing to point them toward — encouragement without example produces children who feel seen but have no picture of what they are being built for. Children without a model of inspired potential tend to either settle far beneath what they carry or chase a version of greatness that has no roots — and in a home without held lines, they have never been taught the discipline that building anything real requires — and they will not know which one they are doing.

Scenario 28

Fractured Pillars: R (Reprover & Wise Mentor) + D (Discipliner)

Solid Pillars: S (Spiritual Leader) + H1 (Husband Who Loves Sacrificially) + E1 (Encourager & Nurturer) + P (Protector & Provider) + H2 (Heart of Integrity) + E2 (Example Who Inspires Potential)

What Happens to the Family:

Six pillars are functioning. Two are not. The cost is not merely subtraction — it is redistribution. His wife has no one in the home willing to tell her the true thing — not in cruelty, but in love; she navigates without the steady voice of a man who knows her and speaks honestly into her life. His wife is holding the lines alone — whatever the father has stopped enforcing, she absorbs, until the weight of being the only authority in the home begins to cost her something she cannot recover. His children are drifting without calibration — no trusted voice that both knows them and tells them the true thing about where they are heading before the consequences arrive. His children are growing up in a home with no held line — not because no one cares, but because the person designed to hold it has stopped; and what a mother holds alone is never quite the same as what a father and mother hold together. He speaks wisdom into his children but enforces nothing — mentorship without discipline produces a child who knows what is right and has learned they do not have to do it. Adults who were never reproved by someone with the authority to do it either resist all correction as attack or accept all correction as truth — neither of which is wisdom, and both of which are expensive.

Section Two

Three Pillars Failing

56 scenarios

Three pillars failing removes an entire dimension from the framework. The home may still function in visible ways — provision continuing, discipline holding in some areas, encouragement present — but the weight now distributed across five pillars instead of eight begins to show. The wife feels it first. The children feel it next, though they will not have words for it until much later.

Scenario 29

Fractured Pillars: S (Spiritual Leader) + H1 (Husband Who Loves Sacrificially) + E1 (Encourager & Nurturer)

Solid Pillars: P (Protector & Provider) + H2 (Heart of Integrity) + E2 (Example Who Inspires Potential) + R (Reprover & Wise Mentor) + D (Discipliner)

What Happens to the Family:

Three of the eight pillars have failed, and the five that remain are beginning to buckle under what they were never designed to carry alone. His wife carries the spiritual weight of the home alone — praying over children her husband will not lead to the altar, covering in faith a family designed to move under his authority. His wife is not being pursued — she is being maintained; the covenant runs on autopilot, and she carries the relational weight of the marriage alone, managing rather than being led. His wife speaks into a silence — there is no voice in the home naming what she carries, affirming who she is, or calling out what God placed in her. His children grow up with a picture of God as ceremonially present and practically irrelevant — faith is what their mother did, not what their father modeled. His children are absorbing a picture of marriage as coexistence — two people occupying the same house — and they will bring that picture into their own relationships before they understand where it came from. No one is speaking the child's design into existence before the world gets there first; their sense of self is built entirely from external mirrors — peer approval, performance, whatever fills the silence. He provides for the family materially but has stopped investing in the marriage — provision without pursuit leaves his wife feeling like a dependent, not a covenant partner. They will reach adulthood without a template for what a man surrendered to something greater than himself actually looks like, and they will not know what they are missing until they are trying to build something themselves.

Scenario 30

Fractured Pillars: S (Spiritual Leader) + H1 (Husband Who Loves Sacrificially) + P (Protector & Provider)

Solid Pillars: E1 (Encourager & Nurturer) + H2 (Heart of Integrity) + E2 (Example Who Inspires Potential) + R (Reprover & Wise Mentor) + D (Discipliner)

What Happens to the Family:

Three pillars are failing. Five remain. The home still functions in visible ways — but the people who live there are carrying more than the outside can see. His wife carries the spiritual weight of the home alone — praying over children her husband will not lead to the altar, covering in faith a family designed to move under his authority. His wife is not being pursued — she is being maintained; the covenant runs on autopilot, and she carries the relational weight of the marriage alone, managing rather than being led. His wife is unprotected — whether the failure is material, emotional, or spiritual; she has learned that the perimeter is unmanned and she cannot rely on him to stand between her and what threatens the home. His children grow up with a picture of God as ceremonially present and practically irrelevant — faith is what their mother did, not what their father modeled. His children are absorbing a picture of marriage as coexistence — two people occupying the same house — and they will bring that picture into their own relationships before they understand where it came from. His children are growing up inside a home with an unlocked door — exposed to whatever fills the vacuum the father has left, and no one standing watch. He provides for the family materially but has stopped investing in the marriage — provision without pursuit leaves his wife feeling like a dependent, not a covenant partner. They will reach adulthood without a template for what a man surrendered to something greater than himself actually looks like, and they will not know what they are missing until they are trying to build something themselves.

Scenario 31

Fractured Pillars: S (Spiritual Leader) + H1 (Husband Who Loves Sacrificially) + H2 (Heart of Integrity)

Solid Pillars: E1 (Encourager & Nurturer) + P (Protector & Provider) + E2 (Example Who Inspires Potential) + R (Reprover & Wise Mentor) + D (Discipliner)

What Happens to the Family:

Three pillars are down. The remaining five are carrying what eight were designed to share — and the home feels the redistribution. His wife carries the spiritual weight of the home alone — praying over children her husband will not lead to the altar, covering in faith a family designed to move under his authority. His wife is not being pursued — she is being maintained; the covenant runs on autopilot, and she carries the relational weight of the marriage alone, managing rather than being led. His wife is married to two men — the one the world sees and the one she lives with; she has learned that the gap between his public commitments and his private behavior is real, and she carries that knowledge alone. His children grow up with a picture of God as ceremonially present and practically irrelevant — faith is what their mother did, not what their father modeled. His children are absorbing a picture of marriage as coexistence — two people occupying the same house — and they will bring that picture into their own relationships before they understand where it came from. His children will find the gap — they always do — and when they do, they will not merely lose respect for their father; they will lose their capacity to trust authority, and sometimes God, for years. He provides for the family materially but has stopped investing in the marriage — provision without pursuit, and integrity withheld in private, leaves his wife feeling like a dependent rather than a covenant partner. They will reach adulthood without a template for what a man surrendered to something greater than himself actually looks like, and they will not know what they are missing until they are trying to build something themselves.

Scenario 32

Fractured Pillars: S (Spiritual Leader) + H1 (Husband Who Loves Sacrificially) + E2 (Example Who Inspires Potential)

Solid Pillars: E1 (Encourager & Nurturer) + P (Protector & Provider) + H2 (Heart of Integrity) + R (Reprover & Wise Mentor) + D (Discipliner)

What Happens to the Family:

Three pillars have failed. The five still standing are doing the work of eight, and the home is beginning to show it. His wife carries the spiritual weight of the home alone — praying over children her husband will not lead to the altar, covering in faith a family designed to move under his authority. His wife is not being pursued — she is being maintained; the covenant runs on autopilot, and she carries the relational weight of the marriage alone, managing rather than being led. His wife sees a man going through the motions of his own life — never fully alive to his design, never modeling what it looks like to pursue the thing God placed in him. His children grow up with a picture of God as ceremonially present and practically irrelevant — faith is what their mother did, not what their father modeled. His children are absorbing a picture of marriage as coexistence — two people occupying the same house — and they will bring that picture into their own relationships before they understand where it came from. His children have no picture of what a man who carries his God-given design actually looks like in daily life; the father's own unlived potential becomes the ceiling the children cannot see past. He speaks into his children but has nothing to point them toward — encouragement without example produces children who feel seen but have no picture of what they are being built for, and without spiritual grounding behind it, even that purpose has no foundation. They will reach adulthood without a template for what a man surrendered to something greater than himself actually looks like, and they will not know what they are missing until they are trying to build something themselves.

Fractured Pillars: S (Spiritual Leader) + H1 (Husband Who Loves Sacrificially) + R (Reprover & Wise Mentor)

Solid Pillars: E1 (Encourager & Nurturer) + P (Protector & Provider) + H2 (Heart of Integrity) + E2 (Example Who Inspires Potential) + D (Discipliner)

What Happens to the Family:

Three of the eight pillars have failed. What remains is real — but five load-bearing points were not designed to carry what eight were built to hold. His wife carries the spiritual weight of the home alone — praying over children her husband will not lead to the altar, covering in faith a family designed to move under his authority. His wife is not being pursued — she is being maintained; the covenant runs on autopilot, and she carries the relational weight of the marriage alone, managing rather than being led. His wife has no one in the home willing to tell her the true thing — not in cruelty, but in love; she navigates without the steady voice of a man who knows her and speaks honestly into her life. His children grow up with a picture of God as ceremonially present and practically irrelevant — faith is what their mother did, not what their father modeled. His children are absorbing a picture of marriage as coexistence — two people occupying the same house — and they will bring that picture into their own relationships before they understand where it came from. His children are drifting without calibration — no trusted voice that both knows them and tells them the true thing about where they are heading before the consequences arrive. He provides for the family materially but has stopped investing in the marriage — provision without pursuit leaves his wife feeling like a dependent, not a covenant partner. They will reach adulthood without a template for what a man surrendered to something greater than himself actually looks like, and they will not know what they are missing until they are trying to build something themselves.

Scenario 34

Fractured Pillars: S (Spiritual Leader) + H1 (Husband Who Loves Sacrificially) + D (Discipliner)

Solid Pillars: E1 (Encourager & Nurturer) + P (Protector & Provider) + H2 (Heart of Integrity) + E2 (Example Who Inspires Potential) + R (Reprover & Wise Mentor)

What Happens to the Family:

Three pillars are failing simultaneously. The five that remain are absorbing the weight of what has been put down. His wife carries the spiritual weight of the home alone — praying over children her husband will not lead to the altar, covering in faith a family designed to move under his authority. His wife is not being pursued — she is being maintained; the covenant runs on autopilot, and she carries the relational weight of the marriage alone, managing rather than being led. His wife is holding the lines alone — whatever the father has stopped enforcing, she absorbs, until the weight of being the only authority in the home begins to cost her something she cannot recover. His children grow up with a picture of God as ceremonially present and practically irrelevant — faith is what their mother did, not what their father modeled. His children are absorbing a picture of marriage as coexistence — two people occupying the same house — and they will bring that picture into their own relationships before they understand where it came from. His children are growing up in a home with no held line — not because no one cares, but because the person designed to hold it has stopped; and what a mother holds alone is never quite the same as what a father and mother hold together. He provides for the family materially but has stopped investing in the marriage — provision without pursuit leaves his wife feeling like a dependent, not a covenant partner. They will reach adulthood without a template for what a man surrendered to something greater than himself actually looks like, and they will not know what they are missing until they are trying to build something themselves.

Scenario 35

Fractured Pillars: S (Spiritual Leader) + E1 (Encourager & Nurturer) + P (Protector & Provider)

Solid Pillars: H1 (Husband Who Loves Sacrificially) + H2 (Heart of Integrity) + E2 (Example Who Inspires Potential) + R (Reprover & Wise Mentor) + D (Discipliner)

What Happens to the Family:

Three pillars down. Five still holding — and the gap between what the home needs and what the framework is currently providing is widening. His wife carries the spiritual weight of the home alone — praying over children her husband will not lead to the altar, covering in faith a family designed to move under his authority. His wife speaks into a silence — there is no voice in the home naming what she carries, affirming who she is, or calling out what God placed in her. His wife is unprotected — whether the failure is material, emotional, or spiritual; she has learned that the perimeter is unmanned and she cannot rely on him to stand between her and what threatens the home. His children grow up with a picture of God as ceremonially present and practically irrelevant — faith is what their mother did, not what their father modeled. No one is speaking the child's design into existence before the world gets there first; their sense of self is built entirely from external mirrors — peer approval, performance, whatever fills the silence. His children are growing up inside a home with an unlocked door — exposed to whatever fills the vacuum the father has left, and no one standing watch. He provides presence without direction — the children can see their father in the room but cannot find God in his example. Adults who were never named by their father spend their lives either achieving to fill the silence or collapsing when achievement fails to do it — and they rarely trace it back to the right source.

Scenario 36

Fractured Pillars: S (Spiritual Leader) + E1 (Encourager & Nurturer) + H2 (Heart of Integrity)

Solid Pillars: H1 (Husband Who Loves Sacrificially) + P (Protector & Provider) + E2 (Example Who Inspires Potential) + R (Reprover & Wise Mentor) + D (Discipliner)

What Happens to the Family:

Three pillars have failed. The remaining five carry what was designed for eight, and the redistribution is felt. His wife carries the spiritual weight of the home alone — praying over children her husband will not lead to the altar, covering in faith a family designed to move under his authority. His wife speaks into a silence — there is no voice in the home naming what she carries, affirming who she is, or calling out what God placed in her. His wife is married to two men — the one the world sees and the one she lives with; she has learned that the gap between his public commitments and his private behavior is real, and she carries that knowledge alone. His children grow up with a picture of God as ceremonially present and practically irrelevant — faith is what their mother did, not what their father modeled. No one is speaking the child's design into existence before the world gets there first; their sense of self is built entirely from external mirrors — peer approval, performance, whatever fills the silence. His children will find the gap — they always do — and when they do, they will not merely lose respect for their father; they will lose their capacity to trust authority, and sometimes God, for years. He provides presence without direction — the children can see their father in the room but cannot find God in his example. The fracture integrity creates is not loud — it is quiet and cumulative; the children do not announce the day they stopped believing him. They simply stop, and he rarely sees it coming.

Scenario 37

Fractured Pillars: S (Spiritual Leader) + E1 (Encourager & Nurturer) + E2 (Example Who Inspires Potential)

Solid Pillars: H1 (Husband Who Loves Sacrificially) + P (Protector & Provider) + H2 (Heart of Integrity) + R (Reprover & Wise Mentor) + D (Discipliner)

What Happens to the Family:

When three pillars fail, the home loses three structural commitments at once. The five that remain are holding — but they were not built to hold alone. His wife carries the spiritual weight of the home alone — praying over children her husband will not lead to the altar, covering in faith a family designed to move under his authority. His wife speaks into a silence — there is no voice in the home naming what she carries, affirming who she is, or calling out what God placed in her. His wife sees a man going through the motions of his own life — never fully alive to his design, never modeling what it looks like to pursue the thing God placed in him. His children grow up with a picture of God as ceremonially present and practically irrelevant — faith is what their mother did, not what their father modeled. No one is speaking the child's design into existence before the world gets there first; their sense of self is built entirely from external mirrors — peer approval, performance, whatever fills the silence. His children have no picture of what a man who carries his God-given design actually looks like in daily life; the father's own unlived potential becomes the ceiling the children cannot see past. He provides presence without direction — the children can see their father in the room but cannot find God in his example. Adults who were never named by their father spend their lives either achieving to fill the silence or collapsing when achievement fails to do it — and they rarely trace it back to the right source.

Scenario 38

Fractured Pillars: S (Spiritual Leader) + E1 (Encourager & Nurturer) + R (Reprover & Wise Mentor)

Solid Pillars: H1 (Husband Who Loves Sacrificially) + P (Protector & Provider) + H2 (Heart of Integrity) + E2 (Example Who Inspires Potential) + D (Discipliner)

What Happens to the Family:

Three pillars are down. The remaining five are carrying what eight were designed to share, and the people inside the home are absorbing the difference. His wife carries the spiritual weight of the home alone — praying over children her husband will not lead to the altar, covering in faith a family designed to move under his authority. His wife speaks into a silence — there is no voice in the home naming what she carries, affirming who she is, or calling out what God placed in her. His wife has no one in the home willing to tell her the true thing — not in cruelty, but in love;

she navigates without the steady voice of a man who knows her and speaks honestly into her life. His children grow up with a picture of God as ceremonially present and practically irrelevant — faith is what their mother did, not what their father modeled. No one is speaking the child's design into existence before the world gets there first; their sense of self is built entirely from external mirrors — peer approval, performance, whatever fills the silence. His children are drifting without calibration — no trusted voice that both knows them and tells them the true thing about where they are heading before the consequences arrive. He provides presence without direction — the children can see their father in the room but cannot find God in his example. Adults who were never named by their father spend their lives either achieving to fill the silence or collapsing when achievement fails to do it — and they rarely trace it back to the right source.

Scenario 39

Fractured Pillars: S (Spiritual Leader) + E1 (Encourager & Nurturer) + D (Discipliner)

Solid Pillars: H1 (Husband Who Loves Sacrificially) + P (Protector & Provider) + H2 (Heart of Integrity) + E2 (Example Who Inspires Potential) + R (Reprover & Wise Mentor)

What Happens to the Family:

Three of the eight pillars have failed, and the five that remain are beginning to buckle under what they were never designed to carry alone. His wife carries the spiritual weight of the home alone — praying over children her husband will not lead to the altar, covering in faith a family designed to move under his authority. His wife speaks into a silence — there is no voice in the home naming what she carries, affirming who she is, or calling out what God placed in her. His wife is holding the lines alone — whatever the father has stopped enforcing, she absorbs, until the weight of being the only authority in the home begins to cost her something she cannot recover. His children grow up with a picture of God as ceremonially present and practically irrelevant — faith is what their mother did, not what their father modeled. No one is speaking the child's design into existence before the world gets there first; their sense of self is built entirely from external mirrors — peer approval, performance, whatever fills the silence. His children are growing up in a home with no held line — not because no one cares, but because the person designed to hold it has stopped; and what a mother holds alone is never quite the same as what a father and mother hold together. He provides presence without direction — the children can see their father in the room but cannot find God in his example. Adults who were never named by their father spend their lives either achieving to fill the silence or collapsing when achievement fails to do it — and they rarely trace it back to the right source.

Scenario 40

Fractured Pillars: S (Spiritual Leader) + P (Protector & Provider) + H2 (Heart of Integrity)

Solid Pillars: H1 (Husband Who Loves Sacrificially) + E1 (Encourager & Nurturer) + E2 (Example Who Inspires Potential) + R (Reprover & Wise Mentor) + D (Discipliner)

What Happens to the Family:

Three pillars are failing. Five remain. The home still functions in visible ways — but the people who live there are carrying more than the outside can see. His wife carries the spiritual weight of the home alone — praying over children her husband will not lead to the altar, covering in faith a family designed to move under his authority. His wife is unprotected — whether the failure is material, emotional, or spiritual; she has learned that the perimeter is unmanned and she cannot rely on him to stand between her and what threatens the home. His wife is married to two men — the one the world sees and the one she lives with; she has learned that the gap between his public commitments and his private behavior is real, and she carries that knowledge alone. His children grow up with a picture of God as ceremonially present and practically irrelevant — faith is what their mother did, not what their father modeled. His children are growing up inside a home with an unlocked door — exposed to whatever fills the vacuum the father has left, and no one standing watch. His children will find the gap — they always do — and when they do, they will not merely lose respect for their father; they will lose their capacity to trust authority, and sometimes God, for years. He provides presence without direction — the children can see their father in the room but cannot find God in his example. The fracture integrity creates is not loud — it is quiet and cumulative; the children do not announce the day they stopped believing him. They simply stop, and he rarely sees it coming.

Scenario 41

Fractured Pillars: S (Spiritual Leader) + P (Protector & Provider) + E2 (Example Who Inspires Potential)

Solid Pillars: H1 (Husband Who Loves Sacrificially) + E1 (Encourager & Nurturer) + H2 (Heart of Integrity) + R (Reprover & Wise Mentor) + D (Discipliner)

What Happens to the Family:

Three pillars are down. The remaining five are carrying what eight were designed to share — and the home feels the redistribution. His wife carries the spiritual weight of the home alone — praying over children her husband will not lead to the altar, covering in faith a family designed to move under his authority. His wife is unprotected — whether the failure is material, emotional, or spiritual; she has learned that the perimeter is unmanned and she cannot rely on him to stand between her and what threatens the home. His wife sees a man going through the motions of his own life — never fully alive to his design, never modeling what it looks like to pursue the thing God placed in him. His children grow up with a picture of God as ceremonially present and practically irrelevant — faith is what their mother did, not what their father modeled. His children are growing up inside a home with an unlocked door — exposed to whatever fills the vacuum the father has left, and no one standing watch. His children have no picture of what a man who carries his God-given design actually looks like in daily life; the father's own unlived potential becomes the ceiling the children cannot see past. He provides presence without direction — the children can see their father in the room but cannot find God in his example. They will reach adulthood without a template for what a man surrendered to something greater than himself actually looks like, and they will not know what they are missing until they are trying to build something themselves.

Scenario 42

Fractured Pillars: S (Spiritual Leader) + P (Protector & Provider) + R (Reprover & Wise Mentor)

Solid Pillars: H1 (Husband Who Loves Sacrificially) + E1 (Encourager & Nurturer) + H2 (Heart of Integrity) + E2 (Example Who Inspires Potential) + D (Discipliner)

What Happens to the Family:

Three pillars have failed. The five still standing are doing the work of eight, and the home is beginning to show it. His wife carries the spiritual weight of the home alone — praying over children her husband will not lead to the altar, covering in faith a family designed to move under his authority. His wife is unprotected — whether the failure is material, emotional, or spiritual; she has learned that the perimeter is unmanned and she cannot rely on him to stand between her and what threatens the home. His wife has no one in the home willing to tell her the true thing — not in cruelty, but in love; she navigates without the steady voice of a man who knows her and speaks honestly into her life. His children grow up with a picture of God as ceremonially present and practically irrelevant — faith is what their mother did, not what their father modeled. His children are growing up inside a home with an unlocked door — exposed to whatever fills the vacuum the father has left, and no one standing watch. His children are drifting without calibration — no trusted voice that both knows them and tells them the true thing about where they are heading before the consequences arrive. He provides presence without direction — the children can see their father in the room but cannot find God in his example. They will reach adulthood without a template for what a man surrendered to something greater than himself actually looks like, and they will not know what they are missing until they are trying to build something themselves.

Scenario 43

Fractured Pillars: S (Spiritual Leader) + P (Protector & Provider) + D (Discipliner)

Solid Pillars: H1 (Husband Who Loves Sacrificially) + E1 (Encourager & Nurturer) + H2 (Heart of Integrity) + E2 (Example Who Inspires Potential) + R (Reprover & Wise Mentor)

What Happens to the Family:

Three of the eight pillars have failed. What remains is

real — but five load-bearing points were not designed to carry what eight were built to hold. His wife carries the spiritual weight of the home alone — praying over children her husband will not lead to the altar, covering in faith a family designed to move under his authority. His wife is unprotected — whether the failure is material, emotional, or spiritual; she has learned that the perimeter is unmanned and she cannot rely on him to stand between her and what threatens the home. His wife is holding the lines alone — whatever the father has stopped enforcing, she absorbs, until the weight of being the only authority in the home begins to cost her something she cannot recover. His children grow up with a picture of God as ceremonially present and practically irrelevant — faith is what their mother did, not what their father modeled. His children are growing up inside a home with an unlocked door — exposed to whatever fills the vacuum the father has left, and no one standing watch. His children are growing up in a home with no held line — not because no one cares, but because the person designed to hold it has stopped; and what a mother holds alone is never quite the same as what a father and mother hold together. He provides presence without direction — the children can see their father in the room but cannot find God in his example. Children who grew up unprotected either over-protect everything in their adult lives, unable to rest, or cannot recognize danger until it has already done its work.

Scenario 44

Fractured Pillars: S (Spiritual Leader) + H2 (Heart of Integrity) + E2 (Example Who Inspires Potential)

Solid Pillars: H1 (Husband Who Loves Sacrificially) + E1 (Encourager & Nurturer) + P (Protector & Provider) + R (Reprover & Wise Mentor) + D (Discipliner)

What Happens to the Family:

Three pillars are failing simultaneously. The five that remain are absorbing the weight of what has been put down. His wife carries the spiritual weight of the home alone — praying over children her husband will not lead to the altar, covering in faith a family designed to move under his authority. His wife is married to two men — the one the world sees and the one she lives with; she has learned that the gap between his public commitments and his private behavior is real, and she carries that knowledge alone. His wife sees a man going through the motions of his own life — never fully alive to his design, never modeling what it looks like to pursue the thing God placed in him. His children grow up with a picture of God as ceremonially present and practically irrelevant — faith is what their mother did, not what their father modeled. His children will find the gap — they always do — and when they do, they will not merely lose respect for their father; they will lose their capacity to trust authority, and sometimes God, for years. His children have no picture of what a man who carries his God-given design actually looks like in daily life; the father's own unlived potential becomes the ceiling the children cannot see past. He provides presence without direction — the children can see their father in the room but cannot find

God in his example. The fracture integrity creates is not loud — it is quiet and cumulative; the children do not announce the day they stopped believing him. They simply stop, and he rarely sees it coming.

Scenario 45

Fractured Pillars: S (Spiritual Leader) + H2 (Heart of Integrity) + R (Reprover & Wise Mentor)

Solid Pillars: H1 (Husband Who Loves Sacrificially) + E1 (Encourager & Nurturer) + P (Protector & Provider) + E2 (Example Who Inspires Potential) + D (Discipliner)

What Happens to the Family:

Three pillars down. Five still holding — and the gap between what the home needs and what the framework is currently providing is widening. His wife carries the spiritual weight of the home alone — praying over children her husband will not lead to the altar, covering in faith a family designed to move under his authority. His wife is married to two men — the one the world sees and the one she lives with; she has learned that the gap between his public commitments and his private behavior is real, and she carries that knowledge alone. His wife has no one in the home willing to tell her the true thing — not in cruelty, but in love; she navigates without the steady voice of a man who knows her and speaks honestly into her life. His children grow up with a picture of God as ceremonially present and practically irrelevant — faith is what their mother did, not what their father modeled. His children will find the gap —

they always do — and when they do, they will not merely lose respect for their father; they will lose their capacity to trust authority, and sometimes God, for years. His children are drifting without calibration — no trusted voice that both knows them and tells them the true thing about where they are heading before the consequences arrive. He provides presence without direction — the children can see their father in the room but cannot find God in his example. The fracture integrity creates is not loud — it is quiet and cumulative; the children do not announce the day they stopped believing him. They simply stop, and he rarely sees it coming.

Scenario 46

Fractured Pillars: S (Spiritual Leader) + H2 (Heart of Integrity) + D (Discipliner)

Solid Pillars: H1 (Husband Who Loves Sacrificially) + E1 (Encourager & Nurturer) + P (Protector & Provider) + E2 (Example Who Inspires Potential) + R (Reprover & Wise Mentor)

What Happens to the Family:

Three pillars have failed. The remaining five carry what was designed for eight, and the redistribution is felt. His wife carries the spiritual weight of the home alone — praying over children her husband will not lead to the altar, covering in faith a family designed to move under his authority. His wife is married to two men — the one the world sees and the one she lives with; she has learned that the gap between his public commitments and his private behavior is real, and she carries that knowledge alone. His wife is holding the lines alone — whatever the father has stopped enforcing, she absorbs, until the weight of being the only authority in the home begins to cost her something she cannot recover. His children grow up with a picture of God as ceremonially present and practically irrelevant — faith is what their mother did, not what their father modeled. His children will find the gap — they always do — and when they do, they will not merely lose respect for their father; they will lose their capacity to trust authority, and sometimes God, for years. His children are growing up in a home with no held line — not because no one cares, but because the person designed to hold it has stopped; and what a mother holds alone is never quite the same as what a father and mother hold together. He provides presence without direction — the children can see their father in the room but cannot find God in his example. The fracture integrity creates is not loud — it is quiet and cumulative; the children do not announce the day they stopped believing him. They simply stop, and he rarely sees it coming.

Scenario 47

Fractured Pillars: S (Spiritual Leader) + E2 (Example Who Inspires Potential) + R (Reprover & Wise Mentor)

Solid Pillars: H1 (Husband Who Loves Sacrificially) + E1 (Encourager & Nurturer) + P (Protector & Provider) + H2 (Heart of Integrity) + D (Discipliner)

What Happens to the Family:

When three pillars fail, the home loses three structural commitments at once. The five that remain are holding — but they were not built to hold alone. His wife carries the spiritual weight of the home alone — praying over children her husband will not lead to the altar, covering in faith a family designed to move under his authority. His wife sees a man going through the motions of his own life — never fully alive to his design, never modeling what it looks like to pursue the thing God placed in him. His wife has no one in the home willing to tell her the true thing — not in cruelty, but in love; she navigates without the steady voice of a man who knows her and speaks honestly into her life. His children grow up with a picture of God as ceremonially present and practically irrelevant — faith is what their mother did, not what their father modeled. His children have no picture of what a man who carries his God-given design actually looks like in daily life; the father's own unlived potential becomes the ceiling the children cannot see past. His children are drifting without calibration — no trusted voice that both knows them and tells them the true thing about where they are heading before the consequences arrive. He provides presence without direction — the children can see their father in the room but cannot find God in his example. They will reach adulthood without a template for what a man surrendered to something greater than himself actually looks like, and they will not know what they are missing until they are trying to build something themselves.

Scenario 48

Fractured Pillars: S (Spiritual Leader) + E2 (Example Who Inspires Potential) + D (Discipliner)

Solid Pillars: H1 (Husband Who Loves Sacrificially) + E1 (Encourager & Nurturer) + P (Protector & Provider) + H2 (Heart of Integrity) + R (Reprover & Wise Mentor)

What Happens to the Family:

Three pillars are down. The remaining five are carrying what eight were designed to share, and the people inside the home are absorbing the difference. His wife carries the spiritual weight of the home alone — praying over children her husband will not lead to the altar, covering in faith a family designed to move under his authority. His wife sees a man going through the motions of his own life — never fully alive to his design, never modeling what it looks like to pursue the thing God placed in him. His wife is holding the lines alone — whatever the father has stopped enforcing, she absorbs, until the weight of being the only authority in the home begins to cost her something she cannot recover. His children grow up with a picture of God as ceremonially present and practically irrelevant — faith is what their mother did, not what their father modeled. His children have no picture of what a man who carries his God-given design actually looks like in daily life; the father's own unlived potential becomes the ceiling the children cannot see past. His children are growing up in a home with no held line — not because no one cares, but because the person designed to hold it has stopped; and what a mother holds alone is never quite the same as what a father and mother hold together. He provides presence without direction — the children can see their father in the room but cannot find God in his example. They will reach adulthood without a template for what a man surrendered to something greater than himself actually looks like, and they will not know what they are missing until they are trying to build something themselves.

Scenario 49

Fractured Pillars: S (Spiritual Leader) + R (Reprover & Wise Mentor) + D (Discipliner)

Solid Pillars: H1 (Husband Who Loves Sacrificially) + E1 (Encourager & Nurturer) + P (Protector & Provider) + H2 (Heart of Integrity) + E2 (Example Who Inspires Potential)

What Happens to the Family:

Three of the eight pillars have failed, and the five that remain are beginning to buckle under what they were never designed to carry alone. His wife carries the spiritual weight of the home alone — praying over children her husband will not lead to the altar, covering in faith a family designed to move under his authority. His wife has no one in the home willing to tell her the true thing — not in cruelty, but in love; she navigates without the steady voice of a man who knows her and speaks honestly into her life. His wife is holding the lines alone — whatever the father has stopped enforcing, she absorbs, until the weight of being the only authority in the home begins to cost her something she cannot recover. His children grow up with a picture of God as ceremonially present and practically irrelevant — faith is what their mother did, not what their father modeled. His children are drifting without calibration — no trusted voice that both knows them and tells them the true thing about where they are heading before the consequences arrive. His children are growing up in a home with no held line — not because no one cares, but because the person designed to hold it has stopped; and what a mother holds alone is never quite the same as what a father and mother hold together. He provides presence without direction — the children can see their father in the room but cannot find God in his example. They will reach adulthood without a template for what a man surrendered to something greater than himself actually looks like, and they will not know what they are missing until they are trying to build something themselves.

Fractured Pillars: H1 (Husband Who Loves Sacrificially) + E1 (Encourager & Nurturer) + P (Protector & Provider)

Solid Pillars: S (Spiritual Leader) + H2 (Heart of Integrity) + E2 (Example Who Inspires Potential) + R (Reprover & Wise Mentor) + D (Discipliner)

What Happens to the Family:

Three pillars are failing. Five remain. The home still functions in visible ways — but the people who live there are carrying more than the outside can see. His wife is not being pursued — she is being maintained; the covenant runs on autopilot, and she carries the relational weight of the marriage alone, managing rather than being led. His wife speaks into a silence — there is no voice in the home naming what she carries, affirming who she is, or calling out what God placed in her. His wife is unprotected — whether the failure is material, emotional, or spiritual; she has learned that the perimeter is unmanned and she cannot rely on him to stand between her and what threatens the home. His children are absorbing a picture of marriage as coexistence — two people occupying the same house — and they will bring that picture into their own relationships before they understand where it came from. No one is speaking the child's design into existence before the world gets there first; their sense of self is built entirely from external mirrors — peer approval, performance, whatever fills the silence. His children are growing up inside a home with an unlocked door — exposed to whatever fills the vacuum the father has left, and no one standing watch. He provides for the home materially but has stopped investing in either the marriage or the people inside it — provision without pursuit, correction without naming, leaves his family feeling managed rather than known. Adults who were never named by their father spend their lives either achieving to fill the silence or collapsing when achievement fails to do it — and they rarely trace it back to the right source.

Scenario 51

Fractured Pillars: H1 (Husband Who Loves Sacrificially) + E1 (Encourager & Nurturer) + H2 (Heart of Integrity)

Solid Pillars: S (Spiritual Leader) + P (Protector & Provider) + E2 (Example Who Inspires Potential) + R (Reprover & Wise Mentor) + D (Discipliner)

What Happens to the Family:

Three pillars are down. The remaining five are carrying what eight were designed to share — and the home feels the redistribution. His wife is not being pursued — she is being maintained; the covenant runs on autopilot, and she carries the relational weight of the marriage alone, managing rather than being led. His wife speaks into a silence — there is no voice in the home naming what she carries, affirming who she is, or calling out what God placed in her. His wife is married to two men — the one the world sees and the one she lives with; she has learned that the gap between his public commitments and his private behavior is real, and she carries that knowledge alone. His children are absorbing a picture of marriage as coexistence — two people occupying the same house — and they will bring that picture into their own relationships before they understand where it came from. No one is speaking the child's design into existence before the world gets there first; their sense of self is built entirely from external mirrors — peer approval, performance, whatever fills the silence. His children will find the gap — they always do — and when they do, they will not merely lose respect for their father; they will lose their capacity to trust authority, and sometimes God, for years. He provides for the home materially but has stopped investing in either the marriage or the people inside it — provision without pursuit, correction without naming, leaves his family feeling managed rather than known. Adults who were never named by their father spend their lives either achieving to fill the silence or collapsing when achievement fails to do it — and they rarely trace it back to the right source.

Scenario 52

Fractured Pillars: H1 (Husband Who Loves Sacrificially) + E1 (Encourager & Nurturer) + E2 (Example Who Inspires Potential)

Solid Pillars: S (Spiritual Leader) + P (Protector & Provider) + H2 (Heart of Integrity) + R (Reprover & Wise Mentor) + D (Discipliner)

What Happens to the Family:

Three pillars have failed. The five still standing are doing the work of eight, and the home is beginning to show it. His wife is not being pursued — she is being maintained; the covenant runs on autopilot, and she carries the relational weight of the marriage alone, managing rather than being led. His wife speaks into a silence — there is no voice in the home naming what she carries, affirming who she is, or calling out what God placed in her. His wife sees a man going through the motions of his own life — never fully alive to his design, never modeling what it looks like to pursue the thing God placed in him. His children are absorbing a picture of marriage as coexistence — two people occupying the same house — and they will bring that picture into their own relationships before they understand where it came from. No one is speaking the child's design into existence before the world gets there first; their sense of self is built entirely from external mirrors — peer approval, performance, whatever fills the silence. His children have no picture of what a man who carries his God-given design actually looks like in daily life; the father's own unlived potential becomes the ceiling the children cannot see past. He provides for the home materially but has stopped investing in either the marriage or the people inside it — provision without pursuit, correction without naming, leaves his family feeling managed rather than known. Adults who were never named by their father spend their lives either achieving to fill the silence or collapsing when achievement fails to do it — and they rarely trace it back to the right source.

Scenario 53

Fractured Pillars: H1 (Husband Who Loves Sacrificially) + E1 (Encourager & Nurturer) + R (Reprover & Wise Mentor)

Solid Pillars: S (Spiritual Leader) + P (Protector & Provider) + H2 (Heart of Integrity) + E2 (Example Who Inspires Potential) + D (Discipliner)

What Happens to the Family:

Three of the eight pillars have failed. What remains is real — but five load-bearing points were not designed to carry what eight were built to hold. His wife is not being pursued — she is being maintained; the covenant runs on autopilot, and she carries the relational weight of the marriage alone, managing rather than being led. His wife speaks into a silence — there is no voice in the home naming what she carries, affirming who she is, or calling out what God placed in her. His wife has no one in the home willing to tell her the true thing — not in cruelty, but in love; she navigates without the steady voice of a man who knows her and speaks honestly into her life. His children are absorbing a picture of marriage as coexistence — two people occupying the same house — and they will bring that picture into their own relationships before they understand where it came from. No one is speaking the child's design into existence before the world gets there first; their sense of self is built entirely from external mirrors — peer approval, performance, whatever fills the silence. His children are drifting without calibration — no trusted voice that both knows them and tells them the true thing about where they are heading before the consequences arrive. He provides for the home materially but has stopped investing in either the marriage or the people inside it — provision without pursuit, correction without naming, leaves his family feeling managed rather than known. Adults who were never named by their father spend their lives either achieving to fill the silence or collapsing when achievement fails to do it — and they rarely trace it back to the right source.

Scenario 54

Fractured Pillars: H1 (Husband Who Loves Sacrificially) + E1 (Encourager & Nurturer) + D (Discipliner)

Solid Pillars: S (Spiritual Leader) + P (Protector & Provider) + H2 (Heart of Integrity) + E2 (Example Who Inspires Potential) + R (Reprover & Wise Mentor)

What Happens to the Family:

Three pillars are failing simultaneously. The five that remain are absorbing the weight of what has been put down. His wife is not being pursued — she is being maintained; the covenant runs on autopilot, and she carries the relational weight of the marriage alone, managing rather than being led. His wife speaks into a silence — there is no voice in the home naming what she carries, affirming who she is, or calling out what God placed in her. His wife is holding the lines alone — whatever the father has stopped enforcing, she absorbs, until the weight of being the only authority in the home begins to cost her something she cannot recover. His children are absorbing a picture of marriage as coexistence — two people occupying the same house — and they will bring that picture into their own relationships before they understand where it came from. No one is speaking the child's design into existence before the world gets there first; their sense of self is built entirely from external mirrors — peer approval, performance, whatever fills the silence. His children are growing up in a home with no held line — not because no one cares, but because the person designed to hold it has stopped; and what a mother holds alone is never quite the same as what a father and mother hold together. He provides for the home materially but has stopped investing in either the marriage or the people inside it — provision without pursuit, correction without naming, leaves his family feeling managed rather than known. Adults who were never named by their father spend their lives either achieving to fill the silence or collapsing when achievement fails to do it — and they rarely trace it back to the right source.

Scenario 55

Fractured Pillars: H1 (Husband Who Loves Sacrificially) + P (Protector & Provider) + H2 (Heart of Integrity)

Solid Pillars: S (Spiritual Leader) + E1 (Encourager & Nurturer) + E2 (Example Who Inspires Potential) + R (Reprover & Wise Mentor) + D (Discipliner)

What Happens to the Family:

Three pillars down. Five still holding — and the gap between what the home needs and what the framework is currently providing is widening. His wife is not being pursued — she is being maintained; the covenant runs on autopilot, and she carries the relational weight of the marriage alone, managing rather than being led. His wife is unprotected — whether the failure is material, emotional, or spiritual; she has learned that the perimeter is unmanned and she cannot rely on him to stand between her and what threatens the home. His wife is married to two men — the one the world sees and the one she lives with; she has learned that the gap between his public commitments and his private behavior is real, and she carries that knowledge alone. His children are absorbing a picture of marriage as coexistence — two people occupying the same house — and they will bring that picture into their own relationships before they understand where it came from. His children are growing up inside a home with an unlocked door — exposed to whatever fills the vacuum the father has left, and no one standing watch. His children will find the gap — they always do — and when they do, they will not merely lose respect for their father; they will lose their capacity to trust authority, and sometimes God, for years. He leads spiritually in appearance but not in private — the vertical commitment he performs on Sunday is contradicted by the man his family sees Monday through Saturday. The fracture integrity creates is not loud — it is quiet and cumulative; the children do not announce the day they stopped believing him. They simply stop, and he rarely sees it coming.

Scenario 56

Fractured Pillars: H1 (Husband Who Loves Sacrificially) + P (Protector & Provider) + E2 (Example Who Inspires Potential)

Solid Pillars: S (Spiritual Leader) + E1 (Encourager & Nurturer) + H2 (Heart of Integrity) + R (Reprover & Wise Mentor) + D (Discipliner)

What Happens to the Family:

Three pillars have failed. The remaining five carry what was designed for eight, and the redistribution is felt. His wife is not being pursued — she is being maintained; the covenant runs on autopilot, and she carries the relational weight of the marriage alone, managing rather than being led. His wife is unprotected — whether the failure is material, emotional, or spiritual; she has learned that the perimeter is unmanned and she cannot rely on him to stand between her and what threatens the home. His wife sees a man going through the motions of his own life — never fully alive to his design, never modeling what it looks like to pursue the thing God placed in him. His children are absorbing a picture of marriage as coexistence — two people occupying the same house — and they will bring that picture into their own relationships before they understand where it came from. His children are growing up inside a home with an unlocked door — exposed to whatever fills the vacuum the father has left, and no one standing watch. His children have no picture of what a man who carries his God-given design actually looks like in daily life; the father's own unlived potential becomes the ceiling the children cannot see past. He provides for the family materially but has stopped investing in the marriage — provision without pursuit leaves his wife feeling like a dependent, not a covenant partner. They will reach adulthood carrying what was missing and not knowing its name — only its weight.

Scenario 57

Fractured Pillars: H1 (Husband Who Loves Sacrificially) + P (Protector & Provider) + R (Reprover & Wise Mentor)

Solid Pillars: S (Spiritual Leader) + E1 (Encourager & Nurturer) + H2 (Heart of Integrity) + E2 (Example Who Inspires Potential) + D (Discipliner)

What Happens to the Family:

When three pillars fail, the home loses three structural commitments at once. The five that remain are holding — but they were not built to hold alone. His wife is not being pursued — she is being maintained; the covenant runs on autopilot, and she carries the relational weight of the marriage alone, managing rather than being led. His wife is unprotected — whether the failure is material, emotional, or spiritual; she has learned that the perimeter is unmanned and she cannot rely on him to stand between her and what threatens the home. His wife has no one in the home willing to tell her the true thing — not in cruelty, but in love; she navigates without the steady voice of a man who knows her and speaks honestly into her life. His children are absorbing a picture of marriage as coexistence — two people occupying the same house — and they will bring that picture into their own relationships before they understand where it came from. His children are growing up inside a home with an unlocked door — exposed to whatever fills the vacuum the father has left, and no one standing watch. His children are drifting without calibration — no trusted voice that both knows them and tells them the true thing about where they are heading before the consequences arrive. He provides for the family materially but has stopped investing in the marriage — provision without pursuit leaves his wife feeling like a dependent, not a covenant partner. They will reach adulthood carrying what was missing and not knowing its name — only its weight.

Scenario 58

Fractured Pillars: H1 (Husband Who Loves Sacrificially) + P (Protector & Provider) + D (Discipliner)

Solid Pillars: S (Spiritual Leader) + E1 (Encourager & Nurturer) + H2 (Heart of Integrity) + E2 (Example Who Inspires Potential) + R (Reprover & Wise Mentor)

What Happens to the Family:

Three pillars are down. The remaining five are carrying what eight were designed to share, and the people inside the home are absorbing the difference. His wife is not being pursued — she is being maintained; the covenant runs on autopilot, and she carries the relational weight of the marriage alone, managing rather than being led. His wife is unprotected — whether the failure is material, emotional, or spiritual; she has learned that the perimeter is unmanned and she cannot rely on him to stand between her and what threatens the home. His wife is holding the lines alone — whatever the father has stopped enforcing, she absorbs, until the weight of being the only authority in the home begins to cost her something she cannot recover. His children are absorbing a picture of marriage as coexistence — two people occupying the same house — and they will bring that picture into their own relationships before they understand where it came from. His children are growing up inside a home with an unlocked door — exposed to whatever fills the vacuum the father has left, and no one standing watch. His children are growing up in a home with no held line — not because no one cares, but because the person designed to hold it has stopped; and what a mother holds alone is never quite the same as what a father and mother hold together. He tries to hold lines in the home but has stopped providing the covering that makes discipline feel like love rather than control — children without protection experience correction as threat. Children who grew up unprotected either over-protect everything in their adult lives, unable to rest, or cannot recognize danger until it has already done its work.

Scenario 59

Fractured Pillars: H1 (Husband Who Loves Sacrificially) + H2 (Heart of Integrity) + E2 (Example Who Inspires Potential)

Solid Pillars: S (Spiritual Leader) + E1 (Encourager & Nurturer) + P (Protector & Provider) + R (Reprover & Wise Mentor) + D (Discipliner)

What Happens to the Family:

Three of the eight pillars have failed, and the five that remain are beginning to buckle under what they were never designed to carry alone. His wife is not being pursued — she is being maintained; the covenant runs on autopilot, and she carries the relational weight of the marriage alone, managing rather than being led. His wife is married to two men — the one the world sees and the one she lives with; she has learned that the gap between his public commitments and his private behavior is real, and she carries that knowledge alone. His wife sees a man going through the motions of his own life — never fully alive to his design, never modeling what it looks like to pursue the thing God placed in him. His children are absorbing a picture of marriage as coexistence — two people occupying the same house — and they will bring that picture into their own relationships before they understand where it came from. His children will find the gap — they always do — and when they do, they will not merely lose respect for their father; they will lose their capacity to trust authority, and sometimes God, for years. His children have no picture of what a man who carries his God-given design actually looks like in daily life; the father's own unlived potential becomes the ceiling the children cannot see past. He leads spiritually in appearance but not in private — the vertical commitment he performs on Sunday is contradicted by the man his family sees Monday through Saturday, and a life not fully lived becomes the only picture of purpose his children have. The fracture integrity creates is not loud — it is quiet and cumulative; the children do not announce the day they stopped believing him. They simply stop, and he rarely sees it coming.

Scenario 60

Fractured Pillars: H1 (Husband Who Loves Sacrificially) + H2 (Heart of Integrity) + R (Reprover & Wise Mentor)

Solid Pillars: S (Spiritual Leader) + E1 (Encourager & Nurturer) + P (Protector & Provider) + E2 (Example Who Inspires Potential) + D (Discipliner)

What Happens to the Family:

Three pillars are failing. Five remain. The home still functions in visible ways — but the people who live there are carrying more than the outside can see. His wife is not being pursued — she is being maintained; the covenant runs on autopilot, and she carries the relational weight of the marriage alone, managing rather than being led. His wife is married to two men — the one the world sees and the one she lives with; she has learned that the gap between his public commitments and his private behavior is real, and she carries that knowledge alone. His wife has no one in the home willing to tell her the true thing — not in cruelty, but in love; she navigates without the steady voice of a man who knows her and speaks honestly into her life. His children are absorbing a picture of marriage as coexistence — two people occupying the same house — and they will bring that picture into their own relationships before they understand where it came from. His children will find the gap — they always do — and when they do, they will not merely lose respect for their father; they will lose their capacity to trust authority, and sometimes God, for years. His children are drifting without calibration — no trusted voice that both knows them and tells them the true thing about where they are heading before the consequences arrive. He leads spiritually in appearance but not in private — the vertical commitment he performs on Sunday is contradicted by the man his family sees Monday through Saturday. The fracture integrity creates is not loud — it is quiet and cumulative; the children do not announce the day they stopped believing him. They simply stop, and he rarely sees it coming.

Scenario 61

Fractured Pillars: H1 (Husband Who Loves Sacrificially) + H2 (Heart of Integrity) + D (Discipliner)

Solid Pillars: S (Spiritual Leader) + E1 (Encourager & Nurturer) + P (Protector & Provider) + E2 (Example Who Inspires Potential) + R (Reprover & Wise Mentor)

What Happens to the Family:

Three pillars are down. The remaining five are carrying what eight were designed to share — and the home feels the redistribution. His wife is not being pursued — she is being maintained; the covenant runs on autopilot, and she carries the relational weight of the marriage alone, managing rather than being led. His wife is married to two men — the one the world sees and the one she lives with; she has learned that the gap between his public commitments and his private behavior is real, and she carries that knowledge alone. His wife is holding the lines alone — whatever the father has stopped enforcing, she absorbs, until the weight of being the only authority in the home begins to cost her something she cannot recover. His children are absorbing a picture of marriage as coexistence — two people occupying the same house — and they will bring that picture into their own relationships before they understand where it came from. His children will find the gap — they always do — and when they do, they will not merely lose respect for their father; they will lose their capacity to trust authority, and sometimes God, for years. His children are growing up in a home with no held line — not because no one cares, but because the person designed to hold it has stopped; and what a mother holds alone is never quite the same as what a father and mother hold together. He leads spiritually in appearance but not in private — the vertical commitment he performs on Sunday is contradicted by the man his family sees Monday through Saturday. The fracture integrity creates is not loud — it is quiet and cumulative; the children do not announce the day they stopped believing him. They simply stop, and he rarely sees it coming.

Scenario 62

Fractured Pillars: H1 (Husband Who Loves Sacrificially) + E2 (Example Who Inspires Potential) + R (Reprover & Wise Mentor)

Solid Pillars: S (Spiritual Leader) + E1 (Encourager & Nurturer) + P (Protector & Provider) + H2 (Heart of Integrity) + D (Discipliner)

What Happens to the Family:

Three pillars have failed. The five still standing are doing the work of eight, and the home is beginning to show it. His wife is not being pursued — she is being maintained; the covenant runs on autopilot, and she carries the relational weight of the marriage alone, managing rather than being led. His wife sees a man going through the motions of his own life — never fully alive to his design, never modeling what it looks like to pursue the thing God placed in him. His wife has no one in the home willing to tell her the true thing — not in cruelty, but in love; she navigates without the steady voice of a man who knows her and speaks honestly into her life. His children are absorbing a picture of marriage as coexistence — two people occupying the same house — and they will bring that picture into their own relationships before they understand where it came from. His children have no picture of what a man who carries his God-given design actually looks like in daily life; the father's own unlived potential becomes the ceiling the children cannot see past. His children are drifting without calibration — no trusted voice that both knows them and tells them the true thing about where they are heading before the consequences arrive. He provides for the family materially but has stopped investing in the marriage — provision without pursuit leaves his wife feeling like a dependent, not a covenant partner. They will reach adulthood carrying what was missing and not knowing its name — only its weight.

Scenario 63

Fractured Pillars: H1 (Husband Who Loves Sacrificially) + E2 (Example Who Inspires Potential) + D (Discipliner)

Solid Pillars: S (Spiritual Leader) + E1 (Encourager & Nurturer) + P (Protector & Provider) + H2 (Heart of Integrity) + R (Reprover & Wise Mentor)

What Happens to the Family:

Three of the eight pillars have failed. What remains is real — but five load-bearing points were not designed to carry what eight were built to hold. His wife is not being pursued — she is being maintained; the covenant runs on autopilot, and she carries the relational weight of the marriage alone, managing rather than being led. His wife sees a man going through the motions of his own life — never fully alive to his design, never modeling what it looks like to pursue the thing God placed in him. His wife is holding the lines alone — whatever the father has stopped enforcing, she absorbs, until the weight of being the only authority in the home begins to cost her something she cannot recover. His children are absorbing a picture of marriage as coexistence — two people occupying the same house — and they will bring that picture into their own relationships before they understand where it came from. His children have no picture of what a man who carries his God-given design actually looks like in daily life; the father's own unlived potential becomes the ceiling the children cannot see past. His children are growing up in a home with no held line — not because no one cares, but because the person designed to hold it has stopped; and what a mother holds alone is never quite the same as what a father and mother hold together. He speaks into his children but has nothing to point them toward — encouragement without example produces children who feel seen but have no picture of what they are being built for. The daughters will accept less than they deserve and not know why; the sons will drift toward the same emotional distance their father modeled and call it normal.

Scenario 64

Fractured Pillars: H1 (Husband Who Loves Sacrificially) + R (Reprover & Wise Mentor) + D (Discipliner)

Solid Pillars: S (Spiritual Leader) + E1 (Encourager & Nurturer) + P (Protector & Provider) + H2 (Heart of Integrity) + E2 (Example Who Inspires Potential)

What Happens to the Family:

Three pillars are failing simultaneously. The five that remain are absorbing the weight of what has been put down. His wife is not being pursued — she is being maintained; the covenant runs on autopilot, and she carries the relational weight of the marriage alone, managing rather than being led. His wife has no one in the home willing to tell her the true thing — not in cruelty, but in love; she navigates without the steady voice of a man who knows her and speaks honestly into her life. His wife is holding the lines alone — whatever the father has stopped enforcing, she absorbs, until the weight of being the only authority in the home begins to cost her something she cannot recover. His children are absorbing a picture of marriage as coexistence — two people occupying the same house — and they will bring that picture into their own relationships before they understand where it came from. His children are drifting without calibration — no trusted voice that both knows them and tells them the true thing about where they are heading before the consequences arrive. His children are growing up in a home with no held line — not because no one cares, but because the person designed to hold it has stopped; and what a mother holds alone is never quite the same as what a father and mother hold together. He speaks wisdom into his children but enforces nothing — mentorship without discipline produces a child who knows what is right and has learned they do not have to do it. The daughters will accept less than they deserve and not know why; the sons will drift toward the same emotional distance their father modeled and call it normal.

Scenario 65

Fractured Pillars: E1 (Encourager & Nurturer) + P (Protector & Provider) + H2 (Heart of Integrity)

Solid Pillars: S (Spiritual Leader) + H1 (Husband Who Loves Sacrificially) + E2 (Example Who Inspires Potential) + R (Reprover & Wise Mentor) + D (Discipliner)

What Happens to the Family:

Three pillars down. Five still holding — and the gap between what the home needs and what the framework is currently providing is widening. His wife speaks into a silence — there is no voice in the home naming what she carries, affirming who she is, or calling out what God placed in her. His wife is unprotected — whether the failure is material, emotional, or spiritual; she has learned that the perimeter is unmanned and she cannot rely on him to stand between her and what threatens the home. His wife is married to two men — the one the world sees and the one she lives with; she has learned that the gap between his public commitments and his private behavior is real, and she carries that knowledge alone. No one is speaking the child's design into existence before the world gets there first; their sense of self is built entirely from external mirrors — peer approval, performance, whatever fills the silence. His children are growing up inside a home with an unlocked door — exposed to whatever fills the vacuum the father has left, and no one standing watch. His children will find the gap — they always do — and when they do, they will not merely lose respect for their father; they will lose their capacity to trust authority, and sometimes God, for years. He leads spiritually in appearance but not in private — the vertical commitment he performs on Sunday is contradicted by the man his family sees Monday through Saturday. The fracture integrity creates is not loud — it is quiet and cumulative; the children do not announce the day they stopped believing him. They simply stop, and he rarely sees it coming.

Scenario 66

Fractured Pillars: E1 (Encourager & Nurturer) + P (Protector & Provider) + E2 (Example Who Inspires Potential)

Solid Pillars: S (Spiritual Leader) + H1 (Husband Who Loves Sacrificially) + H2 (Heart of Integrity) + R (Reprover & Wise Mentor) + D (Discipliner)

What Happens to the Family:

Three pillars have failed. The remaining five carry what was designed for eight, and the redistribution is felt. His wife speaks into a silence — there is no voice in the home naming what she carries, affirming who she is, or calling out what God placed in her. His wife is unprotected — whether the failure is material, emotional, or spiritual; she has learned that the perimeter is unmanned and she cannot rely on him to stand between her and what threatens the home. His wife sees a man going through the motions of his own life — never fully alive to his design, never modeling what it looks like to pursue the thing God placed in him. No one is speaking the child's design into existence before the world gets there first; their sense of self is built entirely from external mirrors — peer approval, performance, whatever fills the silence. His children are growing up inside a home with an unlocked door — exposed to whatever fills the vacuum the father has left, and no one standing watch. His children have no picture of what a man who carries his God-given design actually looks like in daily life; the father's own unlived potential becomes the ceiling the children cannot see past. He corrects his children but never names them — reproof without encouragement produces a child who knows what they did wrong and has no idea who they are. Adults who were never named by their father spend their lives either achieving to fill the silence or collapsing when achievement fails to do it — and they rarely trace it back to the right source.

Scenario 67

Fractured Pillars: E1 (Encourager & Nurturer) + P (Protector & Provider) + R (Reprover & Wise Mentor)

Solid Pillars: S (Spiritual Leader) + H1 (Husband Who Loves Sacrificially) + H2 (Heart of Integrity) + E2 (Example Who Inspires Potential) + D (Discipliner)

What Happens to the Family:

When three pillars fail, the home loses three structural commitments at once. The five that remain are holding — but they were not built to hold alone. His wife speaks into a silence — there is no voice in the home naming what she carries, affirming who she is, or calling out what God placed in her. His wife is unprotected — whether the failure is material, emotional, or spiritual; she has learned that the perimeter is unmanned and she cannot rely on him to stand between her and what threatens the home. His wife has no one in the home willing to tell her the true thing — not in cruelty, but in love; she navigates without the steady voice of a man who knows her and speaks honestly into her life. No one is speaking the child's design into existence before the world gets there first; their sense of self is built entirely from external mirrors — peer approval, performance, whatever fills the silence. His children are growing up inside a home with an unlocked door — exposed to whatever fills the vacuum the father has left, and no one standing watch. His children are drifting without calibration — no trusted voice that both knows them and tells them the true thing about where they are heading before the consequences arrive. He disciplines his children but offers neither naming nor wisdom with it — correction without encouragement or mentorship teaches a child what the line is, but not who they are or why the line matters. Adults who were never named by their father spend their lives either achieving to fill the silence or collapsing when achievement fails to do it — and they rarely trace it back to the right source.

Scenario 68

Fractured Pillars: E1 (Encourager & Nurturer) + P (Protector & Provider) + D (Discipliner)

Solid Pillars: S (Spiritual Leader) + H1 (Husband Who Loves Sacrificially) + H2 (Heart of Integrity) + E2 (Example Who Inspires Potential) + R (Reprover & Wise Mentor)

What Happens to the Family:

Three pillars are down. The remaining five are carrying what eight were designed to share, and the people inside the home are absorbing the difference. His wife speaks into a silence — there is no voice in the home naming what she carries, affirming who she is, or calling out what God placed in her. His wife is unprotected — whether the failure is material, emotional, or spiritual; she has learned that the perimeter is unmanned and she cannot rely on him to stand between her and what threatens the home. His wife is holding the lines alone — whatever the father has stopped enforcing, she absorbs, until the weight of being the only authority in the home begins to cost her something she cannot recover. No one is speaking the child's design into existence before the world gets there first; their sense of self is built entirely from external mirrors — peer approval, performance, whatever fills the silence. His children are growing up inside a home with an unlocked door — exposed to whatever fills the vacuum the father has left, and no one standing watch. His children are growing up in a home with no held line — not because no one cares, but because the person designed to hold it has stopped; and what a mother holds alone is never quite the same as what a father and mother hold together. He tries to hold lines in the home but has stopped providing the covering that makes discipline feel like love rather than control — children without protection experience correction as threat. Children who grew up unprotected either over-protect everything in their adult lives, unable to rest, or cannot recognize danger until it has already done its work.

Scenario 69

Fractured Pillars: E1 (Encourager & Nurturer) + H2 (Heart of Integrity) + E2 (Example Who Inspires Potential)

Solid Pillars: S (Spiritual Leader) + H1 (Husband Who Loves Sacrificially) + P (Protector & Provider) + R (Reprover & Wise Mentor) + D (Discipliner)

What Happens to the Family:

Three of the eight pillars have failed, and the five that remain are beginning to buckle under what they were never designed to carry alone. His wife speaks into a silence — there is no voice in the home naming what she carries, affirming who she is, or calling out what God placed in her. His wife is married to two men — the one the world sees and the one she lives with; she has learned that the gap between his public commitments and his private behavior is real, and she carries that knowledge alone. His wife sees a man going through the motions of his own life — never fully alive to his design, never modeling what it looks like to pursue the thing God placed in him. No one is speaking the child's design into existence before the world gets there first; their sense of self is built entirely from external mirrors — peer approval, performance, whatever fills the silence. His children will find the gap — they always do — and when they do, they will not merely lose respect for their father; they will lose their capacity to trust authority, and sometimes God, for years. His children have no picture of what a man who carries his God-given design actually looks like in daily life; the father's own unlived potential becomes the ceiling the children cannot see past. He leads spiritually in appearance but not in private — the vertical commitment he performs on Sunday is contradicted by the man his family sees Monday through Saturday, and a life not fully lived becomes the only picture of purpose his children have. The fracture integrity creates is not loud — it is quiet and cumulative; the children do not announce the day they stopped believing him. They simply stop, and he rarely sees it coming.

Scenario 70

Fractured Pillars: E1 (Encourager & Nurturer) + H2 (Heart of Integrity) + R (Reprover & Wise Mentor)

Solid Pillars: S (Spiritual Leader) + H1 (Husband Who Loves Sacrificially) + P (Protector & Provider) + E2 (Example Who Inspires Potential) + D (Discipliner)

What Happens to the Family:

Three pillars are failing. Five remain. The home still functions in visible ways — but the people who live there are carrying more than the outside can see. His wife speaks into a silence — there is no voice in the home naming what she carries, affirming who she is, or calling out what God placed in her. His wife is married to two men — the one the world sees and the one she lives with; she has learned that the gap between his public commitments and his private behavior is real, and she carries that knowledge alone. His wife has no one in the home willing to tell her the true thing — not in cruelty, but in love; she navigates without the steady voice of a man who knows her and speaks honestly into her life. No one is speaking the child's design into existence before the world gets there first; their sense of self is built entirely from external mirrors — peer approval, performance, whatever fills the silence. His children will find the gap — they always do — and when they do, they will not merely lose respect for their father; they will lose their capacity to trust authority, and sometimes God, for years. His children are drifting without calibration — no trusted voice that both knows them and tells them the true thing about where they are heading before the consequences arrive. He leads spiritually in appearance but not in private — the vertical commitment he performs on Sunday is contradicted by the man his family sees Monday through Saturday. The fracture integrity creates is not loud — it is quiet and cumulative; the children do not announce the day they stopped believing him. They simply stop, and he rarely sees it coming.

Scenario 71

Fractured Pillars: E1 (Encourager & Nurturer) + H2 (Heart of Integrity) + D (Discipliner)

Solid Pillars: S (Spiritual Leader) + H1 (Husband Who Loves Sacrificially) + P (Protector & Provider) + E2 (Example Who Inspires Potential) + R (Reprover & Wise Mentor)

What Happens to the Family:

Three pillars are down. The remaining five are carrying what eight were designed to share — and the home feels the redistribution. His wife speaks into a silence — there is no voice in the home naming what she carries, affirming who she is, or calling out what God placed in her. His wife is married to two men — the one the world sees and the one she lives with; she has learned that the gap between his public commitments and his private behavior is real, and she carries that knowledge alone. His wife is holding the lines alone — whatever the father has stopped enforcing, she absorbs, until the weight of being the only authority in the home begins to cost her something she cannot recover. No one is speaking the child's design into existence before the world gets there first; their sense of self is built entirely from external mirrors — peer approval, performance, whatever fills the silence. His children will find the gap — they always do — and when they do, they will not merely lose respect for their father; they will lose their capacity to trust authority, and sometimes God, for years. His children are growing up in a home with no held line — not because no one cares, but because the person designed to hold it has stopped; and what a mother holds alone is never quite the same as what a father and mother hold together. He leads spiritually in appearance but not in private — the vertical commitment he performs on Sunday is contradicted by the man his family sees Monday through Saturday. The fracture integrity creates is not loud — it is quiet and cumulative; the children do not announce the day they stopped believing him. They simply stop, and he rarely sees it coming.

Scenario 72

Fractured Pillars: E1 (Encourager & Nurturer) + E2 (Example Who Inspires Potential) + R (Reprover & Wise Mentor)

Solid Pillars: S (Spiritual Leader) + H1 (Husband Who Loves Sacrificially) + P (Protector & Provider) + H2 (Heart of Integrity) + D (Discipliner)

What Happens to the Family:

Three pillars have failed. The five still standing are doing the work of eight, and the home is beginning to show it. His wife speaks into a silence — there is no voice in the home naming what she carries, affirming who she is, or calling out what God placed in her. His wife sees a man going through the motions of his own life — never fully alive to his design, never modeling what it looks like to pursue the thing God placed in him. His wife has no one in the home willing to tell her the true thing — not in cruelty, but in love; she navigates without the steady voice of a man who knows her and speaks honestly into her life. No one is speaking the child's design into existence before the world gets there first; their sense of self is built entirely from external mirrors — peer approval, performance, whatever fills the silence. His children have no picture of what a man who carries his God-given design actually looks like in daily life; the father's own unlived potential becomes the ceiling the children cannot see past. His children are drifting without calibration — no trusted voice that both knows them and tells them the true thing about where they are heading before the consequences arrive. He disciplines his children but offers neither naming nor wisdom with it — correction without encouragement or mentorship teaches a child what the line is, but not who they are or why the line matters.

Adults who were never named by their father spend their lives either achieving to fill the silence or collapsing when achievement fails to do it — and they rarely trace it back to the right source.

Scenario 73

Fractured Pillars: E1 (Encourager & Nurturer) + E2 (Example Who Inspires Potential) + D (Discipliner)

Solid Pillars: S (Spiritual Leader) + H1 (Husband Who Loves Sacrificially) + P (Protector & Provider) + H2 (Heart of Integrity) + R (Reprover & Wise Mentor)

What Happens to the Family:

Three of the eight pillars have failed. What remains is real — but five load-bearing points were not designed to carry what eight were built to hold. His wife speaks into a silence — there is no voice in the home naming what she carries, affirming who she is, or calling out what God placed in her. His wife sees a man going through the motions of his own life — never fully alive to his design, never modeling what it looks like to pursue the thing God placed in him. His wife is holding the lines alone — whatever the father has stopped enforcing, she absorbs, until the weight of being the only authority in the home begins to cost her something she cannot recover. No one is speaking the child's design into existence before the world gets there first; their sense of self is built entirely from external mirrors — peer approval, performance, whatever fills the silence. His children have no picture of what a man who carries his

God-given design actually looks like in daily life; the father's own unlived potential becomes the ceiling the children cannot see past. His children are growing up in a home with no held line — not because no one cares, but because the person designed to hold it has stopped; and what a mother holds alone is never quite the same as what a father and mother hold together. He corrects his children but never names them — reproof without encouragement produces a child who knows what they did wrong and has no idea who they are. Adults who were never named by their father spend their lives either achieving to fill the silence or collapsing when achievement fails to do it — and they rarely trace it back to the right source.

Scenario 74

Fractured Pillars: E1 (Encourager & Nurturer) + R (Reprover & Wise Mentor) + D (Discipliner)

Solid Pillars: S (Spiritual Leader) + H1 (Husband Who Loves Sacrificially) + P (Protector & Provider) + H2 (Heart of Integrity) + E2 (Example Who Inspires Potential)

What Happens to the Family:

Three pillars are failing simultaneously. The five that remain are absorbing the weight of what has been put down. His wife speaks into a silence — there is no voice in the home naming what she carries, affirming who she is, or calling out what God placed in her. His wife has no one in the home willing to tell her the true thing — not in cruelty, but in love; she navigates without the steady voice of a man who knows her and speaks honestly into her life. His wife is holding the lines alone — whatever the father has stopped enforcing, she absorbs, until the weight of being the only authority in the home begins to cost her something she cannot recover. No one is speaking the child's design into existence before the world gets there first; their sense of self is built entirely from external mirrors — peer approval, performance, whatever fills the silence. His children are drifting without calibration — no trusted voice that both knows them and tells them the true thing about where they are heading before the consequences arrive. His children are growing up in a home with no held line — not because no one cares, but because the person designed to hold it has stopped; and what a mother holds alone is never quite the same as what a father and mother hold together. He disciplines his children but offers neither naming nor wisdom with it — correction without encouragement or mentorship teaches a child what the line is, but not who they are or why the line matters. Adults who were never named by their father spend their lives either achieving to fill the silence or collapsing when achievement fails to do it — and they rarely trace it back to the right source.

Scenario 75

Fractured Pillars: P (Protector & Provider) + H2 (Heart of Integrity) + E2 (Example Who Inspires Potential)

Solid Pillars: S (Spiritual Leader) + H1 (Husband Who Loves Sacrificially) + E1 (Encourager & Nurturer) + R (Reprover & Wise Mentor) + D (Discipliner)

What Happens to the Family:

Three pillars down. Five still holding — and the gap between what the home needs and what the framework is currently providing is widening. His wife is unprotected — whether the failure is material, emotional, or spiritual; she has learned that the perimeter is unmanned and she cannot rely on him to stand between her and what threatens the home. His wife is married to two men — the one the world sees and the one she lives with; she has learned that the gap between his public commitments and his private behavior is real, and she carries that knowledge alone. His wife sees a man going through the motions of his own life — never fully alive to his design, never modeling what it looks like to pursue the thing God placed in him. His children are growing up inside a home with an unlocked door — exposed to whatever fills the vacuum the father has left, and no one standing watch. His children will find the gap — they always do — and when they do, they will not merely lose respect for their father; they will lose their capacity to trust authority, and sometimes God, for years. His children have no picture of what a man who carries his God-given design actually looks like in daily life; the father's own unlived potential becomes the ceiling the children cannot see past. He leads spiritually in appearance but not in private — the vertical commitment he performs on Sunday is contradicted by the man his family sees Monday through Saturday, and a life not fully lived becomes the only picture of purpose his children have. The fracture integrity creates is not loud — it is quiet and cumulative; the children do not announce the day they stopped believing him. They simply stop, and he rarely sees it coming.

Scenario 76

Fractured Pillars: P (Protector & Provider) + H2 (Heart of Integrity) + R (Reprover & Wise Mentor)

Solid Pillars: S (Spiritual Leader) + H1 (Husband Who Loves Sacrificially) + E1 (Encourager & Nurturer) + E2 (Example Who Inspires Potential) + D (Discipliner)

What Happens to the Family:

Three pillars have failed. The remaining five carry what was designed for eight, and the redistribution is felt. His wife is unprotected — whether the failure is material, emotional, or spiritual; she has learned that the perimeter is unmanned and she cannot rely on him to stand between her and what threatens the home. His wife is married to two men — the one the world sees and the one she lives with; she has learned that the gap between his public commitments and his private behavior is real, and she carries that knowledge alone. His wife has no one in the home willing to tell her the true thing — not in cruelty, but in love; she navigates without the steady voice of a man who knows her and speaks honestly into her life. His children are growing up inside a home with an unlocked door — exposed to whatever fills the vacuum the father has left, and no one standing watch. His children will find the gap — they always do — and when they do, they will not merely lose respect for their father; they will lose their capacity to trust authority, and sometimes God, for years. His children are drifting without calibration — no trusted voice that both knows them and tells them the true thing about where they are heading before the consequences arrive. He leads spiritually in appearance but not in private — the vertical commitment he performs on Sunday is contradicted by the man his family sees Monday through Saturday. The fracture integrity creates is not loud — it is quiet and cumulative; the children do not announce the day they stopped believing him. They simply stop, and he rarely sees it coming.

Scenario 77

Fractured Pillars: P (Protector & Provider) + H2 (Heart of Integrity) + D (Discipliner)

Solid Pillars: S (Spiritual Leader) + H1 (Husband Who Loves Sacrificially) + E1 (Encourager & Nurturer) + E2 (Example Who Inspires Potential) + R (Reprover & Wise Mentor)

What Happens to the Family:

When three pillars fail, the home loses three structural commitments at once. The five that remain are holding — but they were not built to hold alone. His wife is unprotected — whether the failure is material, emotional, or spiritual; she has learned that the perimeter is unmanned and she cannot rely on him to stand between her and what threatens the home. His wife is married to two men — the one the world sees and the one she lives with; she has learned that the gap between his public commitments and his private behavior is real, and she carries that knowledge alone. His wife is holding the lines alone — whatever the father has stopped enforcing, she absorbs, until the weight of being the only authority in the home begins to cost her something she cannot recover. His children are growing up inside a home with an unlocked door — exposed to whatever fills the vacuum the father has left, and no one standing watch. His children will find the gap — they always do — and when they do, they will not merely lose respect for their father; they will lose their capacity to trust authority, and sometimes God, for years. His children are growing up in a home with no held line — not because no one cares, but because the person designed to hold it has stopped; and what a mother holds alone is never quite the same as what a father and mother hold together. He leads spiritually in appearance but not in private — the vertical commitment he performs on Sunday is contradicted by the man his family sees Monday through Saturday. The fracture integrity creates is not loud — it is quiet and cumulative; the children do not announce the day they stopped believing him. They simply stop, and he rarely sees it coming.

Scenario 78

Fractured Pillars: P (Protector & Provider) + E2 (Example Who Inspires Potential) + R (Reprover & Wise Mentor)

Solid Pillars: S (Spiritual Leader) + H1 (Husband Who Loves Sacrificially) + E1 (Encourager & Nurturer) + H2 (Heart of Integrity) + D (Discipliner)

What Happens to the Family:

Three pillars are down. The remaining five are carrying what eight were designed to share, and the people inside the home are absorbing the difference. His wife is unprotected — whether the failure is material, emotional, or spiritual; she has learned that the perimeter is unmanned and she cannot rely on him to stand between her and what threatens the home. His wife sees a man going through the motions of his own life — never fully alive to his design, never modeling what it looks like to pursue the thing God placed in him. His wife has no one in the home willing to tell her the true thing — not in cruelty, but in love; she navigates without the steady voice of a man who knows her and speaks honestly into her life. His children are growing up inside a home with an unlocked door — exposed to whatever fills the vacuum the father has left, and no one standing watch. His children have no picture of what a man who carries his God-given design actually looks like in daily life; the father's own unlived potential becomes the ceiling the children cannot see past. His children are drifting without calibration — no trusted voice that both knows them and tells them the true thing about where they are heading before the consequences arrive. He disciplines his children but offers no wisdom with it — correction without mentorship teaches a child what the line is but not why it matters or who they become by holding it. They will reach adulthood carrying what was missing and not knowing its name — only its weight.

Scenario 79

Fractured Pillars: P (Protector & Provider) + E2 (Example Who Inspires Potential) + D (Discipliner)

Solid Pillars: S (Spiritual Leader) + H1 (Husband Who Loves Sacrificially) + E1 (Encourager & Nurturer) + H2 (Heart of Integrity) + R (Reprover & Wise Mentor)

What Happens to the Family:

Three of the eight pillars have failed, and the five that remain are beginning to buckle under what they were never designed to carry alone. His wife is unprotected — whether the failure is material, emotional, or spiritual; she has learned that the perimeter is unmanned and she cannot rely on him to stand between her and what threatens the home. His wife sees a man going through the motions of his own life — never fully alive to his design, never modeling what it looks like to pursue the thing God placed in him. His wife is holding the lines alone — whatever the father has stopped enforcing, she absorbs, until the weight of being the only authority in the home begins to cost her something she cannot recover. His children are growing up inside a home with an unlocked door — exposed to whatever fills the vacuum the father has left, and no one standing watch. His children have no picture of what a man who carries his God-given design actually looks like in daily life; the father's own unlived potential becomes the ceiling the children cannot see past. His children are growing up in a home with no held line — not because no one cares, but because the person designed to hold it has stopped; and what a mother holds alone is never quite the same as what a father and mother hold together. He tries to hold lines in the home but has stopped providing the covering that makes discipline feel like love rather than control — children without protection experience correction as threat. Children who grew up unprotected either over-protect everything in their adult lives, unable to rest, or cannot recognize danger until it has already done its work.

Scenario 80

Fractured Pillars: P (Protector & Provider) + R (Reprover & Wise Mentor) + D (Discipliner)

Solid Pillars: S (Spiritual Leader) + H1 (Husband Who Loves Sacrificially) + E1 (Encourager & Nurturer) + H2 (Heart of Integrity) + E2 (Example Who Inspires Potential)

What Happens to the Family:

Three pillars are failing. Five remain. The home still functions in visible ways — but the people who live there are carrying more than the outside can see. His wife is unprotected — whether the failure is material, emotional, or spiritual; she has learned that the perimeter is unmanned and she cannot rely on him to stand between her and what threatens the home. His wife has no one in the home willing to tell her the true thing — not in cruelty, but in love; she navigates without the steady voice of a man who knows her and speaks honestly into her life. His wife is holding the lines alone — whatever the father has stopped enforcing, she absorbs, until the weight of being the only authority in the home begins to cost her something she cannot recover. His children are growing up inside a home with an unlocked door — exposed to whatever fills the vacuum the father has left, and no one standing watch. His children are drifting without calibration — no trusted voice that both knows them and tells them the true thing about where they are heading before the consequences arrive. His children are growing up in a home with no held line — not because no one cares, but because the person designed to hold it has stopped; and what a mother holds alone is never quite the same as what a father and mother hold together. He tries to hold lines in the home but has stopped providing the covering that makes discipline feel like love rather than control — children without protection experience correction as threat. Children who grew up unprotected either over-protect everything in their adult lives, unable to rest, or cannot recognize danger until it has already done its work.

Scenario 81

Fractured Pillars: H2 (Heart of Integrity) + E2 (Example Who Inspires Potential) + R (Reprover & Wise Mentor)

Solid Pillars: S (Spiritual Leader) + H1 (Husband Who Loves Sacrificially) + E1 (Encourager & Nurturer) + P (Protector & Provider) + D (Discipliner)

What Happens to the Family:

Three pillars are down. The remaining five are carrying what eight were designed to share — and the home feels the redistribution. His wife is married to two men — the one the world sees and the one she lives with; she has learned that the gap between his public commitments and his private behavior is real, and she carries that knowledge alone. His wife sees a man going through the motions of his own life — never fully alive to his design, never modeling what it looks like to pursue the thing God placed in him. His wife has no one in the home willing to tell her the true thing — not in cruelty, but in love; she navigates without the steady voice of a man who knows her and speaks honestly into her life. His children will find the gap — they always do — and when they do, they will not merely lose respect for their father; they will lose their capacity to trust authority, and sometimes God, for years. His children have no picture of what a man who carries his God-given design actually looks like in daily life; the father's own unlived potential becomes the ceiling the children cannot see past. His children are drifting without calibration — no trusted voice that both knows them and tells them the true thing about where they are heading before the consequences arrive. He leads spiritually in appearance but not in private — the vertical commitment he performs on Sunday is contradicted by the man his family sees Monday through Saturday, and a life not fully lived becomes the only picture of purpose his children have. The fracture integrity creates is not loud — it is quiet and cumulative; the children do not announce the day they stopped believing him. They simply stop, and he rarely sees it coming.

Scenario 82

Fractured Pillars: H2 (Heart of Integrity) + E2 (Example Who Inspires Potential) + D (Discipliner)

Solid Pillars: S (Spiritual Leader) + H1 (Husband Who Loves Sacrificially) + E1 (Encourager & Nurturer) + P (Protector & Provider) + R (Reprover & Wise Mentor)

What Happens to the Family:

Three pillars have failed. The five still standing are doing the work of eight, and the home is beginning to show it. His wife is married to two men — the one the world sees and the one she lives with; she has learned that the gap between his public commitments and his private behavior is real, and she carries that knowledge alone. His wife sees a man going through the motions of his own life — never fully alive to his design, never modeling what it looks like to pursue the thing God placed in him. His wife is holding the lines alone — whatever the father has stopped enforcing, she absorbs, until the weight of being the only authority in the home begins to cost her something she cannot recover. His children will find the gap — they always do — and when they do, they will not merely lose respect for their father; they will lose their capacity to trust authority, and sometimes God, for years. His children have no picture of what a man who carries his God-given design actually looks like in daily life; the father's own unlived potential becomes the ceiling the children cannot see past. His children are growing up in a home with no held line — not because no one cares, but because the person designed to hold it has stopped; and what a mother holds alone is never quite the same as what a father and mother hold together. He leads spiritually in appearance but not in private — the vertical commitment he performs on Sunday is contradicted by the man his family sees Monday through Saturday, and a life not fully lived becomes the only picture of purpose his children have. The fracture integrity creates is not loud — it is quiet and cumulative; the children do not announce the day they stopped believing him. They simply stop, and he rarely sees it coming.

Scenario 83

Fractured Pillars: H2 (Heart of Integrity) + R (Reprover & Wise Mentor) + D (Discipliner)

Solid Pillars: S (Spiritual Leader) + H1 (Husband Who Loves Sacrificially) + E1 (Encourager & Nurturer) + P (Protector & Provider) + E2 (Example Who Inspires Potential)

What Happens to the Family:

Three of the eight pillars have failed. What remains is real — but five load-bearing points were not designed to carry what eight were built to hold. His wife is married to two men — the one the world sees and the one she lives with; she has learned that the gap between his public commitments and his private behavior is real, and she carries that knowledge alone. His wife has no one in the home willing to tell her the true thing — not in cruelty, but in love; she navigates without the steady voice of a man who knows her and speaks honestly into her life. His wife is holding the lines alone — whatever the father has stopped enforcing, she absorbs, until the weight of being the only authority in the home begins to cost her something she cannot recover. His children will find the gap — they always do — and when they do, they will not merely lose respect for their father; they will lose their capacity to trust authority, and sometimes God, for years. His children are drifting without calibration — no trusted voice that both knows them and tells them the true thing about where they are heading before the consequences arrive. His children are growing up in a home with no held line — not because no one cares, but because the person designed to hold it has stopped; and what a mother holds alone is never quite the same as what a father and mother hold together. He leads spiritually in appearance but not in private — the vertical commitment he performs on Sunday is contradicted by the man his family sees Monday through Saturday. The fracture integrity creates is not loud — it is quiet and cumulative; the children do not announce the day they stopped believing him. They simply stop, and he rarely sees it coming.

Scenario 84

Fractured Pillars: E2 (Example Who Inspires Potential) + R (Reprover & Wise Mentor) + D (Discipliner)

Solid Pillars: S (Spiritual Leader) + H1 (Husband Who Loves Sacrificially) + E1 (Encourager & Nurturer) + P (Protector & Provider) + H2 (Heart of Integrity)

What Happens to the Family:

Three pillars are failing simultaneously. The five that remain are absorbing the weight of what has been put down. His wife sees a man going through the motions of his own life — never fully alive to his design, never modeling what it looks like to pursue the thing God placed in him. His wife has no one in the home willing to tell her the true thing — not in cruelty, but in love; she navigates without the steady voice of a man who knows her and speaks honestly into her life. His wife is holding the lines alone — whatever the father has stopped enforcing, she absorbs, until the weight of being the only authority in the home begins to cost her something she cannot recover. His children have no picture of what a man who carries his God-given design actually looks like in daily life; the father's own unlived potential becomes the ceiling the children cannot see past. His children are drifting without calibration — no trusted voice that both knows them and tells them the true thing about where they are heading before the consequences arrive. His children are growing up in a home with no held line — not because no one cares, but because the person designed to hold it has stopped; and what a mother holds alone is never quite the same as what a father and mother hold together. He speaks wisdom into his children but enforces nothing — mentorship without discipline produces a child who knows what is right and has learned they do not have to do it. They will reach adulthood carrying what was missing and not knowing its name — only its weight.

Four Pillars Failing

70 scenarios

Half the framework has failed. The home operates on four structural commitments where eight were designed to work in concert. At this level, the visible architecture of fatherhood may still appear intact to the outside world. Inside the home, the people who live there know something is missing, even if they cannot name it.

Scenario 85

Fractured Pillars: S (Spiritual Leader) + H1 (Husband Who Loves Sacrificially) + E1 (Encourager & Nurturer) + P (Protector & Provider)

Solid Pillars: H2 (Heart of Integrity) + E2 (Example Who Inspires Potential) + R (Reprover & Wise Mentor) + D (Discipliner)

What Happens to the Family:

Half the framework has collapsed. What remains is working — but it is four pillars doing the work of eight, and it shows. His wife carries the spiritual weight of the home alone — praying over children her husband will not lead to the altar, covering in faith a family designed to move under his authority. At the same time, his wife is not being pursued — she is being maintained; the covenant runs on autopilot, and she carries the relational weight of the marriage alone, managing rather than being led. His children grow up with a picture of God as ceremonially present and practically irrelevant — faith is what their mother did, not what their father modeled. His children are absorbing a picture of marriage as coexistence — two people occupying the same house — and they will bring that picture into their own relationships before they understand where it came from. His wife speaks into a silence — there is no voice in the home naming what she carries, affirming who she is, or calling out what God placed in her. Compounding this, his wife is unprotected — whether the failure is material, emotional, or spiritual; she has learned that the perimeter is unmanned and she cannot rely on him to stand between her and what threatens the home. No one is speaking the child's design into existence before the world gets there first; their sense of self is built entirely from external mirrors — peer approval, performance, whatever fills the silence. His children are growing up inside a home with an unlocked door — exposed to whatever fills the vacuum the father has left, and no one standing watch. He provides for the family materially but has stopped investing in the marriage — provision without pursuit leaves his wife feeling like a dependent, not a covenant partner. What his children are building their picture of fatherhood from is what remains — and the Protector & Provider they needed is one of the things they are not getting. They will reach adulthood without a template for what a man surrendered to something greater than himself actually looks like, and they will not know what they are missing until they are trying to build something themselves.

Scenario 86

Fractured Pillars: S (Spiritual Leader) + H1 (Husband Who Loves Sacrificially) + E1 (Encourager & Nurturer) + H2 (Heart of Integrity)

Solid Pillars: P (Protector & Provider) + E2 (Example Who Inspires Potential) + R (Reprover & Wise Mentor) + D (Discipliner)

What Happens to the Family:

Four of the eight pillars have failed. The home is operating at half its structural capacity, and the family is living inside the gap. His wife carries the spiritual weight of the home alone — praying over children her husband will not lead to the altar, covering in faith a family designed to move under his authority. At the same time, his wife is not being pursued — she is being maintained; the covenant runs on autopilot, and she carries the relational weight of the marriage alone, managing rather than being led. His children grow up with a picture of God as ceremonially present and practically irrelevant — faith is what their mother did, not what their father modeled. His children are absorbing a picture of marriage as coexistence — two people occupying the same house — and they will bring that picture into their own relationships before they understand where it came from. His wife speaks into a silence — there is no voice in the home naming what she carries, affirming who she is, or calling out what God placed in her. Compounding this, his wife is married to two men — the one the world sees and the one she lives with; she has learned that the gap between his public commitments and his private behavior is real, and she carries that knowledge alone. No one is speaking the child's design into existence before the world gets there first; their sense of self is built entirely from external mirrors — peer approval, performance, whatever fills the silence. His children will find the gap — they always do — and when they do, they will not merely lose respect for their father; they will lose their capacity to trust authority, and sometimes God, for years. He provides for the family materially but has stopped investing in the marriage — provision without pursuit, and integrity withheld in private, leaves his wife feeling like a dependent rather than a covenant partner. What his children are building their picture of fatherhood from is what remains — and the Heart of Integrity they needed is one of the things they are not getting. They will reach adulthood without a template for what a man surrendered to something greater than himself actually looks like, and they will not know what they are missing until they are trying to build something themselves.

Scenario 87

Fractured Pillars: S (Spiritual Leader) + H1 (Husband Who Loves Sacrificially) + E1 (Encourager & Nurturer) + E2 (Example Who Inspires Potential)

Solid Pillars: P (Protector & Provider) + H2 (Heart of Integrity) + R (Reprover & Wise Mentor) + D (Discipliner)

What Happens to the Family:

Half the framework has failed, and the four pillars still standing are carrying what was designed for a complete structure. His wife carries the spiritual weight of the home alone — praying over children her husband will not lead to the altar, covering in faith a family designed to move under his authority. At the same time, his wife is not being pursued — she is being maintained; the covenant runs on autopilot, and she carries the relational weight of the marriage alone, managing rather than being led. His children grow up with a picture of God as ceremonially present and practically irrelevant — faith is what their mother did, not what their father modeled. His children are absorbing a picture of marriage as coexistence — two people occupying the same house — and they will bring that picture into their own relationships before they understand where it came from. His wife speaks into a silence — there is no voice in the home naming what she carries, affirming who she is, or calling out what God placed in her. Compounding this, his wife sees a man going through the motions of his own life — never fully alive to his design, never modeling what it looks like to pursue the thing God placed in him. No one is speaking the child's design into existence before the world gets there first; their sense of self is built entirely from external mirrors — peer approval, performance, whatever fills the silence. His children have no picture of what a man who carries his God-given design actually looks like in daily life; the father's own unlived potential becomes the ceiling the children cannot see past. He speaks into his children but has nothing to point them toward — encouragement without example produces children who feel seen but have no picture of what they are being built for, and without spiritual grounding behind it, even that purpose has no foundation. What his children are

building their picture of fatherhood from is what remains —
and the Example Who Inspires Potential they needed is one
of the things they are not getting. They will reach adulthood
without a template for what a man surrendered to
something greater than himself actually looks like, and they
will not know what they are missing until they are trying to
build something themselves.

Scenario 88

**Fractured Pillars: S (Spiritual Leader) + H1 (Husband Who Loves
Sacrificially) + E1 (Encourager & Nurturer) + R (Reprover & Wise Mentor)**

**Solid Pillars: P (Protector & Provider) + H2 (Heart of Integrity) + E2 (Example
Who Inspires Potential) + D (Discipliner)**

What Happens to the Family:

Four pillars down. Four still standing. At this level, the
family can see what is missing even if they cannot yet name
it. His wife carries the spiritual weight of the home alone —
praying over children her husband will not lead to the altar,
covering in faith a family designed to move under his
authority. At the same time, his wife is not being pursued —
she is being maintained; the covenant runs on autopilot, and
she carries the relational weight of the marriage alone,
managing rather than being led. His children grow up with a
picture of God as ceremonially present and practically
irrelevant — faith is what their mother did, not what their
father modeled. His children are absorbing a picture of
marriage as coexistence — two people occupying the same
house — and they will bring that picture into their own

relationships before they understand where it came from. His wife speaks into a silence — there is no voice in the home naming what she carries, affirming who she is, or calling out what God placed in her. Compounding this, his wife has no one in the home willing to tell her the true thing — not in cruelty, but in love; she navigates without the steady voice of a man who knows her and speaks honestly into her life. No one is speaking the child's design into existence before the world gets there first; their sense of self is built entirely from external mirrors — peer approval, performance, whatever fills the silence. His children are drifting without calibration — no trusted voice that both knows them and tells them the true thing about where they are heading before the consequences arrive. He disciplines his children but offers neither naming nor wisdom with it — correction without encouragement or mentorship teaches a child what the line is, but not who they are or why the line matters. What his children are building their picture of fatherhood from is what remains — and the Reprover & Wise Mentor they needed is one of the things they are not getting. They will reach adulthood without a template for what a man surrendered to something greater than himself actually looks like, and they will not know what they are missing until they are trying to build something themselves.

Scenario 89

Fractured Pillars: S (Spiritual Leader) + H1 (Husband Who Loves Sacrificially) + E1 (Encourager & Nurturer) + D (Discipliner)

Solid Pillars: P (Protector & Provider) + H2 (Heart of Integrity) + E2 (Example Who Inspires Potential) + R (Reprover & Wise Mentor)

What Happens to the Family:

Half the framework has failed. The visible architecture of fatherhood may still appear intact from the outside. Inside the home, the people who live there know something is missing. His wife carries the spiritual weight of the home alone — praying over children her husband will not lead to the altar, covering in faith a family designed to move under his authority. At the same time, his wife is not being pursued — she is being maintained; the covenant runs on autopilot, and she carries the relational weight of the marriage alone, managing rather than being led. His children grow up with a picture of God as ceremonially present and practically irrelevant — faith is what their mother did, not what their father modeled. His children are absorbing a picture of marriage as coexistence — two people occupying the same house — and they will bring that picture into their own relationships before they understand where it came from. His wife speaks into a silence — there is no voice in the home naming what she carries, affirming who she is, or calling out what God placed in her. Compounding this, his wife is holding the lines alone — whatever the father has stopped enforcing, she absorbs, until the weight of being the only authority in the home begins to cost her something she cannot recover. No one is speaking the child's design into existence before the world gets there first; their sense of self is built entirely from external mirrors — peer approval, performance, whatever fills the silence. His children are growing up in a home with no held line — not because no one cares, but because the person designed to hold it has stopped; and what a mother holds alone is never quite the same as what a father and mother hold together. He corrects his children but never names them — reproof without encouragement produces a child who knows what they did wrong and has no idea who they are. What his children are building their picture of fatherhood from is what remains — and the Discipliner they needed is one of the things they are not getting. They will reach adulthood without a template for what a man surrendered to something greater than himself actually looks like, and they will not know what they are missing until they are trying to build something themselves.

Scenario 90

Fractured Pillars: S (Spiritual Leader) + H1 (Husband Who Loves Sacrificially) + P (Protector & Provider) + H2 (Heart of Integrity)

Solid Pillars: E1 (Encourager & Nurturer) + E2 (Example Who Inspires Potential) + R (Reprover & Wise Mentor) + D (Discipliner)

What Happens to the Family:

Four pillars have failed. The remaining four are doing the work of eight — and the home bears the weight of that imbalance. His wife carries the spiritual weight of the home alone — praying over children her husband will not lead to the altar, covering in faith a family designed to move under his authority. At the same time, his wife is not being pursued — she is being maintained; the covenant runs on autopilot, and she carries the relational weight of the marriage alone, managing rather than being led. His children grow up with a picture of God as ceremonially present and practically irrelevant — faith is what their mother did, not what their father modeled. His children are absorbing a picture of marriage as coexistence — two people occupying the same house — and they will bring that picture into their own relationships before they understand where it came from. His wife is unprotected — whether the failure is material, emotional, or spiritual; she has learned that the perimeter is unmanned and she cannot rely on him to stand between her and what threatens the home. Compounding this, his wife is married to two men — the one the world sees and the one she lives with; she has learned that the gap between his public commitments and his private behavior is real, and she carries that knowledge alone. His children are growing up inside a home with an unlocked door — exposed to whatever fills the vacuum the father has left, and no one standing watch. His children will find the gap — they always do — and when they do, they will not merely lose respect for their father; they will lose their capacity to trust authority, and sometimes God, for years. He provides for the family materially but has stopped investing in the marriage — provision without pursuit leaves his wife feeling like a dependent, not a covenant partner. What his children are building their picture of fatherhood from is what remains — and the Heart of Integrity they needed is one of the things they are not getting. They will reach adulthood without a template for what a man surrendered to something greater than himself actually looks like, and they will not know what they are missing until they are trying to build something themselves.

Scenario 91

Fractured Pillars: S (Spiritual Leader) + H1 (Husband Who Loves Sacrificially) + P (Protector & Provider) + E2 (Example Who Inspires Potential)

Solid Pillars: E1 (Encourager & Nurturer) + H2 (Heart of Integrity) + R (Reprover & Wise Mentor) + D (Discipliner)

What Happens to the Family:

Half the framework has failed. The home operates on four structural commitments where eight were designed to work in concert. His wife carries the spiritual weight of the home alone — praying over children her husband will not lead to the altar, covering in faith a family designed to move under his authority. At the same time, his wife is not being pursued — she is being maintained; the covenant runs on autopilot, and she carries the relational weight of the marriage alone, managing rather than being led. His children grow up with a picture of God as ceremonially present and practically irrelevant — faith is what their mother did, not what their father modeled. His children are absorbing a picture of marriage as coexistence — two people occupying the same house — and they will bring that picture into their own relationships before they understand where it came from. His wife is unprotected — whether the failure is material, emotional, or spiritual; she has learned that the perimeter is unmanned and she cannot rely on him to stand between her and what threatens the home. Compounding this, his wife sees a man going through the motions of his own life — never fully alive to his design, never modeling what it looks like to pursue the thing God placed in him. His children are growing up inside a home with an unlocked door — exposed to whatever fills the vacuum the father has left, and no one standing watch. His children have no picture of what a man who carries his God-given design actually looks like in daily life; the father's own unlived potential becomes the ceiling the children cannot see past. He speaks into his children but has nothing to point them toward — encouragement without example produces children who feel seen but have no picture of what they are being built for, and without spiritual grounding behind it, even that purpose has no foundation. What his children are building their picture of fatherhood from is what remains — and the Example Who Inspires Potential they needed is one of the things they are not getting. They will reach adulthood without a template for what a man surrendered to something greater than himself actually looks like, and they will not know what they are missing until they are trying to build something themselves.

Scenario 92

Fractured Pillars: S (Spiritual Leader) + H1 (Husband Who Loves Sacrificially) + P (Protector & Provider) + R (Reprover & Wise Mentor)

Solid Pillars: E1 (Encourager & Nurturer) + H2 (Heart of Integrity) + E2 (Example Who Inspires Potential) + D (Discipliner)

What Happens to the Family:

Four pillars have failed. What remains — four load-bearing points where eight were designed — is carrying the weight of what has been put down. His wife carries the spiritual weight of the home alone — praying over children her husband will not lead to the altar, covering in faith a family designed to move under his authority. At the same time, his wife is not being pursued — she is being maintained; the covenant runs on autopilot, and she carries the relational weight of the marriage alone, managing rather than being led. His children grow up with a picture of God as ceremonially present and practically irrelevant — faith is what their mother did, not what their father modeled. His children are absorbing a picture of marriage as coexistence — two people occupying the same house — and they will bring that picture into their own relationships before they understand where it came from. His wife is unprotected — whether the failure is material, emotional, or spiritual; she has learned that the perimeter is unmanned and she cannot rely on him to stand between her and what threatens the home. Compounding this, his wife has no one in the home willing to tell her the true thing — not in cruelty, but in love; she navigates without the steady voice of a man who knows her and speaks honestly into her life. His children are growing up inside a home with an unlocked door — exposed to whatever fills the vacuum the father has left, and no one standing watch. His children are drifting without calibration — no trusted voice that both knows them and tells them the true thing about where they are heading before the consequences arrive. He provides for the family materially but has stopped investing in the marriage — provision without pursuit leaves his wife feeling like a dependent, not a covenant partner. What his children are building their picture of fatherhood from is what remains — and the Reprover & Wise Mentor they needed is one of the things they are not getting. They will reach adulthood without a template for what a man surrendered to something greater than himself actually looks like, and they will not know what they are missing until they are trying to build something themselves.

Scenario 93

Fractured Pillars: S (Spiritual Leader) + H1 (Husband Who Loves Sacrificially) + P (Protector & Provider) + D (Discipliner)

Solid Pillars: E1 (Encourager & Nurturer) + H2 (Heart of Integrity) + E2 (Example Who Inspires Potential) + R (Reprover & Wise Mentor)

What Happens to the Family:

Half the framework is down. The four pillars still standing are real, but they were not designed to carry the home alone. His wife carries the spiritual weight of the home alone — praying over children her husband will not lead to the altar, covering in faith a family designed to move under his authority. At the same time, his wife is not being pursued — she is being maintained; the covenant runs on autopilot, and she carries the relational weight of the marriage alone, managing rather than being led. His children grow up with a picture of God as ceremonially present and practically irrelevant — faith is what their mother did, not what their father modeled. His children are absorbing a picture of marriage as coexistence — two people occupying the same house — and they will bring that picture into their own relationships before they understand where it came from. His wife is unprotected — whether the failure is material, emotional, or spiritual; she has learned that the perimeter is unmanned and she cannot rely on him to stand between her and what threatens the home. Compounding this, his wife is holding the lines alone — whatever the father has stopped enforcing, she absorbs, until the weight of being the only authority in the home begins to cost her something she cannot recover. His children are growing up inside a home with an unlocked door — exposed to whatever fills the vacuum the father has left, and no one standing watch. His children are growing up in a home with no held line — not because no one cares, but because the person designed to hold it has stopped; and what a mother holds alone is never quite the same as what a father and mother hold together. He tries to hold lines in the home but has stopped providing the covering that makes discipline feel like love rather than control — children without protection experience correction as threat. What his children are building their picture of fatherhood from is what remains — and the Discipliner they needed is one of the things they are not getting. They will reach adulthood without a template for what a man surrendered to something greater than himself actually looks like, and they will not know what they are missing until they are trying to build something themselves.

Scenario 94

Fractured Pillars: S (Spiritual Leader) + H1 (Husband Who Loves Sacrificially) + H2 (Heart of Integrity) + E2 (Example Who Inspires Potential)

Solid Pillars: E1 (Encourager & Nurturer) + P (Protector & Provider) + R (Reprover & Wise Mentor) + D (Discipliner)

What Happens to the Family:

Four pillars have failed. Four remain. The home may still look functional from the outside; inside, the people who live there know something is wrong. His wife carries the spiritual weight of the home alone — praying over children her husband will not lead to the altar, covering in faith a family designed to move under his authority. At the same time, his wife is not being pursued — she is being maintained; the covenant runs on autopilot, and she carries the relational weight of the marriage alone, managing rather than being led. His children grow up with a picture of God as ceremonially present and practically irrelevant — faith is what their mother did, not what their father modeled. His children are absorbing a picture of marriage as coexistence — two people occupying the same house — and they will bring that picture into their own relationships before they understand where it came from. His wife is married to two men — the one the world sees and the one she lives with;

she has learned that the gap between his public commitments and his private behavior is real, and she carries that knowledge alone. Compounding this, his wife sees a man going through the motions of his own life — never fully alive to his design, never modeling what it looks like to pursue the thing God placed in him. His children will find the gap — they always do — and when they do, they will not merely lose respect for their father; they will lose their capacity to trust authority, and sometimes God, for years. His children have no picture of what a man who carries his God-given design actually looks like in daily life; the father's own unlived potential becomes the ceiling the children cannot see past. He leads spiritually in appearance but not in private — the vertical commitment he performs on Sunday is contradicted by the man his family sees Monday through Saturday, and a life not fully lived becomes the only picture of purpose his children have. What his children are building their picture of fatherhood from is what remains — and the Example Who Inspires Potential they needed is one of the things they are not getting. They will reach adulthood without a template for what a man surrendered to something greater than himself actually looks like, and they will not know what they are missing until they are trying to build something themselves.

Scenario 95

Fractured Pillars: S (Spiritual Leader) + H1 (Husband Who Loves Sacrificially) + H2 (Heart of Integrity) + R (Reprover & Wise Mentor)

Solid Pillars: E1 (Encourager & Nurturer) + P (Protector & Provider) + E2 (Example Who Inspires Potential) + D (Discipliner)

What Happens to the Family:

Half the framework has collapsed. What remains is working — but it is four pillars doing the work of eight, and it shows. His wife carries the spiritual weight of the home alone — praying over children her husband will not lead to the altar, covering in faith a family designed to move under his authority. At the same time, his wife is not being pursued — she is being maintained; the covenant runs on autopilot, and she carries the relational weight of the marriage alone, managing rather than being led. His children grow up with a picture of God as ceremonially present and practically irrelevant — faith is what their mother did, not what their father modeled. His children are absorbing a picture of marriage as coexistence — two people occupying the same house — and they will bring that picture into their own relationships before they understand where it came from. His wife is married to two men — the one the world sees and the one she lives with; she has learned that the gap between his public commitments and his private behavior is real, and she carries that knowledge alone. Compounding this, his wife has no one in the home willing to tell her the true thing — not in cruelty, but in love; she navigates without the steady voice of a man who knows her and speaks honestly into her life. His children will find the gap — they always do — and when they do, they will not merely lose respect for their father; they will lose their capacity to trust authority, and sometimes God, for years. His children are drifting without calibration — no trusted voice that both knows them and tells them the true thing about where they are heading before the consequences arrive. He provides for the family materially but has stopped investing in the marriage — provision without pursuit, and integrity withheld in private, leaves his wife feeling like a dependent rather than a covenant partner. What his children are building their picture of fatherhood from is what remains — and the Reprover & Wise Mentor they needed is one of the things they are not getting. They will reach adulthood without a template for what a man surrendered to something greater than himself actually looks like, and they will not know what they are missing until they are trying to build something themselves.

Scenario 96

Fractured Pillars: S (Spiritual Leader) + H1 (Husband Who Loves Sacrificially) + H2 (Heart of Integrity) + D (Discipliner)

Solid Pillars: E1 (Encourager & Nurturer) + P (Protector & Provider) + E2 (Example Who Inspires Potential) + R (Reprover & Wise Mentor)

What Happens to the Family:

Four of the eight pillars have failed. The home is operating at half its structural capacity, and the family is living inside the gap. His wife carries the spiritual weight of the home alone — praying over children her husband will not lead to the altar, covering in faith a family designed to move under his authority. At the same time, his wife is not being pursued — she is being maintained; the covenant runs on autopilot, and she carries the relational weight of the marriage alone, managing rather than being led. His children grow up with a picture of God as ceremonially present and practically irrelevant — faith is what their mother did, not what their father modeled. His children are absorbing a picture of marriage as coexistence — two people occupying the same house — and they will bring that picture into their own relationships before they understand where it came from. His wife is married to two men — the one the world sees and the one she lives with; she has learned that the gap between his public commitments and his private behavior is real, and she carries that knowledge alone. Compounding this, his wife is holding the lines alone — whatever the father has stopped enforcing, she absorbs, until the weight of being the only authority in the home begins to cost her something she cannot recover. His children will find the gap — they always do — and when they do, they will not merely lose respect for their father; they will lose their capacity to trust authority, and sometimes God, for years. His children are growing up in a home with no held line — not because no one cares, but because the person designed to hold it has stopped; and what a mother holds alone is never quite the same as what a father and mother hold together. He provides for the family materially but has stopped investing in the marriage — provision without pursuit, and integrity withheld in private, leaves his wife feeling like a dependent rather than a covenant partner. What his children are building their picture of fatherhood from is what remains — and the Discipliner they needed is one of the things they are not getting. They will reach adulthood without a template for what a man surrendered to something greater than himself actually looks like, and they will not know what they are missing until they are trying to build something themselves.

Scenario 97

Fractured Pillars: S (Spiritual Leader) + H1 (Husband Who Loves Sacrificially) + E2 (Example Who Inspires Potential) + R (Reprover & Wise Mentor)

Solid Pillars: E1 (Encourager & Nurturer) + P (Protector & Provider) + H2 (Heart of Integrity) + D (Discipliner)

What Happens to the Family:

Half the framework has failed, and the four pillars still standing are carrying what was designed for a complete structure. His wife carries the spiritual weight of the home alone — praying over children her husband will not lead to the altar, covering in faith a family designed to move under his authority. At the same time, his wife is not being pursued — she is being maintained; the covenant runs on autopilot, and she carries the relational weight of the marriage alone, managing rather than being led. His children grow up with a picture of God as ceremonially present and practically irrelevant — faith is what their mother did, not what their father modeled. His children are absorbing a picture of marriage as coexistence — two people occupying the same house — and they will bring that picture into their own relationships before they understand where it came from. His wife sees a man going through the motions of his own life — never fully alive to his design, never modeling what it looks like to pursue the thing God placed in him. Compounding this, his wife has no one in the home willing to tell her the true thing — not in cruelty, but in love; she navigates without the steady voice of a man who knows her and speaks honestly into her life. His children have no picture of what a man who carries his God-given design actually looks like in daily life; the father's own unlived potential becomes the ceiling the children cannot see past. His children are drifting without calibration — no trusted voice that both knows them and tells them the true thing about where they are heading before the consequences arrive. He speaks into his children but has nothing to point them toward — encouragement without example produces children who feel seen but have no picture of what they are being built for, and without spiritual grounding behind it, even that purpose has no foundation. What his children are building their picture of fatherhood from is what remains — and the Reprover & Wise Mentor they needed is one of the things they are not getting. They will reach adulthood without a template for what a man surrendered to something greater than himself actually looks like, and they will not know what they are missing until they are trying to build something themselves.

Scenario 98

Fractured Pillars: S (Spiritual Leader) + H1 (Husband Who Loves Sacrificially) + E2 (Example Who Inspires Potential) + D (Discipliner)

Solid Pillars: E1 (Encourager & Nurturer) + P (Protector & Provider) + H2 (Heart of Integrity) + R (Reprover & Wise Mentor)

What Happens to the Family:

Four pillars down. Four still standing. At this level, the family can see what is missing even if they cannot yet name it. His wife carries the spiritual weight of the home alone — praying over children her husband will not lead to the altar, covering in faith a family designed to move under his authority. At the same time, his wife is not being pursued — she is being maintained; the covenant runs on autopilot, and she carries the relational weight of the marriage alone, managing rather than being led. His children grow up with a picture of God as ceremonially present and practically irrelevant — faith is what their mother did, not what their father modeled. His children are absorbing a picture of marriage as coexistence — two people occupying the same house — and they will bring that picture into their own relationships before they understand where it came from. His wife sees a man going through the motions of his own life — never fully alive to his design, never modeling what it looks like to pursue the thing God placed in him. Compounding this, his wife is holding the lines alone — whatever the father has stopped enforcing, she absorbs, until the weight of being the only authority in the home begins to cost her something she cannot recover. His children have no picture of what a man who carries his God-given design actually looks like in daily life; the father's own unlived potential becomes the ceiling the children cannot see past. His children are growing up in a home with no held line — not because no one cares, but because the person designed to hold it has stopped; and what a mother holds alone is never quite the same as what a father and mother hold together. He speaks into his children but has nothing to point them toward — encouragement without example produces children who feel seen but have no picture of what they are being built for, and without spiritual grounding behind it, even that purpose has no foundation. What his children are building their picture of fatherhood from is what remains — and the Discipliner they needed is one of the things they are not getting. They will reach adulthood without a template for what a man surrendered to something greater than himself actually looks like, and they will not know what they are missing until they are trying to build something themselves.

Scenario 99

Fractured Pillars: S (Spiritual Leader) + H1 (Husband Who Loves Sacrificially) + R (Reprover & Wise Mentor) + D (Discipliner)

Solid Pillars: E1 (Encourager & Nurturer) + P (Protector & Provider) + H2 (Heart of Integrity) + E2 (Example Who Inspires Potential)

What Happens to the Family:

Half the framework has failed. The visible architecture of fatherhood may still appear intact from the outside. Inside the home, the people who live there know something is missing. His wife carries the spiritual weight of the home alone — praying over children her husband will not lead to the altar, covering in faith a family designed to move under his authority. At the same time, his wife is not being pursued — she is being maintained; the covenant runs on autopilot, and she carries the relational weight of the marriage alone, managing rather than being led. His children grow up with a picture of God as ceremonially present and practically irrelevant — faith is what their mother did, not what their father modeled. His children are absorbing a picture of marriage as coexistence — two people occupying the same house — and they will bring that picture into their own relationships before they understand where it came from. His wife has no one in the home willing to tell her the true thing — not in cruelty, but in love; she navigates without the steady voice of a man who knows her and speaks honestly into her life. Compounding this, his wife is holding the lines alone — whatever the father has stopped enforcing, she absorbs, until the weight of being the only authority in the home begins to cost her something she cannot recover. His children are drifting without calibration — no trusted voice that both knows them and tells them the true thing about where they are heading before the consequences arrive. His children are growing up in a home with no held line — not because no one cares, but because the person designed to hold it has stopped; and what a mother holds alone is never quite the same as what a father and mother hold together. He speaks wisdom into his children but enforces nothing — mentorship without discipline produces a child who knows what is right and has learned they do not have to do it. What his children are

building their picture of fatherhood from is what remains —
and the Discipliner they needed is one of the things they are
not getting. They will reach adulthood without a template
for what a man surrendered to something greater than
himself actually looks like, and they will not know what they
are missing until they are trying to build something
themselves.

Scenario 100

Fractured Pillars: S (Spiritual Leader) + E1 (Encourager & Nurturer) + P (Protector & Provider) + H2 (Heart of Integrity)

Solid Pillars: H1 (Husband Who Loves Sacrificially) + E2 (Example Who Inspires Potential) + R (Reprover & Wise Mentor) + D (Discipliner)

What Happens to the Family:

Four pillars have failed. The remaining four are doing the
work of eight — and the home bears the weight of that
imbalance. His wife carries the spiritual weight of the home
alone — praying over children her husband will not lead to
the altar, covering in faith a family designed to move under
his authority. At the same time, his wife speaks into a
silence — there is no voice in the home naming what she
carries, affirming who she is, or calling out what God placed
in her. His children grow up with a picture of God as
ceremonially present and practically irrelevant — faith is
what their mother did, not what their father modeled. No
one is speaking the child's design into existence before the
world gets there first; their sense of self is built entirely
from external mirrors — peer approval, performance,

whatever fills the silence. His wife is unprotected — whether the failure is material, emotional, or spiritual; she has learned that the perimeter is unmanned and she cannot rely on him to stand between her and what threatens the home. Compounding this, his wife is married to two men — the one the world sees and the one she lives with; she has learned that the gap between his public commitments and his private behavior is real, and she carries that knowledge alone. His children are growing up inside a home with an unlocked door — exposed to whatever fills the vacuum the father has left, and no one standing watch. His children will find the gap — they always do — and when they do, they will not merely lose respect for their father; they will lose their capacity to trust authority, and sometimes God, for years. He corrects his children but never names them — reproof without encouragement produces a child who knows what they did wrong and has no idea who they are. What his children are building their picture of fatherhood from is what remains — and the Heart of Integrity they needed is one of the things they are not getting. The fracture integrity creates is not loud — it is quiet and cumulative; the children do not announce the day they stopped believing him. They simply stop, and he rarely sees it coming.

Scenario 101

Fractured Pillars: S (Spiritual Leader) + E1 (Encourager & Nurturer) + P (Protector & Provider) + E2 (Example Who Inspires Potential)

Solid Pillars: H1 (Husband Who Loves Sacrificially) + H2 (Heart of Integrity) + R (Reprover & Wise Mentor) + D (Discipliner)

What Happens to the Family:

Half the framework has failed. The home operates on four structural commitments where eight were designed to work in concert. His wife carries the spiritual weight of the home alone — praying over children her husband will not lead to the altar, covering in faith a family designed to move under his authority. At the same time, his wife speaks into a silence — there is no voice in the home naming what she carries, affirming who she is, or calling out what God placed in her. His children grow up with a picture of God as ceremonially present and practically irrelevant — faith is what their mother did, not what their father modeled. No one is speaking the child's design into existence before the world gets there first; their sense of self is built entirely from external mirrors — peer approval, performance, whatever fills the silence. His wife is unprotected — whether the failure is material, emotional, or spiritual; she has learned that the perimeter is unmanned and she cannot rely on him to stand between her and what threatens the home. Compounding this, his wife sees a man going through the motions of his own life — never fully alive to his design, never modeling what it looks like to pursue the thing God placed in him. His children are growing up inside a home with an unlocked door — exposed to whatever fills the vacuum the father has left, and no one standing watch. His children have no picture of what a man who carries his God-given design actually looks like in daily life; the father's own unlived potential becomes the ceiling the children cannot see past. He speaks into his children but has nothing to point them toward — encouragement without example produces children who feel seen but have no picture of what they are being built for, and without spiritual grounding behind it, even that purpose has no foundation. What his children are building their picture of fatherhood from is what remains — and the Example Who Inspires Potential they needed is one of the things they are not getting. Adults who were never named by their father spend their lives either achieving to fill the silence or collapsing when achievement fails to do it — and they rarely trace it back to the right source.

Scenario 102

Fractured Pillars: S (Spiritual Leader) + E1 (Encourager & Nurturer) + P (Protector & Provider) + R (Reprover & Wise Mentor)

Solid Pillars: H1 (Husband Who Loves Sacrificially) + H2 (Heart of Integrity) + E2 (Example Who Inspires Potential) + D (Discipliner)

What Happens to the Family:

Four pillars have failed. What remains — four load-bearing points where eight were designed — is carrying the weight of what has been put down. His wife carries the spiritual weight of the home alone — praying over children her husband will not lead to the altar, covering in faith a family designed to move under his authority. At the same time, his wife speaks into a silence — there is no voice in the home naming what she carries, affirming who she is, or calling out what God placed in her. His children grow up with a picture of God as ceremonially present and practically irrelevant — faith is what their mother did, not what their father modeled. No one is speaking the child's design into existence before the world gets there first; their sense of self is built entirely from external mirrors — peer approval, performance, whatever fills the silence. His wife is unprotected — whether the failure is material, emotional, or spiritual; she has learned that the perimeter is unmanned and she cannot rely on him to stand between her and what threatens the home. Compounding this, his wife has no one in the home willing to tell her the true thing — not in cruelty, but in love; she navigates without the steady voice of a man who knows her and speaks honestly into her life. His children are growing up inside a home with an unlocked door — exposed to whatever fills the vacuum the father has left, and no one standing watch. His children are drifting without calibration — no trusted voice that both knows them and tells them the true thing about where they are heading before the consequences arrive. He disciplines his children but offers neither naming nor wisdom with it — correction without encouragement or mentorship teaches a child what the line is, but not who they are or why the line matters. What his children are building their picture of fatherhood from is what remains — and the Reprover & Wise Mentor they needed is one of the things they are not getting. Adults who were never named by their father spend their lives either achieving to fill the silence or collapsing when achievement fails to do it — and they rarely trace it back to the right source.

Scenario 103

Fractured Pillars: S (Spiritual Leader) + E1 (Encourager & Nurturer) + P (Protector & Provider) + D (Discipliner)

Solid Pillars: H1 (Husband Who Loves Sacrificially) + H2 (Heart of Integrity) + E2 (Example Who Inspires Potential) + R (Reprover & Wise Mentor)

What Happens to the Family:

Half the framework is down. The four pillars still standing are real, but they were not designed to carry the home alone. His wife carries the spiritual weight of the home alone — praying over children her husband will not lead to the altar, covering in faith a family designed to move under his authority. At the same time, his wife speaks into a silence — there is no voice in the home naming what she carries, affirming who she is, or calling out what God placed in her. His children grow up with a picture of God as ceremonially present and practically irrelevant — faith is what their mother did, not what their father modeled. No one is speaking the child's design into existence before the world gets there first; their sense of self is built entirely from external mirrors — peer approval, performance, whatever fills the silence. His wife is unprotected — whether the failure is material, emotional, or spiritual; she has learned that the perimeter is unmanned and she cannot rely on him to stand between her and what threatens the home. Compounding this, his wife is holding the lines alone —

whatever the father has stopped enforcing, she absorbs, until the weight of being the only authority in the home begins to cost her something she cannot recover. His children are growing up inside a home with an unlocked door — exposed to whatever fills the vacuum the father has left, and no one standing watch. His children are growing up in a home with no held line — not because no one cares, but because the person designed to hold it has stopped; and what a mother holds alone is never quite the same as what a father and mother hold together. He tries to hold lines in the home but has stopped providing the covering that makes discipline feel like love rather than control — children without protection experience correction as threat. What his children are building their picture of fatherhood from is what remains — and the Discipliner they needed is one of the things they are not getting. Adults who were never named by their father spend their lives either achieving to fill the silence or collapsing when achievement fails to do it — and they rarely trace it back to the right source.

Scenario 104

Fractured Pillars: S (Spiritual Leader) + E1 (Encourager & Nurturer) + H2 (Heart of Integrity) + E2 (Example Who Inspires Potential)

Solid Pillars: H1 (Husband Who Loves Sacrificially) + P (Protector & Provider) + R (Reprover & Wise Mentor) + D (Discipliner)

What Happens to the Family:

Four pillars have failed. Four remain. The home may still look functional from the outside; inside, the people who live there know something is wrong. His wife carries the spiritual weight of the home alone — praying over children her husband will not lead to the altar, covering in faith a family designed to move under his authority. At the same time, his wife speaks into a silence — there is no voice in the home naming what she carries, affirming who she is, or calling out what God placed in her. His children grow up with a picture of God as ceremonially present and practically irrelevant — faith is what their mother did, not what their father modeled. No one is speaking the child's design into existence before the world gets there first; their sense of self is built entirely from external mirrors — peer approval, performance, whatever fills the silence. His wife is married to two men — the one the world sees and the one she lives with; she has learned that the gap between his public commitments and his private behavior is real, and she carries that knowledge alone. Compounding this, his wife sees a man going through the motions of his own life — never fully alive to his design, never modeling what it looks like to pursue the thing God placed in him. His children will find the gap — they always do — and when they do, they will not merely lose respect for their father; they will lose their capacity to trust authority, and sometimes God, for years. His children have no picture of what a man who carries his God-given design actually looks like in daily life; the father's own unlived potential becomes the ceiling the children cannot see past. He leads spiritually in appearance but not in private — the vertical commitment he performs on Sunday is contradicted by the man his family sees Monday through Saturday, and a life not fully lived becomes the only picture of purpose his children have. What his children are building their picture of fatherhood from is what remains — and the Example Who Inspires Potential they needed is one of the things they are not getting. The fracture integrity creates is not loud — it is quiet and cumulative; the children do not announce the day they stopped believing him. They simply stop, and a life not fully lived becomes the only template of purpose they were given.

Scenario 105

Fractured Pillars: S (Spiritual Leader) + E1 (Encourager & Nurturer) + H2 (Heart of Integrity) + R (Reprover & Wise Mentor)

Solid Pillars: H1 (Husband Who Loves Sacrificially) + P (Protector & Provider) + E2 (Example Who Inspires Potential) + D (Discipliner)

What Happens to the Family:

Half the framework has collapsed. What remains is working — but it is four pillars doing the work of eight, and it shows. His wife carries the spiritual weight of the home alone — praying over children her husband will not lead to the altar, covering in faith a family designed to move under his authority. At the same time, his wife speaks into a silence — there is no voice in the home naming what she carries, affirming who she is, or calling out what God placed in her. His children grow up with a picture of God as ceremonially present and practically irrelevant — faith is what their mother did, not what their father modeled. No one is speaking the child's design into existence before the world gets there first; their sense of self is built entirely from external mirrors — peer approval, performance, whatever fills the silence. His wife is married to two men — the one the world sees and the one she lives with; she has learned that the gap between his public commitments and his private behavior is real, and she carries that knowledge alone. Compounding this, his wife has no one in the home willing to tell her the true thing — not in cruelty, but in love; she navigates without the steady voice of a man who knows her and speaks honestly into her life. His children will find the gap — they always do — and when they do, they will not merely lose respect for their father; they will lose their capacity to trust authority, and sometimes God, for years. His children are drifting without calibration — no trusted voice that both knows them and tells them the true thing about where they are heading before the consequences arrive. He disciplines his children but offers neither naming nor wisdom with it — correction without encouragement or mentorship teaches a child what the line is, but not who they are or why the line matters. What his children are building their picture of fatherhood from is what remains — and the Reprover & Wise Mentor they needed is one of the things they are not getting. The fracture integrity creates is not loud — it is quiet and cumulative; the children do not announce the day they stopped believing him. They simply stop, and he rarely sees it coming.

Scenario 106

Fractured Pillars: S (Spiritual Leader) + E1 (Encourager & Nurturer) + H2 (Heart of Integrity) + D (Discipliner)

Solid Pillars: H1 (Husband Who Loves Sacrificially) + P (Protector & Provider) + E2 (Example Who Inspires Potential) + R (Reprover & Wise Mentor)

What Happens to the Family:

Four of the eight pillars have failed. The home is operating at half its structural capacity, and the family is living inside the gap. His wife carries the spiritual weight of the home alone — praying over children her husband will not lead to the altar, covering in faith a family designed to move under his authority. At the same time, his wife speaks into a silence — there is no voice in the home naming what she carries, affirming who she is, or calling out what God placed in her. His children grow up with a picture of God as ceremonially present and practically irrelevant — faith is what their mother did, not what their father modeled. No one is speaking the child's design into existence before the world gets there first; their sense of self is built entirely from external mirrors — peer approval, performance, whatever fills the silence. His wife is married to two men — the one the world sees and the one she lives with; she has learned that the gap between his public commitments and his private behavior is real, and she carries that knowledge alone. Compounding this, his wife is holding the lines alone — whatever the father has stopped enforcing, she absorbs, until the weight of being the only authority in the home begins to cost her something she cannot recover. His children will find the gap — they always do — and when they do, they will not merely lose respect for their father; they will lose their capacity to trust authority, and sometimes God, for years. His children are growing up in a home with no held line — not because no one cares, but because the person designed to hold it has stopped; and what a mother holds alone is never quite the same as what a father and mother hold together. He corrects his children but never names them — reproof without encouragement produces a child who knows what they did wrong and has no idea who they are. What his children are building their picture of fatherhood from is what remains — and the Discipliner they needed is one of the things they are not getting. The fracture integrity creates is not loud — it is quiet and cumulative; the children do not announce the day they stopped believing him. They simply stop, and he rarely sees it coming.

Scenario 107

Fractured Pillars: S (Spiritual Leader) + E1 (Encourager & Nurturer) + E2 (Example Who Inspires Potential) + R (Reprover & Wise Mentor)

Solid Pillars: H1 (Husband Who Loves Sacrificially) + P (Protector & Provider) + H2 (Heart of Integrity) + D (Discipliner)

What Happens to the Family:

Half the framework has failed, and the four pillars still standing are carrying what was designed for a complete structure. His wife carries the spiritual weight of the home alone — praying over children her husband will not lead to the altar, covering in faith a family designed to move under his authority. At the same time, his wife speaks into a silence — there is no voice in the home naming what she carries, affirming who she is, or calling out what God placed in her. His children grow up with a picture of God as ceremonially present and practically irrelevant — faith is what their mother did, not what their father modeled. No one is speaking the child's design into existence before the world gets there first; their sense of self is built entirely from external mirrors — peer approval, performance, whatever fills the silence. His wife sees a man going through the motions of his own life — never fully alive to his design, never modeling what it looks like to pursue the thing God placed in him. Compounding this, his wife has no one in the home willing to tell her the true thing — not in cruelty, but in love; she navigates without the steady voice of a man who knows her and speaks honestly into her life. His children have no picture of what a man who carries his God-given design actually looks like in daily life; the father's own unlived potential becomes the ceiling the children cannot see past. His children are drifting without calibration — no trusted voice that both knows them and tells them the true thing about where they are heading before the consequences arrive. He speaks into his children but has nothing to point them toward — encouragement without example produces children who feel seen but have no picture of what they are being built for, and without spiritual grounding behind it, even that purpose has no foundation. What his children are building their picture of fatherhood from is what remains — and the Reprover & Wise Mentor they needed is one of the things they are not getting. Adults who were never named by their father spend their lives either achieving to fill the silence or collapsing when achievement fails to do it — and they rarely trace it back to the right source.

Scenario 108

Fractured Pillars: S (Spiritual Leader) + E1 (Encourager & Nurturer) + E2 (Example Who Inspires Potential) + D (Discipliner)

Solid Pillars: H1 (Husband Who Loves Sacrificially) + P (Protector & Provider) + H2 (Heart of Integrity) + R (Reprover & Wise Mentor)

What Happens to the Family:

Four pillars down. Four still standing. At this level, the family can see what is missing even if they cannot yet name it. His wife carries the spiritual weight of the home alone — praying over children her husband will not lead to the altar, covering in faith a family designed to move under his authority. At the same time, his wife speaks into a silence — there is no voice in the home naming what she carries, affirming who she is, or calling out what God placed in her. His children grow up with a picture of God as ceremonially present and practically irrelevant — faith is what their mother did, not what their father modeled. No one is speaking the child's design into existence before the world gets there first; their sense of self is built entirely from external mirrors — peer approval, performance, whatever fills the silence. His wife sees a man going through the motions of his own life — never fully alive to his design, never modeling what it looks like to pursue the thing God placed in him. Compounding this, his wife is holding the lines alone — whatever the father has stopped enforcing, she absorbs, until the weight of being the only authority in the home begins to cost her something she cannot recover. His children have no picture of what a man who carries his God-given design actually looks like in daily life; the father's own unlived potential becomes the ceiling the children cannot see past. His children are growing up in a home with no held line — not because no one cares, but because the person designed to hold it has stopped; and what a mother holds alone is never quite the same as what a father and mother hold together. He speaks into his children but has nothing to point them toward — encouragement without example produces children who feel seen but have no picture of what they are being built for, and without spiritual grounding behind it, even that purpose has no foundation. What his children are building their picture of fatherhood from is what remains — and the Discipliner they needed is one of the things they are not getting. Adults who were never named by their father spend their lives either achieving to fill the silence or collapsing when achievement fails to do it — and they rarely trace it back to the right source.

Scenario 109

Fractured Pillars: S (Spiritual Leader) + E1 (Encourager & Nurturer) + R (Reprover & Wise Mentor) + D (Discipliner)

Solid Pillars: H1 (Husband Who Loves Sacrificially) + P (Protector & Provider) + H2 (Heart of Integrity) + E2 (Example Who Inspires Potential)

What Happens to the Family:

Half the framework has failed. The visible architecture of fatherhood may still appear intact from the outside. Inside the home, the people who live there know something is missing. His wife carries the spiritual weight of the home alone — praying over children her husband will not lead to the altar, covering in faith a family designed to move under his authority. At the same time, his wife speaks into a silence — there is no voice in the home naming what she carries, affirming who she is, or calling out what God placed in her. His children grow up with a picture of God as ceremonially present and practically irrelevant — faith is what their mother did, not what their father modeled. No one is speaking the child's design into existence before the world gets there first; their sense of self is built entirely from external mirrors — peer approval, performance, whatever fills the silence. His wife has no one in the home willing to tell her the true thing — not in cruelty, but in love; she navigates without the steady voice of a man who knows her and speaks honestly into her life. Compounding this, his wife is holding the lines alone — whatever the father has stopped enforcing, she absorbs, until the weight of being the only authority in the home begins to cost her something she cannot recover. His children are drifting without calibration — no trusted voice that both knows them and tells them the true thing about where they are heading before the consequences arrive. His children are growing up in a home with no held line — not because no one cares, but because the person designed to hold it has stopped; and what a mother holds alone is never quite the same as what a father and mother hold together. He disciplines his children but offers neither naming nor wisdom with it — correction without encouragement or mentorship teaches a child what the line is, but not who they are or why the line matters. What his children are building their picture of fatherhood from is what remains — and the Discipliner they needed is one of the things they are not getting. Adults who were never named by their father spend their lives either achieving to fill the silence or collapsing when achievement fails to do it — and they rarely trace it back to the right source.

Scenario 110

Fractured Pillars: S (Spiritual Leader) + P (Protector & Provider) + H2 (Heart of Integrity) + E2 (Example Who Inspires Potential)

Solid Pillars: H1 (Husband Who Loves Sacrificially) + E1 (Encourager & Nurturer) + R (Reprover & Wise Mentor) + D (Discipliner)

What Happens to the Family:

Four pillars have failed. The remaining four are doing the work of eight — and the home bears the weight of that imbalance. His wife carries the spiritual weight of the home alone — praying over children her husband will not lead to the altar, covering in faith a family designed to move under his authority. At the same time, his wife is unprotected — whether the failure is material, emotional, or spiritual; she has learned that the perimeter is unmanned and she cannot rely on him to stand between her and what threatens the home. His children grow up with a picture of God as ceremonially present and practically irrelevant — faith is what their mother did, not what their father modeled. His children are growing up inside a home with an unlocked door — exposed to whatever fills the vacuum the father has left, and no one standing watch. His wife is married to two men — the one the world sees and the one she lives with; she has learned that the gap between his public commitments and his private behavior is real, and she carries that knowledge alone. Compounding this, his wife sees a man going through the motions of his own life — never fully alive to his design, never modeling what it looks like to pursue the thing God placed in him. His children will find the gap — they always do — and when they do, they will not merely lose respect for their father; they will lose their capacity to trust authority, and sometimes God, for years. His children have no picture of what a man who carries his God-given design actually looks like in daily life; the father's own unlived potential becomes the ceiling the children cannot see past. He leads spiritually in appearance but not in private — the vertical commitment he performs on Sunday is contradicted by the man his family sees Monday through Saturday, and a life not fully lived becomes the only picture of purpose his children have. What his children are

building their picture of fatherhood from is what remains —
and the Example Who Inspires Potential they needed is one
of the things they are not getting. The fracture integrity
creates is not loud — it is quiet and cumulative; the children
do not announce the day they stopped believing him. They
simply stop, and a life not fully lived becomes the only
template of purpose they were given.

Scenario 111

Fractured Pillars: S (Spiritual Leader) + P (Protector & Provider) + H2 (Heart of Integrity) + R (Reprover & Wise Mentor)

Solid Pillars: H1 (Husband Who Loves Sacrificially) + E1 (Encourager & Nurturer) + E2 (Example Who Inspires Potential) + D (Discipliner)

What Happens to the Family:

Half the framework has failed. The home operates on
four structural commitments where eight were designed to
work in concert. His wife carries the spiritual weight of the
home alone — praying over children her husband will not
lead to the altar, covering in faith a family designed to move
under his authority. At the same time, his wife is
unprotected — whether the failure is material, emotional, or
spiritual; she has learned that the perimeter is unmanned
and she cannot rely on him to stand between her and what
threatens the home. His children grow up with a picture of
God as ceremonially present and practically irrelevant —
faith is what their mother did, not what their father
modeled. His children are growing up inside a home with an
unlocked door — exposed to whatever fills the vacuum the

father has left, and no one standing watch. His wife is married to two men — the one the world sees and the one she lives with; she has learned that the gap between his public commitments and his private behavior is real, and she carries that knowledge alone. Compounding this, his wife has no one in the home willing to tell her the true thing — not in cruelty, but in love; she navigates without the steady voice of a man who knows her and speaks honestly into her life. His children will find the gap — they always do — and when they do, they will not merely lose respect for their father; they will lose their capacity to trust authority, and sometimes God, for years. His children are drifting without calibration — no trusted voice that both knows them and tells them the true thing about where they are heading before the consequences arrive. He disciplines his children but offers no wisdom with it — correction without mentorship teaches a child what the line is but not why it matters or who they become by holding it. What his children are building their picture of fatherhood from is what remains — and the Reprover & Wise Mentor they needed is one of the things they are not getting. The fracture integrity creates is not loud — it is quiet and cumulative; the children do not announce the day they stopped believing him. They simply stop, and he rarely sees it coming.

Scenario 112

Fractured Pillars: S (Spiritual Leader) + P (Protector & Provider) + H2 (Heart of Integrity) + D (Discipliner)

Solid Pillars: H1 (Husband Who Loves Sacrificially) + E1 (Encourager & Nurturer) + E2 (Example Who Inspires Potential) + R (Reprover & Wise Mentor)

What Happens to the Family:

Four pillars have failed. What remains — four load-bearing points where eight were designed — is carrying the weight of what has been put down. His wife carries the spiritual weight of the home alone — praying over children her husband will not lead to the altar, covering in faith a family designed to move under his authority. At the same time, his wife is unprotected — whether the failure is material, emotional, or spiritual; she has learned that the perimeter is unmanned and she cannot rely on him to stand between her and what threatens the home. His children grow up with a picture of God as ceremonially present and practically irrelevant — faith is what their mother did, not what their father modeled. His children are growing up inside a home with an unlocked door — exposed to whatever fills the vacuum the father has left, and no one standing watch. His wife is married to two men — the one the world sees and the one she lives with; she has learned that the gap between his public commitments and his private behavior is real, and she carries that knowledge alone. Compounding this, his wife is holding the lines alone — whatever the father has stopped enforcing, she absorbs, until the weight of being the only authority in the home begins to cost her something she cannot recover. His children will find the gap — they always do — and when they do, they will not merely lose respect for their father; they will lose their capacity to trust authority, and sometimes God, for years. His children are growing up in a home with no held line — not because no one cares, but because the person designed to hold it has stopped; and what a mother holds alone is never quite the same as what a father and mother hold together. He tries to hold lines in the home but has stopped providing the covering that makes discipline feel like love rather than control — children without protection experience correction as threat. What his children are building their picture of fatherhood from is what remains — and the Discipliner they needed is one of the things they are not getting. The fracture integrity creates is not loud — it is quiet and cumulative; the children do not announce the day they stopped believing him. They simply stop, and he rarely sees it coming.

Scenario 113

Fractured Pillars: S (Spiritual Leader) + P (Protector & Provider) + E2 (Example Who Inspires Potential) + R (Reprover & Wise Mentor)

Solid Pillars: H1 (Husband Who Loves Sacrificially) + E1 (Encourager & Nurturer) + H2 (Heart of Integrity) + D (Discipliner)

What Happens to the Family:

Half the framework is down. The four pillars still standing are real, but they were not designed to carry the home alone. His wife carries the spiritual weight of the home alone — praying over children her husband will not lead to the altar, covering in faith a family designed to move under his authority. At the same time, his wife is unprotected — whether the failure is material, emotional, or spiritual; she has learned that the perimeter is unmanned and she cannot rely on him to stand between her and what threatens the home. His children grow up with a picture of God as ceremonially present and practically irrelevant — faith is what their mother did, not what their father modeled. His children are growing up inside a home with an unlocked door — exposed to whatever fills the vacuum the father has left, and no one standing watch. His wife sees a man going through the motions of his own life — never fully alive to his design, never modeling what it looks like to pursue the thing God placed in him. Compounding this, his wife has no one in the home willing to tell her the true thing — not in cruelty, but in love; she navigates without the steady voice of a man who knows her and speaks honestly into her life. His children have no picture of what a man who carries his God-given design actually looks like in daily life; the father's own unlived potential becomes the ceiling the children cannot see past. His children are drifting without calibration — no trusted voice that both knows them and tells them the true thing about where they are heading before the consequences arrive. He speaks into his children but has nothing to point them toward — encouragement without example produces children who feel seen but have no picture of what they are being built for, and without spiritual grounding behind it, even that purpose has no foundation. What his children are building their picture of fatherhood from is what remains — and the Reprover &

Wise Mentor they needed is one of the things they are not getting. They will reach adulthood without a template for what a man surrendered to something greater than himself actually looks like, and they will not know what they are missing until they are trying to build something themselves.

Scenario 114

Fractured Pillars: S (Spiritual Leader) + P (Protector & Provider) + E2 (Example Who Inspires Potential) + D (Discipliner)

Solid Pillars: H1 (Husband Who Loves Sacrificially) + E1 (Encourager & Nurturer) + H2 (Heart of Integrity) + R (Reprover & Wise Mentor)

What Happens to the Family:

Four pillars have failed. Four remain. The home may still look functional from the outside; inside, the people who live there know something is wrong. His wife carries the spiritual weight of the home alone — praying over children her husband will not lead to the altar, covering in faith a family designed to move under his authority. At the same time, his wife is unprotected — whether the failure is material, emotional, or spiritual; she has learned that the perimeter is unmanned and she cannot rely on him to stand between her and what threatens the home. His children grow up with a picture of God as ceremonially present and practically irrelevant — faith is what their mother did, not what their father modeled. His children are growing up inside a home with an unlocked door — exposed to whatever fills the vacuum the father has left, and no one standing watch. His wife sees a man going through the motions of his own life — never fully alive to his design, never modeling what it looks like to pursue the thing God placed in him. Compounding this, his wife is holding the lines alone — whatever the father has stopped enforcing, she absorbs, until the weight of being the only authority in the home begins to cost her something she cannot recover. His children have no picture of what a man who carries his God-given design actually looks like in daily life; the father's own unlived potential becomes the ceiling the children cannot see past. His children are growing up in a home with no held line — not because no one cares, but because the person designed to hold it has stopped; and what a mother holds alone is never quite the same as what a father and mother hold together. He speaks into his children but has nothing to point them toward — encouragement without example produces children who feel seen but have no picture of what they are being built for, and without spiritual grounding behind it, even that purpose has no foundation. What his children are building their picture of fatherhood from is what remains — and the Discipliner they needed is one of the things they are not getting. They will reach adulthood without a template for what a man surrendered to something greater than himself actually looks like, and they will not know what they are missing until they are trying to build something themselves.

Scenario 115

Fractured Pillars: S (Spiritual Leader) + P (Protector & Provider) + R (Reprover & Wise Mentor) + D (Discipliner)

Solid Pillars: H1 (Husband Who Loves Sacrificially) + E1 (Encourager & Nurturer) + H2 (Heart of Integrity) + E2 (Example Who Inspires Potential)

What Happens to the Family:

Half the framework has collapsed. What remains is working — but it is four pillars doing the work of eight, and it shows. His wife carries the spiritual weight of the home alone — praying over children her husband will not lead to the altar, covering in faith a family designed to move under his authority. At the same time, his wife is unprotected — whether the failure is material, emotional, or spiritual; she has learned that the perimeter is unmanned and she cannot rely on him to stand between her and what threatens the home. His children grow up with a picture of God as ceremonially present and practically irrelevant — faith is what their mother did, not what their father modeled. His children are growing up inside a home with an unlocked door — exposed to whatever fills the vacuum the father has left, and no one standing watch. His wife has no one in the home willing to tell her the true thing — not in cruelty, but in love; she navigates without the steady voice of a man who knows her and speaks honestly into her life. Compounding this, his wife is holding the lines alone — whatever the father has stopped enforcing, she absorbs, until the weight of being the only authority in the home begins to cost her something she cannot recover. His children are drifting without calibration — no trusted voice that both knows them and tells them the true thing about where they are heading before the consequences arrive. His children are growing up in a home with no held line — not because no one cares, but because the person designed to hold it has stopped; and what a mother holds alone is never quite the same as what a father and mother hold together. He tries to hold lines in the home but has stopped providing the covering that makes discipline feel like love rather than control — children without protection experience correction as threat. What his children are building their picture of fatherhood from is what remains — and the Discipliner they needed is one of the things they are not getting. They will reach adulthood without a template for what a man surrendered to something greater than himself actually looks like, and they will not know what they are missing until they are trying to build something themselves.

Scenario 116

Fractured Pillars: S (Spiritual Leader) + H2 (Heart of Integrity) + E2 (Example Who Inspires Potential) + R (Reprover & Wise Mentor)

Solid Pillars: H1 (Husband Who Loves Sacrificially) + E1 (Encourager & Nurturer) + P (Protector & Provider) + D (Discipliner)

What Happens to the Family:

Four of the eight pillars have failed. The home is operating at half its structural capacity, and the family is living inside the gap. His wife carries the spiritual weight of the home alone — praying over children her husband will not lead to the altar, covering in faith a family designed to move under his authority. At the same time, his wife is married to two men — the one the world sees and the one she lives with; she has learned that the gap between his public commitments and his private behavior is real, and she carries that knowledge alone. His children grow up with a picture of God as ceremonially present and practically irrelevant — faith is what their mother did, not what their father modeled. His children will find the gap — they always do — and when they do, they will not merely lose respect for their father; they will lose their capacity to trust authority, and sometimes God, for years. His wife sees a man going through the motions of his own life — never fully alive to his design, never modeling what it looks like to pursue the thing God placed in him. Compounding this, his wife has no one in the home willing to tell her the true thing — not in cruelty, but in love; she navigates without the steady voice of a man who knows her and speaks honestly into her life. His children have no picture of what a man who carries his God-given design actually looks like in daily life; the father's own unlived potential becomes the ceiling the children cannot see past. His children are drifting without calibration — no trusted voice that both knows them and tells them the true thing about where they are heading before the consequences arrive. He leads spiritually in appearance but not in private — the vertical commitment he performs on Sunday is contradicted by the man his family sees Monday through Saturday, and a life not fully lived becomes the only picture of purpose his children have. What his children are building their picture of fatherhood from is what remains — and the Reprover & Wise Mentor they needed is one of the things they are not getting. The fracture integrity creates is not loud — it is quiet and cumulative; the children do not announce the day they stopped believing him. They simply stop, and a life not fully lived becomes the only template of purpose they were given.

Scenario 117

Fractured Pillars: S (Spiritual Leader) + H2 (Heart of Integrity) + E2 (Example Who Inspires Potential) + D (Discipliner)

Solid Pillars: H1 (Husband Who Loves Sacrificially) + E1 (Encourager & Nurturer) + P (Protector & Provider) + R (Reprover & Wise Mentor)

What Happens to the Family:

Half the framework has failed, and the four pillars still standing are carrying what was designed for a complete structure. His wife carries the spiritual weight of the home alone — praying over children her husband will not lead to the altar, covering in faith a family designed to move under his authority. At the same time, his wife is married to two men — the one the world sees and the one she lives with; she has learned that the gap between his public commitments and his private behavior is real, and she carries that knowledge alone. His children grow up with a picture of God as ceremonially present and practically irrelevant — faith is what their mother did, not what their father modeled. His children will find the gap — they always do — and when they do, they will not merely lose respect for their father; they will lose their capacity to trust authority, and sometimes God, for years. His wife sees a man going through the motions of his own life — never fully alive to his design, never modeling what it looks like to pursue the thing God placed in him. Compounding this, his wife is holding the lines alone — whatever the father has stopped enforcing, she absorbs, until the weight of being the only authority in the home begins to cost her something she cannot recover. His children have no picture of what a man who carries his God-given design actually looks like in daily life; the father's own unlived potential becomes the ceiling the children cannot see past. His children are growing up in a home with no held line — not because no one cares, but because the person designed to hold it has stopped; and what a mother holds alone is never quite the same as what a father and mother hold together. He leads spiritually in appearance but not in private — the vertical commitment he performs on Sunday is contradicted by the man his family sees Monday through Saturday, and a life not fully lived becomes the only picture of purpose his children have. What his children are building their picture of fatherhood from is what remains — and the Discipliner they needed is one of the things they are not getting. The fracture integrity creates is not loud — it is quiet and cumulative; the children do not announce the day they stopped believing him. They simply stop, and a life not fully lived becomes the only template of purpose they were given.

Fractured Pillars: S (Spiritual Leader) + H2 (Heart of Integrity) + R (Reprover & Wise Mentor) + D (Discipliner)

Solid Pillars: H1 (Husband Who Loves Sacrificially) + E1 (Encourager & Nurturer) + P (Protector & Provider) + E2 (Example Who Inspires Potential)

What Happens to the Family:

Four pillars down. Four still standing. At this level, the family can see what is missing even if they cannot yet name it. His wife carries the spiritual weight of the home alone — praying over children her husband will not lead to the altar, covering in faith a family designed to move under his authority. At the same time, his wife is married to two men — the one the world sees and the one she lives with; she has learned that the gap between his public commitments and his private behavior is real, and she carries that knowledge alone. His children grow up with a picture of God as ceremonially present and practically irrelevant — faith is what their mother did, not what their father modeled. His children will find the gap — they always do — and when they do, they will not merely lose respect for their father; they will lose their capacity to trust authority, and sometimes God, for years. His wife has no one in the home willing to tell her the true thing — not in cruelty, but in love; she navigates without the steady voice of a man who knows her and speaks honestly into her life. Compounding this, his wife is holding the lines alone — whatever the father has stopped enforcing, she absorbs, until the weight of being the only authority in the home begins to cost her something she cannot recover. His children are drifting without calibration — no trusted voice that both knows them and tells them the true thing about where they are heading before the consequences arrive. His children are growing up in a home with no held line — not because no one cares, but because the person designed to hold it has stopped; and what a mother holds alone is never quite the same as what a father and mother hold together. He speaks wisdom into his children but enforces nothing — mentorship without discipline produces a child who knows what is right and has learned they do not have to do it. What his children are building their picture of fatherhood from is what remains — and the Discipliner they needed is one of the things they are not getting. The fracture integrity creates is not loud — it is quiet and cumulative; the children do not announce the day they stopped believing him. They simply stop, and he rarely sees it coming.

Scenario 119

Fractured Pillars: S (Spiritual Leader) + E2 (Example Who Inspires Potential) + R (Reprover & Wise Mentor) + D (Discipliner)

Solid Pillars: H1 (Husband Who Loves Sacrificially) + E1 (Encourager & Nurturer) + P (Protector & Provider) + H2 (Heart of Integrity)

What Happens to the Family:

Half the framework has failed. The visible architecture of fatherhood may still appear intact from the outside. Inside the home, the people who live there know something is missing. His wife carries the spiritual weight of the home alone — praying over children her husband will not lead to the altar, covering in faith a family designed to move under his authority. At the same time, his wife sees a man going through the motions of his own life — never fully alive to his design, never modeling what it looks like to pursue the thing God placed in him. His children grow up with a picture of God as ceremonially present and practically irrelevant — faith is what their mother did, not what their father modeled. His children have no picture of what a man who carries his God-given design actually looks like in daily life; the father's own unlived potential becomes the ceiling the children cannot see past. His wife has no one in the home willing to tell her the true thing — not in cruelty, but in love; she navigates without the steady voice of a man who knows her and speaks honestly into her life. Compounding this, his wife is holding the lines alone — whatever the father has stopped enforcing, she absorbs, until the weight of being the only authority in the home begins to cost her something she cannot recover. His children are drifting without calibration — no trusted voice that both knows them and tells them the true thing about where they are heading before the consequences arrive. His children are growing up in a home with no held line — not because no one cares, but because the person designed to hold it has stopped; and what a mother holds alone is never quite the same as what a father and mother hold together. He speaks into his children but has nothing to point them toward — encouragement without example produces children who feel seen but have no picture of what they are being built for, and without spiritual grounding behind it, even that purpose has no foundation. What his children are building their picture of fatherhood from is what remains — and the Discipliner they needed is one of the things they are not getting. They will reach adulthood without a template for what a man surrendered to something greater than himself actually looks like, and they will not know what they are missing until they are trying to build something themselves.

Scenario 120

Fractured Pillars: H1 (Husband Who Loves Sacrificially) + E1 (Encourager & Nurturer) + P (Protector & Provider) + H2 (Heart of Integrity)

Solid Pillars: S (Spiritual Leader) + E2 (Example Who Inspires Potential) + R (Reprover & Wise Mentor) + D (Discipliner)

What Happens to the Family:

Four pillars have failed. The remaining four are doing the work of eight — and the home bears the weight of that imbalance. His wife is not being pursued — she is being maintained; the covenant runs on autopilot, and she carries the relational weight of the marriage alone, managing rather than being led. At the same time, his wife speaks into a silence — there is no voice in the home naming what she carries, affirming who she is, or calling out what God placed in her. His children are absorbing a picture of marriage as coexistence — two people occupying the same house — and they will bring that picture into their own relationships before they understand where it came from. No one is speaking the child's design into existence before the world gets there first; their sense of self is built entirely from external mirrors — peer approval, performance, whatever fills the silence. His wife is unprotected — whether the failure is material, emotional, or spiritual; she has learned that the perimeter is unmanned and she cannot rely on him to stand between her and what threatens the home. Compounding this, his wife is married to two men — the one the world sees and the one she lives with; she has learned that the gap between his public commitments and his private behavior is real, and she carries that knowledge alone. His children are growing up inside a home with an unlocked door — exposed to whatever fills the vacuum the father has left, and no one standing watch. His children will find the gap — they always do — and when they do, they will not merely lose respect for their father; they will lose their capacity to trust authority, and sometimes God, for years. He provides for the home materially but has stopped investing in either the marriage or the people inside it — provision without pursuit, correction without naming, leaves his family feeling managed rather than known. What his children are building their picture of fatherhood from is what remains — and the Heart of Integrity they needed is one of the things they are not getting. The fracture integrity creates is not loud — it is quiet and cumulative; the children do not announce the day they stopped believing him. They simply stop, and he rarely sees it coming.

Scenario 121

Fractured Pillars: H1 (Husband Who Loves Sacrificially) + E1 (Encourager & Nurturer) + P (Protector & Provider) + E2 (Example Who Inspires Potential)

Solid Pillars: S (Spiritual Leader) + H2 (Heart of Integrity) + R (Reprover & Wise Mentor) + D (Discipliner)

What Happens to the Family:

Half the framework has failed. The home operates on four structural commitments where eight were designed to work in concert. His wife is not being pursued — she is being maintained; the covenant runs on autopilot, and she carries the relational weight of the marriage alone, managing rather than being led. At the same time, his wife speaks into a silence — there is no voice in the home naming what she carries, affirming who she is, or calling out what God placed in her. His children are absorbing a picture of marriage as coexistence — two people occupying the same house — and they will bring that picture into their own relationships before they understand where it came from. No one is speaking the child's design into existence before the world gets there first; their sense of self is built entirely from external mirrors — peer approval, performance, whatever fills the silence. His wife is unprotected — whether the failure is material, emotional, or spiritual; she has learned that the perimeter is unmanned and she cannot rely on him to stand between her and what threatens the home. Compounding this, his wife sees a man going through the motions of his own life — never fully alive to his design, never modeling what it looks like to pursue the thing God placed in him. His children are growing up inside a home with an unlocked door — exposed to whatever fills the vacuum the father has left, and no one standing watch. His children have no picture of what a man who carries his God-given design actually looks like in daily life; the father's own unlived potential becomes the ceiling the children cannot see past. He provides for the home materially but has stopped investing in either the marriage or the people inside it — provision without pursuit, correction without naming, leaves his family feeling managed rather than known. What his children are building their picture of fatherhood from is what remains — and the Example Who Inspires Potential they needed is one of the things they are not getting. Adults who were never named by their father spend their lives either achieving to fill the silence or collapsing when achievement fails to do it — and they rarely trace it back to the right source.

Scenario 122

Fractured Pillars: H1 (Husband Who Loves Sacrificially) + E1 (Encourager & Nurturer) + P (Protector & Provider) + R (Reprover & Wise Mentor)

Solid Pillars: S (Spiritual Leader) + H2 (Heart of Integrity) + E2 (Example Who Inspires Potential) + D (Discipliner)

What Happens to the Family:

Four pillars have failed. What remains — four load-bearing points where eight were designed — is carrying the weight of what has been put down. His wife is not being pursued — she is being maintained; the covenant runs on autopilot, and she carries the relational weight of the marriage alone, managing rather than being led. At the same time, his wife speaks into a silence — there is no voice in the home naming what she carries, affirming who she is, or calling out what God placed in her. His children are absorbing a picture of marriage as coexistence — two people occupying the same house — and they will bring that picture into their own relationships before they understand where it came from. No one is speaking the child's design into existence before the world gets there first; their sense of self is built entirely from external mirrors — peer approval, performance, whatever fills the silence. His wife is unprotected — whether the failure is material, emotional, or spiritual; she has learned that the perimeter is unmanned and she cannot rely on him to stand between her and what threatens the home. Compounding this, his wife has no one in the home willing to tell her the true thing — not in cruelty, but in love; she navigates without the steady voice of a man who knows her and speaks honestly into her life. His children are growing up inside a home with an unlocked door — exposed to whatever fills the vacuum the father has left, and no one standing watch. His children are drifting without calibration — no trusted voice that both knows them and tells them the true thing about where they are heading before the consequences arrive. He provides for the home materially but has stopped investing in either the marriage or the people inside it — provision without pursuit, correction without naming, leaves his family feeling managed rather than known. What his children are building their picture of fatherhood from is what remains — and the Reprover & Wise Mentor they needed is one of the things they are not getting. Adults who were never named by their father spend their lives either achieving to fill the silence or collapsing when achievement fails to do it — and they rarely trace it back to the right source.

Scenario 123

Fractured Pillars: H1 (Husband Who Loves Sacrificially) + E1 (Encourager & Nurturer) + P (Protector & Provider) + D (Discipliner)

Solid Pillars: S (Spiritual Leader) + H2 (Heart of Integrity) + E2 (Example Who Inspires Potential) + R (Reprover & Wise Mentor)

What Happens to the Family:

Half the framework is down. The four pillars still standing are real, but they were not designed to carry the home alone. His wife is not being pursued — she is being maintained; the covenant runs on autopilot, and she carries the relational weight of the marriage alone, managing rather than being led. At the same time, his wife speaks into a silence — there is no voice in the home naming what she carries, affirming who she is, or calling out what God placed in her. His children are absorbing a picture of marriage as coexistence — two people occupying the same house — and they will bring that picture into their own relationships before they understand where it came from. No one is speaking the child's design into existence before the world gets there first; their sense of self is built entirely from external mirrors — peer approval, performance, whatever fills the silence. His wife is unprotected — whether the failure is material, emotional, or spiritual; she has learned that the perimeter is unmanned and she cannot rely on him to stand between her and what threatens the home. Compounding this, his wife is holding the lines alone — whatever the father has stopped enforcing, she absorbs, until the weight of being the only authority in the home begins to cost her something she cannot recover. His children are growing up inside a home with an unlocked door — exposed to whatever fills the vacuum the father has left, and no one standing watch. His children are growing up in a home with no held line — not because no one cares, but because the person designed to hold it has stopped; and what a mother holds alone is never quite the same as what a father and mother hold together. He provides for the home materially but has stopped investing in either the marriage or the people inside it — provision without pursuit, correction without naming, leaves his family feeling managed rather than known. What his children are building their picture of fatherhood from is what remains — and the Discipliner they needed is one of the things they are not getting. The daughters will accept less than they deserve and not know why; the sons will drift toward the same emotional distance their father modeled and call it normal.

Scenario 124

Fractured Pillars: H1 (Husband Who Loves Sacrificially) + E1 (Encourager & Nurturer) + H2 (Heart of Integrity) + E2 (Example Who Inspires Potential)

Solid Pillars: S (Spiritual Leader) + P (Protector & Provider) + R (Reprover & Wise Mentor) + D (Discipliner)

What Happens to the Family:

Four pillars have failed. Four remain. The home may still look functional from the outside; inside, the people who live there know something is wrong. His wife is not being pursued — she is being maintained; the covenant runs on autopilot, and she carries the relational weight of the marriage alone, managing rather than being led. At the same time, his wife speaks into a silence — there is no voice in the home naming what she carries, affirming who she is, or calling out what God placed in her. His children are absorbing a picture of marriage as coexistence — two people occupying the same house — and they will bring that picture into their own relationships before they understand where it came from. No one is speaking the child's design into existence before the world gets there first; their sense of self is built entirely from external mirrors — peer approval, performance, whatever fills the silence. His wife is married to two men — the one the world sees and the one she lives with; she has learned that the gap between his public commitments and his private behavior is real, and she carries that knowledge alone. Compounding this, his wife sees a man going through the motions of his own life — never fully alive to his design, never modeling what it looks like to pursue the thing God placed in him. His children will find the gap — they always do — and when they do, they will not merely lose respect for their father; they will lose their capacity to trust authority, and sometimes God, for years. His children have no picture of what a man who carries his God-given design actually looks like in daily life; the father's own unlived potential becomes the ceiling the children cannot see past. He provides for the home materially but has stopped investing in either the marriage or the people inside it — provision without pursuit, correction without naming, leaves his family feeling managed rather than known. What his children are building their picture of fatherhood from is what remains — and the Example Who Inspires Potential they needed is one of the things they are not getting. The fracture integrity creates is not loud — it is quiet and cumulative; the children do not announce the day they stopped believing him. They simply stop, and a life not fully lived becomes the only template of purpose they were given.

Scenario 125

Fractured Pillars: H1 (Husband Who Loves Sacrificially) + E1 (Encourager & Nurturer) + H2 (Heart of Integrity) + R (Reprover & Wise Mentor)

Solid Pillars: S (Spiritual Leader) + P (Protector & Provider) + E2 (Example Who Inspires Potential) + D (Discipliner)

What Happens to the Family:

Half the framework has collapsed. What remains is working — but it is four pillars doing the work of eight, and it shows. His wife is not being pursued — she is being maintained; the covenant runs on autopilot, and she carries the relational weight of the marriage alone, managing rather than being led. At the same time, his wife speaks into a silence — there is no voice in the home naming what she carries, affirming who she is, or calling out what God placed in her. His children are absorbing a picture of marriage as coexistence — two people occupying the same house — and they will bring that picture into their own relationships before they understand where it came from. No one is speaking the child's design into existence before the world gets there first; their sense of self is built entirely from external mirrors — peer approval, performance, whatever fills the silence. His wife is married to two men — the one the world sees and the one she lives with; she has learned that the gap between his public commitments and his private behavior is real, and she carries that knowledge alone. Compounding this, his wife has no one in the home willing to tell her the true thing — not in cruelty, but in love; she navigates without the steady voice of a man who knows her and speaks honestly into her life. His children will find the gap — they always do — and when they do, they will not merely lose respect for their father; they will lose their capacity to trust authority, and sometimes God, for years. His children are drifting without calibration — no trusted voice that both knows them and tells them the true thing about where they are heading before the consequences arrive. He provides for the home materially but has stopped investing in either the marriage or the people inside it — provision without pursuit, correction without naming, leaves his family feeling managed rather than known. What his children are building their picture of fatherhood from is what remains — and the Reprover & Wise Mentor they needed is one of the things they are not getting. The fracture integrity creates is not loud — it is quiet and cumulative; the children do not announce the day they stopped believing him. They simply stop, and he rarely sees it coming.

Scenario 126

Fractured Pillars: H1 (Husband Who Loves Sacrificially) + E1 (Encourager & Nurturer) + H2 (Heart of Integrity) + D (Discipliner)

Solid Pillars: S (Spiritual Leader) + P (Protector & Provider) + E2 (Example Who Inspires Potential) + R (Reprover & Wise Mentor)

What Happens to the Family:

Four of the eight pillars have failed. The home is operating at half its structural capacity, and the family is living inside the gap. His wife is not being pursued — she is being maintained; the covenant runs on autopilot, and she carries the relational weight of the marriage alone, managing rather than being led. At the same time, his wife speaks into a silence — there is no voice in the home naming what she carries, affirming who she is, or calling out what God placed in her. His children are absorbing a picture of marriage as coexistence — two people occupying the same house — and they will bring that picture into their own relationships before they understand where it came from. No one is speaking the child's design into existence before the world gets there first; their sense of self is built entirely from external mirrors — peer approval, performance, whatever fills the silence. His wife is married to two men — the one the world sees and the one she lives with; she has learned that the gap between his public commitments and his private behavior is real, and she carries that knowledge alone. Compounding this, his wife is holding the lines alone — whatever the father has stopped enforcing, she absorbs, until the weight of being the only authority in the home begins to cost her something she cannot recover. His children will find the gap — they always do — and when they do, they will not merely lose respect for their father; they will lose their capacity to trust authority, and sometimes God, for years. His children are growing up in a home with no held line — not because no one cares, but because the person designed to hold it has stopped; and what a mother holds alone is never quite the same as what a father and mother hold together. He provides for the home materially but has stopped investing in either the marriage or the people inside it — provision without pursuit, correction without naming, leaves his family feeling managed rather than known. What his children are building their picture of fatherhood from is what remains — and the Discipliner they needed is one of the things they are not getting. The daughters will accept less than they deserve and not know why; the sons will drift toward the same emotional distance their father modeled and call it normal.

Scenario 127

Fractured Pillars: H1 (Husband Who Loves Sacrificially) + E1 (Encourager & Nurturer) + E2 (Example Who Inspires Potential) + R (Reprover & Wise Mentor)

Solid Pillars: S (Spiritual Leader) + P (Protector & Provider) + H2 (Heart of Integrity) + D (Discipliner)

What Happens to the Family:

Half the framework has failed, and the four pillars still standing are carrying what was designed for a complete structure. His wife is not being pursued — she is being maintained; the covenant runs on autopilot, and she carries the relational weight of the marriage alone, managing rather than being led. At the same time, his wife speaks into a silence — there is no voice in the home naming what she carries, affirming who she is, or calling out what God placed in her. His children are absorbing a picture of marriage as coexistence — two people occupying the same house — and they will bring that picture into their own relationships before they understand where it came from. No one is speaking the child's design into existence before the world gets there first; their sense of self is built entirely from external mirrors — peer approval, performance, whatever fills the silence. His wife sees a man going through the motions of his own life — never fully alive to his design, never modeling what it looks like to pursue the thing God placed in him. Compounding this, his wife has no one in the home willing to tell her the true thing — not in cruelty, but in love; she navigates without the steady voice of a man who knows her and speaks honestly into her life. His children have no picture of what a man who carries his God-given design actually looks like in daily life; the father's own unlived potential becomes the ceiling the children cannot see past. His children are drifting without calibration — no trusted voice that both knows them and tells them the true thing about where they are heading before the consequences arrive. He provides for the home materially but has stopped investing in either the marriage or the people inside it — provision without pursuit, correction without naming, leaves his family feeling managed rather than known. What his children are building their picture of fatherhood from is what remains — and the Reprover & Wise Mentor they needed is one of the things they are not getting. Adults who were never named by their father spend their lives either achieving to fill the silence or collapsing when achievement fails to do it — and they rarely trace it back to the right source.

Scenario 128

Fractured Pillars: H1 (Husband Who Loves Sacrificially) + E1 (Encourager & Nurturer) + E2 (Example Who Inspires Potential) + D (Discipliner)

Solid Pillars: S (Spiritual Leader) + P (Protector & Provider) + H2 (Heart of Integrity) + R (Reprover & Wise Mentor)

What Happens to the Family:

Four pillars down. Four still standing. At this level, the family can see what is missing even if they cannot yet name it. His wife is not being pursued — she is being maintained; the covenant runs on autopilot, and she carries the relational weight of the marriage alone, managing rather than being led. At the same time, his wife speaks into a silence — there is no voice in the home naming what she carries, affirming who she is, or calling out what God placed in her. His children are absorbing a picture of marriage as coexistence — two people occupying the same house — and they will bring that picture into their own relationships before they understand where it came from. No one is speaking the child's design into existence before the world gets there first; their sense of self is built entirely from external mirrors — peer approval, performance, whatever fills the silence. His wife sees a man going through the motions of his own life — never fully alive to his design, never modeling what it looks like to pursue the thing God placed in him. Compounding this, his wife is holding the lines alone — whatever the father has stopped enforcing, she absorbs, until the weight of being the only authority in the home begins to cost her something she cannot recover. His children have no picture of what a man who carries his God-given design actually looks like in daily life; the father's own unlived potential becomes the ceiling the children cannot see past. His children are growing up in a home with no held line — not because no one cares, but because the person designed to hold it has stopped; and what a mother holds alone is never quite the same as what a father and mother hold together. He provides for the home materially but has stopped investing in either the marriage or the people inside it — provision without pursuit, correction without naming, leaves his family feeling managed rather than known. What his children are building their picture of fatherhood from is what remains — and the Discipliner they needed is one of the things they are not getting. The daughters will accept less than they deserve and not know why; the sons will drift toward the same emotional distance their father modeled and call it normal.

***

Scenario 129

Fractured Pillars: H1 (Husband Who Loves Sacrificially) + E1 (Encourager & Nurturer) + R (Reprover & Wise Mentor) + D (Discipliner)

Solid Pillars: S (Spiritual Leader) + P (Protector & Provider) + H2 (Heart of Integrity) + E2 (Example Who Inspires Potential)

What Happens to the Family:

Half the framework has failed. The visible architecture of fatherhood may still appear intact from the outside. Inside the home, the people who live there know something is missing. His wife is not being pursued — she is being maintained; the covenant runs on autopilot, and she carries the relational weight of the marriage alone, managing rather than being led. At the same time, his wife speaks into a silence — there is no voice in the home naming what she carries, affirming who she is, or calling out what God placed in her. His children are absorbing a picture of marriage as coexistence — two people occupying the same house — and they will bring that picture into their own relationships before they understand where it came from. No one is speaking the child's design into existence before the world gets there first; their sense of self is built entirely from external mirrors — peer approval, performance, whatever fills the silence. His wife has no one in the home willing to tell her the true thing — not in cruelty, but in love; she navigates without the steady voice of a man who knows her and speaks honestly into her life. Compounding this, his wife is holding the lines alone — whatever the father has stopped enforcing, she absorbs, until the weight of being the only authority in the home begins to cost her something she cannot recover. His children are drifting without calibration — no trusted voice that both knows them and tells them the true thing about where they are heading before the consequences arrive. His children are growing up in a home with no held line — not because no one cares, but because the person designed to hold it has stopped; and what a mother holds alone is never quite the same as what a father and mother hold together. He provides for the home materially but has stopped investing in either the marriage or the people inside it — provision without pursuit, correction without naming, leaves his family feeling managed rather than known. What his children are building their picture of fatherhood from is what remains — and the Discipliner they needed is one of the things they are not getting. The daughters will accept less than they deserve and not know why; the sons will drift toward the same emotional distance their father modeled and call it normal.

Scenario 130

Fractured Pillars: H1 (Husband Who Loves Sacrificially) + P (Protector & Provider) + H2 (Heart of Integrity) + E2 (Example Who Inspires Potential)

Solid Pillars: S (Spiritual Leader) + E1 (Encourager & Nurturer) + R (Reprover & Wise Mentor) + D (Discipliner)

What Happens to the Family:

Four pillars have failed. The remaining four are doing the work of eight — and the home bears the weight of that imbalance. His wife is not being pursued — she is being maintained; the covenant runs on autopilot, and she carries the relational weight of the marriage alone, managing rather than being led. At the same time, his wife is unprotected — whether the failure is material, emotional, or spiritual; she has learned that the perimeter is unmanned and she cannot rely on him to stand between her and what threatens the home. His children are absorbing a picture of marriage as coexistence — two people occupying the same house — and they will bring that picture into their own relationships before they understand where it came from. His children are growing up inside a home with an unlocked door — exposed to whatever fills the vacuum the father has left, and no one standing watch. His wife is married to two men — the one the world sees and the one she lives with; she has learned that the gap between his public commitments and his private behavior is real, and she carries that knowledge alone. Compounding this, his wife sees a man going through the motions of his own life — never fully alive to his design, never modeling what it looks like to pursue the thing God placed in him. His children will find the gap — they always do — and when they do, they will not merely lose respect for their father; they will lose their capacity to trust authority, and sometimes God, for years. His children have no picture of what a man who carries his God-given design actually looks like in daily life; the father's own unlived potential becomes the ceiling the children cannot see past. He leads spiritually in appearance but not in private — the vertical commitment he performs on Sunday is contradicted by the man his family sees Monday through Saturday, and a life not fully lived becomes the only picture of purpose his children have. What his children are building their picture of fatherhood from is what remains — and the Example Who Inspires Potential they needed is one of the things they are not getting. The fracture integrity creates is not loud — it is quiet and cumulative; the children do not announce the day they stopped believing him. They simply stop, and a life not fully lived becomes the only template of purpose they were given.

Scenario 131

Fractured Pillars: H1 (Husband Who Loves Sacrificially) + P (Protector & Provider) + H2 (Heart of Integrity) + R (Reprover & Wise Mentor)

Solid Pillars: S (Spiritual Leader) + E1 (Encourager & Nurturer) + E2 (Example Who Inspires Potential) + D (Discipliner)

What Happens to the Family:

Half the framework has failed. The home operates on four structural commitments where eight were designed to work in concert. His wife is not being pursued — she is being maintained; the covenant runs on autopilot, and she carries the relational weight of the marriage alone, managing rather than being led. At the same time, his wife is unprotected — whether the failure is material, emotional, or spiritual; she has learned that the perimeter is unmanned and she cannot rely on him to stand between her and what threatens the home. His children are absorbing a picture of marriage as coexistence — two people occupying the same house — and they will bring that picture into their own relationships before they understand where it came from. His children are growing up inside a home with an unlocked door — exposed to whatever fills the vacuum the father has left, and no one standing watch. His wife is married to two men — the one the world sees and the one she lives with; she has learned that the gap between his public commitments and his private behavior is real, and she carries that knowledge alone. Compounding this, his wife has no one in the home willing to tell her the true thing — not in cruelty, but in love; she navigates without the steady voice of a man who knows her and speaks honestly into her life. His children will find the gap — they always do — and when they do, they will not merely lose respect for their father; they will lose their capacity to trust authority, and sometimes God, for years. His children are drifting without calibration — no trusted voice that both knows them and tells them the true thing about where they are heading before the consequences arrive. He leads spiritually in appearance but not in private — the vertical commitment he performs on Sunday is contradicted by the man his family sees Monday through Saturday. What his children are building their picture of fatherhood from is what remains —

and the Reprover & Wise Mentor they needed is one of the things they are not getting. The fracture integrity creates is not loud — it is quiet and cumulative; the children do not announce the day they stopped believing him. They simply stop, and he rarely sees it coming.

Scenario 132

Fractured Pillars: H1 (Husband Who Loves Sacrificially) + P (Protector & Provider) + H2 (Heart of Integrity) + D (Discipliner)

Solid Pillars: S (Spiritual Leader) + E1 (Encourager & Nurturer) + E2 (Example Who Inspires Potential) + R (Reprover & Wise Mentor)

What Happens to the Family:

Four pillars have failed. What remains — four load-bearing points where eight were designed — is carrying the weight of what has been put down. His wife is not being pursued — she is being maintained; the covenant runs on autopilot, and she carries the relational weight of the marriage alone, managing rather than being led. At the same time, his wife is unprotected — whether the failure is material, emotional, or spiritual; she has learned that the perimeter is unmanned and she cannot rely on him to stand between her and what threatens the home. His children are absorbing a picture of marriage as coexistence — two people occupying the same house — and they will bring that picture into their own relationships before they understand where it came from. His children are growing up inside a home with an unlocked door — exposed to whatever fills the vacuum the father has left, and no one standing watch. His wife is married to two men — the one the world sees and the one she lives with; she has learned that the gap between his public commitments and his private behavior is real, and she carries that knowledge alone. Compounding this, his wife is holding the lines alone — whatever the father has stopped enforcing, she absorbs, until the weight of being the only authority in the home begins to cost her something she cannot recover. His children will find the gap — they always do — and when they do, they will not merely lose respect for their father; they will lose their capacity to trust authority, and sometimes God, for years. His children are growing up in a home with no held line — not because no one cares, but because the person designed to hold it has stopped; and what a mother holds alone is never quite the same as what a father and mother hold together. He leads spiritually in appearance but not in private — the vertical commitment he performs on Sunday is contradicted by the man his family sees Monday through Saturday. What his children are building their picture of fatherhood from is what remains — and the Discipliner they needed is one of the things they are not getting. The daughters will accept less than they deserve and not know why; the sons will drift toward the same emotional distance their father modeled and call it normal.

Scenario 133

Fractured Pillars: H1 (Husband Who Loves Sacrificially) + P (Protector & Provider) + E2 (Example Who Inspires Potential) + R (Reprover & Wise Mentor)

Solid Pillars: S (Spiritual Leader) + E1 (Encourager & Nurturer) + H2 (Heart of Integrity) + D (Discipliner)

What Happens to the Family:

Half the framework is down. The four pillars still standing are real, but they were not designed to carry the home alone. His wife is not being pursued — she is being maintained; the covenant runs on autopilot, and she carries the relational weight of the marriage alone, managing rather than being led. At the same time, his wife is unprotected — whether the failure is material, emotional, or spiritual; she has learned that the perimeter is unmanned and she cannot rely on him to stand between her and what threatens the home. His children are absorbing a picture of marriage as coexistence — two people occupying the same house — and they will bring that picture into their own relationships before they understand where it came from. His children are growing up inside a home with an unlocked door — exposed to whatever fills the vacuum the father has left, and no one standing watch. His wife sees a man going through the motions of his own life — never fully alive to his design, never modeling what it looks like to pursue the thing God placed in him. Compounding this, his wife has no one in the home willing to tell her the true thing — not in cruelty, but in love; she navigates without the steady voice of a man who knows her and speaks honestly into her life. His children have no picture of what a man who carries his God-given design actually looks like in daily life; the father's own unlived potential becomes the ceiling the children cannot see past. His children are drifting without calibration — no trusted voice that both knows them and tells them the true thing about where they are heading before the consequences arrive. He provides for the family materially but has stopped investing in the marriage — provision without pursuit leaves his wife feeling like a dependent, not a covenant partner. What his children are building their picture of fatherhood from is what remains — and the Reprover & Wise Mentor they needed is one of the things they are not getting. They will reach adulthood without a template for what a man surrendered to something greater than himself actually looks like, and they will not know what they are missing until they are trying to build something themselves.

Scenario 134

Fractured Pillars: H1 (Husband Who Loves Sacrificially) + P (Protector & Provider) + E2 (Example Who Inspires Potential) + D (Discipliner)

Solid Pillars: S (Spiritual Leader) + E1 (Encourager & Nurturer) + H2 (Heart of Integrity) + R (Reprover & Wise Mentor)

What Happens to the Family:

Four pillars have failed. Four remain. The home may still look functional from the outside; inside, the people who live there know something is wrong. His wife is not being pursued — she is being maintained; the covenant runs on autopilot, and she carries the relational weight of the marriage alone, managing rather than being led. At the same time, his wife is unprotected — whether the failure is material, emotional, or spiritual; she has learned that the perimeter is unmanned and she cannot rely on him to stand between her and what threatens the home. His children are absorbing a picture of marriage as coexistence — two people occupying the same house — and they will bring that picture into their own relationships before they understand where it came from. His children are growing up inside a home with an unlocked door — exposed to whatever fills the vacuum the father has left, and no one standing watch. His wife sees a man going through the motions of his own life — never fully alive to his design, never modeling what it looks like to pursue the thing God placed in him. Compounding this, his wife is holding the lines alone — whatever the father has stopped enforcing, she absorbs, until the weight of being the only authority in the home begins to cost her something she cannot recover. His children have no picture of what a man who carries his God-given design actually looks like in daily life; the father's own unlived potential becomes the ceiling the children cannot see past. His children are growing up in a home with no held line — not because no one cares, but because the person designed to hold it has stopped; and what a mother holds alone is never quite the same as what a father and mother hold together. He tries to hold lines in the home but has stopped providing the covering that makes discipline feel like love rather than control — children without protection experience correction as threat. What his children are building their picture of fatherhood from is what remains — and the

Discipliner they needed is one of the things they are not getting. The daughters will accept less than they deserve and not know why; the sons will drift toward the same emotional distance their father modeled and call it normal.

Scenario 135

Fractured Pillars: H1 (Husband Who Loves Sacrificially) + P (Protector & Provider) + R (Reprover & Wise Mentor) + D (Discipliner)

Solid Pillars: S (Spiritual Leader) + E1 (Encourager & Nurturer) + H2 (Heart of Integrity) + E2 (Example Who Inspires Potential)

What Happens to the Family:

Half the framework has collapsed. What remains is working — but it is four pillars doing the work of eight, and it shows. His wife is not being pursued — she is being maintained; the covenant runs on autopilot, and she carries the relational weight of the marriage alone, managing rather than being led. At the same time, his wife is unprotected — whether the failure is material, emotional, or spiritual; she has learned that the perimeter is unmanned and she cannot rely on him to stand between her and what threatens the home. His children are absorbing a picture of marriage as coexistence — two people occupying the same house — and they will bring that picture into their own relationships before they understand where it came from. His children are growing up inside a home with an unlocked door — exposed to whatever fills the vacuum the father has left, and no one standing watch. His wife has no one in the home willing to tell her the true thing — not in cruelty, but in love;

she navigates without the steady voice of a man who knows her and speaks honestly into her life. Compounding this, his wife is holding the lines alone — whatever the father has stopped enforcing, she absorbs, until the weight of being the only authority in the home begins to cost her something she cannot recover. His children are drifting without calibration — no trusted voice that both knows them and tells them the true thing about where they are heading before the consequences arrive. His children are growing up in a home with no held line — not because no one cares, but because the person designed to hold it has stopped; and what a mother holds alone is never quite the same as what a father and mother hold together. He tries to hold lines in the home but has stopped providing the covering that makes discipline feel like love rather than control — children without protection experience correction as threat. What his children are building their picture of fatherhood from is what remains — and the Discipliner they needed is one of the things they are not getting. The daughters will accept less than they deserve and not know why; the sons will drift toward the same emotional distance their father modeled and call it normal.

Scenario 136

Fractured Pillars: H1 (Husband Who Loves Sacrificially) + H2 (Heart of Integrity) + E2 (Example Who Inspires Potential) + R (Reprover & Wise Mentor)

Solid Pillars: S (Spiritual Leader) + E1 (Encourager & Nurturer) + P (Protector & Provider) + D (Discipliner)

What Happens to the Family:

Four of the eight pillars have failed. The home is operating at half its structural capacity, and the family is living inside the gap. His wife is not being pursued — she is being maintained; the covenant runs on autopilot, and she carries the relational weight of the marriage alone, managing rather than being led. At the same time, his wife is married to two men — the one the world sees and the one she lives with; she has learned that the gap between his public commitments and his private behavior is real, and she carries that knowledge alone. His children are absorbing a picture of marriage as coexistence — two people occupying the same house — and they will bring that picture into their own relationships before they understand where it came from. His children will find the gap — they always do — and when they do, they will not merely lose respect for their father; they will lose their capacity to trust authority, and sometimes God, for years. His wife sees a man going through the motions of his own life — never fully alive to his design, never modeling what it looks like to pursue the thing God placed in him. Compounding this, his wife has no one in the home willing to tell her the true thing — not in cruelty, but in love; she navigates without the steady voice of a man who knows her and speaks honestly into her life. His children have no picture of what a man who carries his God-given design actually looks like in daily life; the father's own unlived potential becomes the ceiling the children cannot see past. His children are drifting without calibration — no trusted voice that both knows them and tells them the true thing about where they are heading before the consequences arrive. He leads spiritually in appearance but not in private — the vertical commitment he performs on Sunday is contradicted by the man his family sees Monday through Saturday, and a life not fully lived becomes the only picture of purpose his children have. What his children are building their picture of fatherhood from is what remains — and the Reprover & Wise Mentor they needed is one of the things they are not getting. The fracture integrity creates is not loud — it is quiet and cumulative; the children do not announce the day they stopped believing him. They simply stop, and a life not fully lived becomes the only template of purpose they were given.

Scenario 137

Fractured Pillars: H1 (Husband Who Loves Sacrificially) + H2 (Heart of Integrity) + E2 (Example Who Inspires Potential) + D (Discipliner)

Solid Pillars: S (Spiritual Leader) + E1 (Encourager & Nurturer) + P (Protector & Provider) + R (Reprover & Wise Mentor)

What Happens to the Family:

Half the framework has failed, and the four pillars still standing are carrying what was designed for a complete structure. His wife is not being pursued — she is being maintained; the covenant runs on autopilot, and she carries the relational weight of the marriage alone, managing rather than being led. At the same time, his wife is married to two men — the one the world sees and the one she lives with; she has learned that the gap between his public commitments and his private behavior is real, and she carries that knowledge alone. His children are absorbing a picture of marriage as coexistence — two people occupying the same house — and they will bring that picture into their own relationships before they understand where it came from. His children will find the gap — they always do — and when they do, they will not merely lose respect for their father; they will lose their capacity to trust authority, and sometimes God, for years. His wife sees a man going through the motions of his own life — never fully alive to his design, never modeling what it looks like to pursue the thing God placed in him. Compounding this, his wife is holding the lines alone — whatever the father has stopped enforcing, she absorbs, until the weight of being the only authority in the home begins to cost her something she cannot recover. His children have no picture of what a man who carries his God-given design actually looks like in daily life; the father's own unlived potential becomes the ceiling the children cannot see past. His children are growing up in a home with no held line — not because no one cares, but because the person designed to hold it has stopped; and what a mother holds alone is never quite the same as what a father and mother hold together. He leads spiritually in appearance but not in private — the vertical commitment he performs on Sunday is contradicted by the man his family sees Monday through Saturday, and a life not fully lived becomes the only picture of purpose his children have. What his children are building their picture of fatherhood from is what remains — and the Discipliner they needed is one of the things they are not getting. The daughters will accept less than they deserve and not know why; the sons will drift toward the same emotional distance their father modeled and call it normal.

Scenario 138

Fractured Pillars: H1 (Husband Who Loves Sacrificially) + H2 (Heart of Integrity) + R (Reprover & Wise Mentor) + D (Discipliner)

Solid Pillars: S (Spiritual Leader) + E1 (Encourager & Nurturer) + P (Protector & Provider) + E2 (Example Who Inspires Potential)

What Happens to the Family:

Four pillars down. Four still standing. At this level, the family can see what is missing even if they cannot yet name it. His wife is not being pursued — she is being maintained; the covenant runs on autopilot, and she carries the relational weight of the marriage alone, managing rather than being led. At the same time, his wife is married to two men — the one the world sees and the one she lives with; she has learned that the gap between his public commitments and his private behavior is real, and she carries that knowledge alone. His children are absorbing a picture of marriage as coexistence — two people occupying the same house — and they will bring that picture into their own relationships before they understand where it came from. His children will find the gap — they always do — and when they do, they will not merely lose respect for their father; they will lose their capacity to trust authority, and sometimes God, for years. His wife has no one in the home willing to tell her the true thing — not in cruelty, but in love; she navigates without the steady voice of a man who knows her and speaks honestly into her life. Compounding this, his wife is holding the lines alone — whatever the father has stopped enforcing, she absorbs, until the weight of being the only authority in the home begins to cost her something she cannot recover. His children are drifting without calibration — no trusted voice that both knows them and tells them the true thing about where they are heading before the consequences arrive. His children are growing up in a home with no held line — not because no one cares, but because the person designed to hold it has stopped; and what a mother holds alone is never quite the same as what a father and mother hold together. He leads spiritually in appearance but not in private — the vertical commitment he performs on Sunday is contradicted by the man his family sees Monday through Saturday. What his children are building their picture of fatherhood from is what remains — and the Discipliner they needed is one of the things they are not getting. The daughters will accept less than they deserve and not know why; the sons will drift toward the same emotional distance their father modeled and call it normal.

Scenario 139

Fractured Pillars: H1 (Husband Who Loves Sacrificially) + E2 (Example Who Inspires Potential) + R (Reprover & Wise Mentor) + D (Discipliner)

Solid Pillars: S (Spiritual Leader) + E1 (Encourager & Nurturer) + P (Protector & Provider) + H2 (Heart of Integrity)

What Happens to the Family:

Half the framework has failed. The visible architecture of fatherhood may still appear intact from the outside. Inside the home, the people who live there know something is missing. His wife is not being pursued — she is being maintained; the covenant runs on autopilot, and she carries the relational weight of the marriage alone, managing rather than being led. At the same time, his wife sees a man going through the motions of his own life — never fully alive to his design, never modeling what it looks like to pursue the thing God placed in him. His children are absorbing a picture of marriage as coexistence — two people occupying the same house — and they will bring that picture into their own relationships before they understand where it came from. His children have no picture of what a man who carries his God-given design actually looks like in daily life; the father's own unlived potential becomes the ceiling the children cannot see past. His wife has no one in the home willing to tell her the true thing — not in cruelty, but in love; she navigates without the steady voice of a man who knows her and speaks honestly into her life. Compounding this, his wife is holding the lines alone — whatever the father has stopped enforcing, she absorbs, until the weight of being the only authority in the home begins to cost her something she cannot recover. His children are drifting without calibration — no trusted voice that both knows them and tells them the true thing about where they are heading before the consequences arrive. His children are growing up in a home with no held line — not because no one cares, but because the person designed to hold it has stopped; and what a mother holds alone is never quite the same as what a father and mother hold together. He speaks wisdom into his children but enforces nothing — mentorship without discipline produces a child who knows what is right and has learned they do not have to do it. What his children are building their picture of fatherhood from is what remains — and the Discipliner they needed is one of the things they are not getting. The daughters will accept less than they deserve and not know why; the sons will drift toward the same emotional distance their father modeled and call it normal.

Scenario 140

Fractured Pillars: E1 (Encourager & Nurturer) + P (Protector & Provider) + H2 (Heart of Integrity) + E2 (Example Who Inspires Potential)

Solid Pillars: S (Spiritual Leader) + H1 (Husband Who Loves Sacrificially) + R (Reprover & Wise Mentor) + D (Discipliner)

What Happens to the Family:

Four pillars have failed. The remaining four are doing the work of eight — and the home bears the weight of that imbalance. His wife speaks into a silence — there is no voice in the home naming what she carries, affirming who she is, or calling out what God placed in her. At the same time, his wife is unprotected — whether the failure is material, emotional, or spiritual; she has learned that the perimeter is unmanned and she cannot rely on him to stand between her and what threatens the home. No one is speaking the child's design into existence before the world gets there first; their sense of self is built entirely from external mirrors — peer approval, performance, whatever fills the silence. His children are growing up inside a home with an unlocked door — exposed to whatever fills the vacuum the father has left, and no one standing watch. His wife is married to two men — the one the world sees and the one she lives with; she has learned that the gap between his public commitments and his private behavior is real, and she carries that knowledge alone. Compounding this, his wife sees a man going through the motions of his own life — never fully alive to his design, never modeling what it looks like to pursue the thing God placed in him. His children will find the gap — they always do — and when they do, they will not merely lose respect for their father; they will lose their capacity to trust authority, and sometimes God, for years. His children have no picture of what a man who carries his God-given design actually looks like in daily life; the father's own unlived potential becomes the ceiling the children cannot see past. He leads spiritually in appearance but not in private — the vertical commitment he performs on Sunday is contradicted by the man his family sees Monday through Saturday, and a life not fully lived becomes the only picture of purpose his children have. What his children are building their picture of fatherhood from is what remains — and the Example Who Inspires Potential they needed is one of the things they are not getting. The fracture integrity creates is not loud — it is quiet and cumulative; the children do not announce the day they stopped believing him. They simply stop, and a life not fully lived becomes the only template of purpose they were given.

Scenario 141

Fractured Pillars: E1 (Encourager & Nurturer) + P (Protector & Provider) + H2 (Heart of Integrity) + R (Reprover & Wise Mentor)

Solid Pillars: S (Spiritual Leader) + H1 (Husband Who Loves Sacrificially) + E2 (Example Who Inspires Potential) + D (Discipliner)

What Happens to the Family:

Half the framework has failed. The home operates on four structural commitments where eight were designed to work in concert. His wife speaks into a silence — there is no voice in the home naming what she carries, affirming who she is, or calling out what God placed in her. At the same time, his wife is unprotected — whether the failure is material, emotional, or spiritual; she has learned that the perimeter is unmanned and she cannot rely on him to stand between her and what threatens the home. No one is speaking the child's design into existence before the world gets there first; their sense of self is built entirely from external mirrors — peer approval, performance, whatever fills the silence. His children are growing up inside a home with an unlocked door — exposed to whatever fills the vacuum the father has left, and no one standing watch. His wife is married to two men — the one the world sees and the one she lives with; she has learned that the gap between his public commitments and his private behavior is real, and she carries that knowledge alone. Compounding this, his wife has no one in the home willing to tell her the true thing — not in cruelty, but in love; she navigates without the steady voice of a man who knows her and speaks honestly into her life. His children will find the gap — they always do — and when they do, they will not merely lose respect for their father; they will lose their capacity to trust authority, and sometimes God, for years. His children are drifting without calibration — no trusted voice that both knows them and tells them the true thing about where they are heading before the consequences arrive. He leads spiritually in appearance but not in private — the vertical commitment he performs on Sunday is contradicted by the man his family sees Monday through Saturday. What his children are building their picture of fatherhood from is what remains — and the Reprover & Wise Mentor they needed is one of the things they are not getting. The fracture integrity creates is not loud — it is quiet and cumulative; the children do not announce the day they stopped believing him. They simply stop, and he rarely sees it coming.

Scenario 142

Fractured Pillars: E1 (Encourager & Nurturer) + P (Protector & Provider) + H2 (Heart of Integrity) + D (Discipliner)

Solid Pillars: S (Spiritual Leader) + H1 (Husband Who Loves Sacrificially) + E2 (Example Who Inspires Potential) + R (Reprover & Wise Mentor)

What Happens to the Family:

Four pillars have failed. What remains — four load-bearing points where eight were designed — is carrying the weight of what has been put down. His wife speaks into a silence — there is no voice in the home naming what she carries, affirming who she is, or calling out what God placed in her. At the same time, his wife is unprotected — whether the failure is material, emotional, or spiritual; she has learned that the perimeter is unmanned and she cannot rely on him to stand between her and what threatens the home. No one is speaking the child's design into existence before the world gets there first; their sense of self is built entirely from external mirrors — peer approval, performance, whatever fills the silence. His children are growing up inside a home with an unlocked door — exposed to whatever fills the vacuum the father has left, and no one standing watch. His wife is married to two men — the one the world sees and the one she lives with; she has learned that the gap between his public commitments and his private behavior is real, and she carries that knowledge alone. Compounding this, his wife is holding the lines alone — whatever the father has stopped enforcing, she absorbs, until the weight of being the only authority in the home begins to cost her something she cannot recover. His children will find the gap — they always do — and when they do, they will not merely lose respect for their father; they will lose their capacity to trust authority, and sometimes God, for years. His children are growing up in a home with no held line — not because no one cares, but because the person designed to hold it has stopped; and what a mother holds alone is never quite the same as what a father and mother hold together. He leads spiritually in appearance but not in private — the vertical commitment he performs on Sunday is contradicted by the man his family sees Monday through Saturday. What his children are building their picture of fatherhood from is what remains — and the Discipliner they needed is one of the things they are not getting. The fracture integrity creates is not loud — it is quiet and cumulative; the children do not announce the day they stopped believing him. They simply stop, and he rarely sees it coming.

Scenario 143

Fractured Pillars: E1 (Encourager & Nurturer) + P (Protector & Provider) + E2 (Example Who Inspires Potential) + R (Reprover & Wise Mentor)

Solid Pillars: S (Spiritual Leader) + H1 (Husband Who Loves Sacrificially) + H2 (Heart of Integrity) + D (Discipliner)

What Happens to the Family:

Half the framework is down. The four pillars still standing are real, but they were not designed to carry the home alone. His wife speaks into a silence — there is no voice in the home naming what she carries, affirming who she is, or calling out what God placed in her. At the same time, his wife is unprotected — whether the failure is material, emotional, or spiritual; she has learned that the perimeter is unmanned and she cannot rely on him to stand between her and what threatens the home. No one is speaking the child's design into existence before the world gets there first; their sense of self is built entirely from external mirrors — peer approval, performance, whatever fills the silence. His children are growing up inside a home with an unlocked door — exposed to whatever fills the vacuum the father has left, and no one standing watch. His wife sees a man going through the motions of his own life — never fully alive to his design, never modeling what it looks like to pursue the thing God placed in him. Compounding this, his wife has no one in the home willing to tell her the true thing — not in cruelty, but in love; she navigates without the steady voice of a man who knows her and speaks honestly into her life. His children have no picture of what a man who carries his God-given design actually looks like in daily life; the father's own unlived potential becomes the ceiling the children cannot see past. His children are drifting without calibration — no trusted voice that both knows them and tells them the true thing about where they are heading before the consequences arrive. He disciplines his children but offers neither naming nor wisdom with it — correction without encouragement or mentorship teaches a child what the line is, but not who they are or why the line matters. What his children are building their picture of fatherhood from is what remains — and the Reprover & Wise Mentor they needed is one of the things they are not getting. Adults who were never named by their father spend their lives either achieving to fill the silence or collapsing when achievement fails to do it — and they rarely trace it back to the right source.

Scenario 144

Fractured Pillars: E1 (Encourager & Nurturer) + P (Protector & Provider) + E2 (Example Who Inspires Potential) + D (Discipliner)

Solid Pillars: S (Spiritual Leader) + H1 (Husband Who Loves Sacrificially) + H2 (Heart of Integrity) + R (Reprover & Wise Mentor)

What Happens to the Family:

Four pillars have failed. Four remain. The home may still look functional from the outside; inside, the people who live there know something is wrong. His wife speaks into a silence — there is no voice in the home naming what she carries, affirming who she is, or calling out what God placed in her. At the same time, his wife is unprotected — whether the failure is material, emotional, or spiritual; she has learned that the perimeter is unmanned and she cannot rely on him to stand between her and what threatens the home. No one is speaking the child's design into existence before the world gets there first; their sense of self is built entirely from external mirrors — peer approval, performance, whatever fills the silence. His children are growing up inside a home with an unlocked door — exposed to whatever fills the vacuum the father has left, and no one standing watch. His wife sees a man going through the motions of his own life — never fully alive to his design, never modeling what it looks like to pursue the thing God placed in him. Compounding this, his wife is holding the lines alone — whatever the father has stopped enforcing, she absorbs, until the weight of being the only authority in the home begins to cost her something she cannot recover. His children have no picture of what a man who carries his God-given design actually looks like in daily life; the father's own unlived potential becomes the ceiling the children cannot see past. His children are growing up in a home with no held line — not because no one cares, but because the person designed to hold it has stopped; and what a mother holds alone is never quite the same as what a father and mother hold together. He tries to hold lines in the home but has stopped providing the covering that makes discipline feel like love rather than control — children without protection experience correction as threat. What his children are building their picture of fatherhood from is what remains — and the Discipliner they needed is one of the things they are not getting. Adults who were never named by their father spend their lives either achieving to fill the silence or collapsing when achievement fails to do it — and they rarely trace it back to the right source.

Scenario 145

Fractured Pillars: E1 (Encourager & Nurturer) + P (Protector & Provider) + R (Reprover & Wise Mentor) + D (Discipliner)

Solid Pillars: S (Spiritual Leader) + H1 (Husband Who Loves Sacrificially) + H2 (Heart of Integrity) + E2 (Example Who Inspires Potential)

What Happens to the Family:

Half the framework has collapsed. What remains is working — but it is four pillars doing the work of eight, and it shows. His wife speaks into a silence — there is no voice in the home naming what she carries, affirming who she is, or calling out what God placed in her. At the same time, his wife is unprotected — whether the failure is material, emotional, or spiritual; she has learned that the perimeter is unmanned and she cannot rely on him to stand between her and what threatens the home. No one is speaking the child's design into existence before the world gets there first; their sense of self is built entirely from external mirrors — peer approval, performance, whatever fills the silence. His children are growing up inside a home with an unlocked door — exposed to whatever fills the vacuum the father has left, and no one standing watch. His wife has no one in the home willing to tell her the true thing — not in cruelty, but in love; she navigates without the steady voice of a man who knows her and speaks honestly into her life. Compounding this, his wife is holding the lines alone — whatever the father has stopped enforcing, she absorbs, until the weight of being the only authority in the home begins to cost her something she cannot recover. His children are drifting without calibration — no trusted voice that both knows them and tells them the true thing about where they are heading before the consequences arrive. His children are growing up in a home with no held line — not because no one cares, but because the person designed to hold it has stopped; and what a mother holds alone is never quite the same as what a father and mother hold together. He disciplines his children but offers neither naming nor wisdom with it — correction without encouragement or mentorship teaches a child what the line is, but not who they are or why the line matters. What his children are building their picture of fatherhood from is what remains — and the Discipliner they needed is one of the things they are not getting. Adults who were never named by their father spend their lives either achieving to fill the silence or collapsing when achievement fails to do it — and they rarely trace it back to the right source.

Scenario 146

Fractured Pillars: E1 (Encourager & Nurturer) + H2 (Heart of Integrity) + E2 (Example Who Inspires Potential) + R (Reprover & Wise Mentor)

Solid Pillars: S (Spiritual Leader) + H1 (Husband Who Loves Sacrificially) + P (Protector & Provider) + D (Discipliner)

What Happens to the Family:

Four of the eight pillars have failed. The home is operating at half its structural capacity, and the family is living inside the gap. His wife speaks into a silence — there is no voice in the home naming what she carries, affirming who she is, or calling out what God placed in her. At the same time, his wife is married to two men — the one the world sees and the one

216

she lives with; she has learned that the gap between his public commitments and his private behavior is real, and she carries that knowledge alone. No one is speaking the child's design into existence before the world gets there first; their sense of self is built entirely from external mirrors — peer approval, performance, whatever fills the silence. His children will find the gap — they always do — and when they do, they will not merely lose respect for their father; they will lose their capacity to trust authority, and sometimes God, for years. His wife sees a man going through the motions of his own life — never fully alive to his design, never modeling what it looks like to pursue the thing God placed in him. Compounding this, his wife has no one in the home willing to tell her the true thing — not in cruelty, but in love; she navigates without the steady voice of a man who knows her and speaks honestly into her life. His children have no picture of what a man who carries his God-given design actually looks like in daily life; the father's own unlived potential becomes the ceiling the children cannot see past. His children are drifting without calibration — no trusted voice that both knows them and tells them the true thing about where they are heading before the consequences arrive. He leads spiritually in appearance but not in private — the vertical commitment he performs on Sunday is contradicted by the man his family sees Monday through Saturday, and a life not fully lived becomes the only picture of purpose his children have. What his children are building their picture of fatherhood from is what remains — and the Reprover & Wise Mentor they needed is one of the things they are not getting. The fracture integrity creates is not loud — it is quiet and cumulative; the children do not announce the day they stopped believing him. They simply stop, and a life not fully lived becomes the only template of purpose they were given.

Scenario 147

Fractured Pillars: E1 (Encourager & Nurturer) + H2 (Heart of Integrity) + E2 (Example Who Inspires Potential) + D (Discipliner)

Solid Pillars: S (Spiritual Leader) + H1 (Husband Who Loves Sacrificially) + P (Protector & Provider) + R (Reprover & Wise Mentor)

What Happens to the Family:

Half the framework has failed, and the four pillars still standing are carrying what was designed for a complete structure. His wife speaks into a silence — there is no voice in the home naming what she carries, affirming who she is, or calling out what God placed in her. At the same time, his wife is married to two men — the one the world sees and the one she lives with; she has learned that the gap between his public commitments and his private behavior is real, and she carries that knowledge alone. No one is speaking the child's design into existence before the world gets there first; their sense of self is built entirely from external mirrors — peer approval, performance, whatever fills the silence. His children will find the gap — they always do — and when they do, they will not merely lose respect for their father; they will lose their capacity to trust authority, and sometimes God, for years. His wife sees a man going through the motions of his own life — never fully alive to his design, never modeling what it looks like to pursue the thing God placed in him. Compounding this, his wife is holding the lines alone — whatever the father has stopped enforcing, she absorbs, until the weight of being the only authority in the home begins to cost her something she cannot recover. His children have no picture of what a man who carries his God-given design actually looks like in daily life; the father's own unlived potential becomes the ceiling the children cannot see past. His children are growing up in a home with no held line — not because no one cares, but because the person designed to hold it has stopped; and what a mother holds alone is never quite the same as what a father and mother hold together. He leads spiritually in appearance but not in private — the vertical commitment he performs on Sunday is contradicted by the man his family sees Monday through Saturday, and a life not fully lived becomes the only picture of purpose his children have. What his children are building their picture of fatherhood from is what remains — and the Discipliner they needed is one of the things they are not getting. The fracture integrity creates is not loud — it is quiet and cumulative; the children do not announce the day they stopped believing him. They simply stop, and a life not fully lived becomes the only template of purpose they were given.

Fractured Pillars: E1 (Encourager & Nurturer) + H2 (Heart of Integrity) + R (Reprover & Wise Mentor) + D (Discipliner)

Solid Pillars: S (Spiritual Leader) + H1 (Husband Who Loves Sacrificially) + P (Protector & Provider) + E2 (Example Who Inspires Potential)

What Happens to the Family:

Four pillars down. Four still standing. At this level, the family can see what is missing even if they cannot yet name it. His wife speaks into a silence — there is no voice in the home naming what she carries, affirming who she is, or calling out what God placed in her. At the same time, his wife is married to two men — the one the world sees and the one she lives with; she has learned that the gap between his public commitments and his private behavior is real, and she carries that knowledge alone. No one is speaking the child's design into existence before the world gets there first; their sense of self is built entirely from external mirrors — peer approval, performance, whatever fills the silence. His children will find the gap — they always do — and when they do, they will not merely lose respect for their father; they will lose their capacity to trust authority, and sometimes God, for years. His wife has no one in the home willing to tell her the true thing — not in cruelty, but in love; she navigates without the steady voice of a man who knows her and speaks honestly into her life. Compounding this, his wife is holding the lines alone — whatever the father has stopped enforcing, she absorbs, until the weight of being the only authority in the home begins to cost her something she cannot recover. His children are drifting without calibration — no trusted voice that both knows them and tells them the true thing about where they are heading before the consequences arrive. His children are growing up in a home with no held line — not because no one cares, but because the person designed to hold it has stopped; and what a mother holds alone is never quite the same as what a father and mother hold together. He leads spiritually in appearance but not in private — the vertical commitment he performs on Sunday is contradicted by the man his family sees Monday through Saturday. What his children are building their picture of fatherhood from is what remains — and the Discipliner they needed is one of the things they are not getting. The fracture integrity creates is not loud — it is quiet and cumulative; the children do not announce the day they stopped believing him. They simply stop, and he rarely sees it coming.

Scenario 149

Fractured Pillars: E1 (Encourager & Nurturer) + E2 (Example Who Inspires Potential) + R (Reprover & Wise Mentor) + D (Discipliner)

Solid Pillars: S (Spiritual Leader) + H1 (Husband Who Loves Sacrificially) + P (Protector & Provider) + H2 (Heart of Integrity)

What Happens to the Family:

Half the framework has failed. The visible architecture of fatherhood may still appear intact from the outside. Inside the home, the people who live there know something is missing. His wife speaks into a silence — there is no voice in the home naming what she carries, affirming who she is, or calling out what God placed in her. At the same time, his wife sees a man going through the motions of his own life — never fully alive to his design, never modeling what it looks like to pursue the thing God placed in him. No one is speaking the child's design into existence before the world gets there first; their sense of self is built entirely from external mirrors — peer approval, performance, whatever fills the silence. His children have no picture of what a man who carries his God-given design actually looks like in daily life; the father's own unlived potential becomes the ceiling the children cannot see past. His wife has no one in the home willing to tell her the true thing — not in cruelty, but in love; she navigates without the steady voice of a man who knows her and speaks honestly into her life. Compounding this, his wife is holding the lines alone — whatever the father has stopped enforcing, she absorbs, until the weight of being the only authority in the home begins to cost her something she cannot recover. His children are drifting without calibration — no trusted voice that both knows them and tells them the true thing about where they are heading before the consequences arrive. His children are growing up in a home with no held line — not because no one cares, but because the person designed to hold it has stopped; and what a mother holds alone is never quite the same as what a father and mother hold together. He disciplines his children but offers neither naming nor wisdom with it — correction without encouragement or mentorship teaches a child what the line is, but not who they are or why the line matters. What his children are building their picture of fatherhood from is what remains — and the Discipliner they needed is one of the things they are not getting. Adults who were never named by their father spend their lives either achieving to fill the silence or collapsing when achievement fails to do it — and they rarely trace it back to the right source.

Scenario 150

Fractured Pillars: P (Protector & Provider) + H2 (Heart of Integrity) + E2 (Example Who Inspires Potential) + R (Reprover & Wise Mentor)

Solid Pillars: S (Spiritual Leader) + H1 (Husband Who Loves Sacrificially) + E1 (Encourager & Nurturer) + D (Discipliner)

What Happens to the Family:

Four pillars have failed. The remaining four are doing the work of eight — and the home bears the weight of that imbalance. His wife is unprotected — whether the failure is material, emotional, or spiritual; she has learned that the perimeter is unmanned and she cannot rely on him to stand between her and what threatens the home. At the same time, his wife is married to two men — the one the world sees and the one she lives with; she has learned that the gap between his public commitments and his private behavior is real, and she carries that knowledge alone. His children are growing up inside a home with an unlocked door — exposed to whatever fills the vacuum the father has left, and no one standing watch. His children will find the gap — they always do — and when they do, they will not merely lose respect for their father; they will lose their capacity to trust authority, and sometimes God, for years. His wife sees a man going through the motions of his own life — never fully alive to his design, never modeling what it looks like to pursue the thing God placed in him. Compounding this, his wife has no one in the home willing to tell her the true thing — not in cruelty, but in love; she navigates without the steady voice of a man who knows her and speaks honestly into her life. His children have no picture of what a man who carries his God-given design actually looks like in daily life; the father's own unlived potential becomes the ceiling the children cannot see past. His children are drifting without calibration — no trusted voice that both knows them and tells them the true thing about where they are heading before the consequences arrive. He leads spiritually in appearance but not in private — the vertical commitment he performs on Sunday is contradicted by the man his family sees Monday through Saturday, and a life not fully lived becomes the only picture of purpose his children have. What his children are building their picture of fatherhood from is what remains — and the Reprover & Wise Mentor they needed is one of the things they are not getting. The fracture integrity creates is not loud — it is quiet and cumulative; the children do not announce the day they stopped believing him. They simply stop, and a life not fully lived becomes the only template of purpose they were given.

Scenario 151

Fractured Pillars: P (Protector & Provider) + H2 (Heart of Integrity) + E2 (Example Who Inspires Potential) + D (Discipliner)

Solid Pillars: S (Spiritual Leader) + H1 (Husband Who Loves Sacrificially) + E1 (Encourager & Nurturer) + R (Reprover & Wise Mentor)

What Happens to the Family:

Half the framework has failed. The home operates on four structural commitments where eight were designed to work in concert. His wife is unprotected — whether the failure is material, emotional, or spiritual; she has learned that the perimeter is unmanned and she cannot rely on him to stand between her and what threatens the home. At the same time, his wife is married to two men — the one the world sees and the one she lives with; she has learned that the gap between his public commitments and his private behavior is real, and she carries that knowledge alone. His children are growing up inside a home with an unlocked door — exposed to whatever fills the vacuum the father has left, and no one standing watch. His children will find the gap — they always do — and when they do, they will not merely lose respect for their father; they will lose their capacity to trust authority, and sometimes God, for years. His wife sees a man going through the motions of his own life — never fully alive to his design, never modeling what it looks like to pursue the thing God placed in him. Compounding this, his wife is holding the lines alone — whatever the father has stopped enforcing, she absorbs, until the weight of being the only authority in the home begins to cost her something she cannot recover. His children have no picture of what a man who carries his

God-given design actually looks like in daily life; the father's own unlived potential becomes the ceiling the children cannot see past. His children are growing up in a home with no held line — not because no one cares, but because the person designed to hold it has stopped; and what a mother holds alone is never quite the same as what a father and mother hold together. He leads spiritually in appearance but not in private — the vertical commitment he performs on Sunday is contradicted by the man his family sees Monday through Saturday, and a life not fully lived becomes the only picture of purpose his children have. What his children are building their picture of fatherhood from is what remains — and the Discipliner they needed is one of the things they are not getting. The fracture integrity creates is not loud — it is quiet and cumulative; the children do not announce the day they stopped believing him. They simply stop, and a life not fully lived becomes the only template of purpose they were given.

Scenario 152

Fractured Pillars: P (Protector & Provider) + H2 (Heart of Integrity) + R (Reprover & Wise Mentor) + D (Discipliner)

Solid Pillars: S (Spiritual Leader) + H1 (Husband Who Loves Sacrificially) + E1 (Encourager & Nurturer) + E2 (Example Who Inspires Potential)

What Happens to the Family:

Four pillars have failed. What remains — four load-bearing points where eight were designed — is carrying the weight of what has been put down. His wife is unprotected

— whether the failure is material, emotional, or spiritual; she has learned that the perimeter is unmanned and she cannot rely on him to stand between her and what threatens the home. At the same time, his wife is married to two men — the one the world sees and the one she lives with; she has learned that the gap between his public commitments and his private behavior is real, and she carries that knowledge alone. His children are growing up inside a home with an unlocked door — exposed to whatever fills the vacuum the father has left, and no one standing watch. His children will find the gap — they always do — and when they do, they will not merely lose respect for their father; they will lose their capacity to trust authority, and sometimes God, for years. His wife has no one in the home willing to tell her the true thing — not in cruelty, but in love; she navigates without the steady voice of a man who knows her and speaks honestly into her life. Compounding this, his wife is holding the lines alone — whatever the father has stopped enforcing, she absorbs, until the weight of being the only authority in the home begins to cost her something she cannot recover. His children are drifting without calibration — no trusted voice that both knows them and tells them the true thing about where they are heading before the consequences arrive. His children are growing up in a home with no held line — not because no one cares, but because the person designed to hold it has stopped; and what a mother holds alone is never quite the same as what a father and mother hold together. He leads spiritually in appearance but not in private — the vertical commitment he performs on Sunday is contradicted by the man his family sees Monday through Saturday. What his children are building their picture of fatherhood from is what remains — and the Discipliner they needed is one of the things they are not getting. The fracture integrity creates is not loud — it is quiet and cumulative; the children do not announce the day they stopped believing him. They simply stop, and he rarely sees it coming.

Scenario 153

Fractured Pillars: P (Protector & Provider) + E2 (Example Who Inspires Potential) + R (Reprover & Wise Mentor) + D (Discipliner)

Solid Pillars: S (Spiritual Leader) + H1 (Husband Who Loves Sacrificially) + E1 (Encourager & Nurturer) + H2 (Heart of Integrity)

What Happens to the Family:

Half the framework is down. The four pillars still standing are real, but they were not designed to carry the home alone. His wife is unprotected — whether the failure is material, emotional, or spiritual; she has learned that the perimeter is unmanned and she cannot rely on him to stand between her and what threatens the home. At the same time, his wife sees a man going through the motions of his own life — never fully alive to his design, never modeling what it looks like to pursue the thing God placed in him. His children are growing up inside a home with an unlocked door — exposed to whatever fills the vacuum the father has left, and no one standing watch. His children have no picture of what a man who carries his God-given design actually looks like in daily life; the father's own unlived potential becomes the ceiling the children cannot see past. His wife has no one in the home willing to tell her the true thing — not in cruelty, but in love; she navigates without the steady voice of a man who knows her and speaks honestly into her life. Compounding this, his wife is holding the lines alone — whatever the father has stopped enforcing, she absorbs, until the weight of being the only authority in the home begins to cost her something she cannot recover. His children are drifting without calibration — no trusted voice that both knows them and tells them the true thing about where they are heading before the consequences arrive. His children are growing up in a home with no held line — not because no one cares, but because the person designed to hold it has stopped; and what a mother holds alone is never quite the same as what a father and mother hold together. He tries to hold lines in the home but has stopped providing the covering that makes discipline feel like love rather than control — children without protection experience correction as threat. What his children are building their picture of fatherhood from is what remains — and the Discipliner they needed is one of the things they are not getting. They will reach adulthood without a template for what a man surrendered to something greater than himself actually looks like, and they will not know what they are missing until they are trying to build something themselves.

Scenario 154

Fractured Pillars: H2 (Heart of Integrity) + E2 (Example Who Inspires Potential) + R (Reprover & Wise Mentor) + D (Discipliner)

Solid Pillars: S (Spiritual Leader) + H1 (Husband Who Loves Sacrificially) + E1 (Encourager & Nurturer) + P (Protector & Provider)

What Happens to the Family:

Four pillars have failed. Four remain. The home may still look functional from the outside; inside, the people who live there know something is wrong. His wife is married to two men — the one the world sees and the one she lives with; she has learned that the gap between his public commitments and his private behavior is real, and she carries that knowledge alone. At the same time, his wife sees a man going through the motions of his own life — never fully alive to his design, never modeling what it looks like to pursue the thing God placed in him. His children will find the gap — they always do — and when they do, they will not merely lose respect for their father; they will lose their capacity to trust authority, and sometimes God, for years. His children have no picture of what a man who carries his God-given design actually looks like in daily life; the father's own unlived potential becomes the ceiling the children cannot see past. His wife has no one in the home willing to tell her the true thing — not in cruelty, but in love; she navigates without the steady voice of a man who knows her and speaks honestly into her life. Compounding this, his wife is holding the lines alone — whatever the father has stopped enforcing, she absorbs, until the weight of being the only authority in the home begins to cost her something she cannot recover. His children are drifting without calibration — no trusted voice that both knows them and tells them the true thing about where they are heading before the consequences arrive. His children are growing up in a home with no held line — not because no one cares, but because the person designed to hold it has stopped; and what a mother holds alone is never quite the same as what a father and mother hold together. He leads spiritually in appearance but not in private — the vertical commitment he performs on Sunday is contradicted by the man his family sees Monday through Saturday, and a life not fully lived becomes the only picture of purpose his children have. What his children are building their picture of fatherhood from is what remains — and the Discipliner they needed is one of the things they are not getting. The fracture integrity creates is not loud — it is quiet and cumulative; the children do not announce the day they stopped believing him. They simply stop, and a life not fully lived becomes the only template of purpose they were given.

Five Pillars Failing

56 scenarios

*Five pillars failing leaves three standing. The father is not absent —
but the version of fatherhood he is providing is three-eighths of
what his family was designed to receive. The three remaining
pillars now carry the full weight of the father's identity in his
children's lives. Everything his children know about fatherhood,
they are learning from what did not fail.*

Scenario 155

Fractured Pillars: S (Spiritual Leader) + H1 (Husband Who Loves Sacrificially) + E1 (Encourager & Nurturer) + P (Protector & Provider) + H2 (Heart of Integrity)

Solid Pillars: E2 (Example Who Inspires Potential) + R (Reprover & Wise Mentor) + D (Discipliner)

What Happens to the Family:

Five pillars are fractured. The three still standing —
Example Who Inspires Potential + Reprover & Wise Mentor
+ Discipliner — have become the entire definition of
fatherhood in this home. His children will grow up believing
this is what fathers do, because it is what their father did.
His wife carries the spiritual weight of the home alone —

praying over children her husband will not lead to the altar, covering in faith a family designed to move under his authority. At the same time, his wife is not being pursued — she is being maintained; the covenant runs on autopilot, and she carries the relational weight of the marriage alone, managing rather than being led. His children are inheriting both deficits simultaneously. His children grow up with a picture of God as ceremonially present and practically irrelevant — faith is what their mother did, not what their father modeled. His children are absorbing a picture of marriage as coexistence — two people occupying the same house — and they will bring that picture into their own relationships before they understand where it came from. His wife speaks into a silence — there is no voice in the home naming what she carries, affirming who she is, or calling out what God placed in her. His wife is unprotected — whether the failure is material, emotional, or spiritual; she has learned that the perimeter is unmanned and she cannot rely on him to stand between her and what threatens the home. No one is speaking the child's design into existence before the world gets there first; their sense of self is built entirely from external mirrors — peer approval, performance, whatever fills the silence. His children are growing up inside a home with an unlocked door — exposed to whatever fills the vacuum the father has left, and no one standing watch. His children will find the gap — they always do — and when they do, they will not merely lose respect for their father; they will lose their capacity to trust authority, and sometimes God, for years. He provides for the family materially but has stopped investing in the marriage — provision without pursuit leaves his wife feeling like a dependent, not a covenant partner. What his children are building their picture of fatherhood from is what remains — and the Heart of Integrity they needed is one of the things they are not getting. The fracture integrity creates is not loud — it is quiet and cumulative; the children do not announce the day they stopped believing him. They simply stop, and he rarely sees it coming.

Scenario 156

Fractured Pillars: S (Spiritual Leader) + H1 (Husband Who Loves Sacrificially) + E1 (Encourager & Nurturer) + P (Protector & Provider) + E2 (Example Who Inspires Potential)

Solid Pillars: H2 (Heart of Integrity) + R (Reprover & Wise Mentor) + D (Discipliner)

What Happens to the Family:

Five of the eight pillars have failed. What remains — Heart of Integrity + Reprover & Wise Mentor + Discipliner — has become the whole picture of fatherhood for this family. His children will grow up believing this is what fathers do. His wife carries the spiritual weight of the home alone — praying over children her husband will not lead to the altar, covering in faith a family designed to move under his authority. At the same time, his wife is not being pursued — she is being maintained; the covenant runs on autopilot, and she carries the relational weight of the marriage alone, managing rather than being led. His children are inheriting both deficits simultaneously. His children grow up with a picture of God as ceremonially present and practically irrelevant — faith is what their mother did, not what their father modeled. His children are absorbing a picture of marriage as coexistence — two people occupying the same house — and they will bring that picture into their own relationships before they understand where it came from. His wife speaks into a silence — there is no voice in the home naming what she carries, affirming who she is, or calling out what God placed in her. His wife is unprotected — whether the failure is material, emotional, or spiritual; she has learned that the perimeter is unmanned and she cannot rely on him to stand between her and what threatens the home. No one is speaking the child's design into existence before the world gets there first; their sense of self is built entirely from external mirrors — peer approval, performance, whatever fills the silence. His children are growing up inside a home with an unlocked door — exposed to whatever fills the vacuum the father has left, and no one standing watch. His children have no picture of what a man who carries his God-given design actually looks like in daily life; the father's own unlived potential becomes the ceiling the children cannot see past. He speaks into his children but has nothing to point them toward — encouragement without example produces children who feel seen but have no picture of what they are being built for, and without spiritual grounding behind it, even that purpose has no foundation. What his children are building their picture of fatherhood from is what remains — and the Example Who Inspires Potential they needed is one of the things they are not getting. Adults who were never named by their father spend their lives either achieving to fill the silence or collapsing when achievement fails to do it — and they rarely trace it back to the right source.

Scenario 157

Fractured Pillars: S (Spiritual Leader) + H1 (Husband Who Loves Sacrificially) + E1 (Encourager & Nurturer) + P (Protector & Provider) + R (Reprover & Wise Mentor)

Solid Pillars: H2 (Heart of Integrity) + E2 (Example Who Inspires Potential) + D (Discipliner)

What Happens to the Family:

Five pillars have failed. Three remain — Heart of Integrity + Example Who Inspires Potential + Discipliner. Those three are not simply holding; they have become everything the children know about what a father is. His wife carries the spiritual weight of the home alone — praying over children her husband will not lead to the altar, covering in faith a family designed to move under his authority. At the same time, his wife is not being pursued — she is being maintained; the covenant runs on autopilot, and she carries the relational weight of the marriage alone, managing rather than being led. His children are inheriting both deficits simultaneously. His children grow up with a picture of God as ceremonially present and practically irrelevant — faith is what their mother did, not what their father modeled. His children are absorbing a picture of marriage as coexistence — two people occupying the same house — and they will bring that picture into their own relationships before they understand where it came from. His wife speaks into a silence — there is no voice in the home naming what she carries, affirming who she is, or calling out what God placed in her. His wife is unprotected — whether the failure is material, emotional, or spiritual; she has learned that the perimeter is unmanned and she cannot rely on him to stand between her and what threatens the home. No one is speaking the child's design into existence before the world gets there first; their sense of self is built entirely from external mirrors — peer approval, performance, whatever fills the silence. His children are growing up inside a home with an unlocked door — exposed to whatever fills the vacuum the father has left, and no one standing watch. His children are drifting without calibration — no trusted voice that both knows them and tells them the true thing about where they are heading before the consequences arrive. He disciplines his children but offers neither naming nor wisdom with it — correction without encouragement or mentorship teaches a child what the line is, but not who they are or why the line matters. What his children are building their picture of fatherhood from is what remains — and the Reprover & Wise Mentor they needed is one of the things they are not getting. Adults who were never named by their father spend their lives either achieving to fill the silence or collapsing when achievement fails to do it — and they rarely trace it back to the right source.

Scenario 158

Fractured Pillars: S (Spiritual Leader) + H1 (Husband Who Loves Sacrificially) + E1 (Encourager & Nurturer) + P (Protector & Provider) + D (Discipliner)

Solid Pillars: H2 (Heart of Integrity) + E2 (Example Who Inspires Potential) + R (Reprover & Wise Mentor)

What Happens to the Family:

Five pillars are down. Three are standing: Heart of Integrity + Example Who Inspires Potential + Reprover & Wise Mentor. And those three have become the entire definition of fatherhood in this home. His wife carries the spiritual weight of the home alone — praying over children her husband will not lead to the altar, covering in faith a family designed to move under his authority. At the same time, his wife is not being pursued — she is being maintained; the covenant runs on autopilot, and she carries the relational weight of the marriage alone, managing rather than being led. His children are inheriting both deficits simultaneously. His children grow up with a picture of God as ceremonially present and practically irrelevant — faith is what their mother did, not what their father modeled. His children are absorbing a picture of marriage as coexistence — two people occupying the same house — and they will bring that picture into their own relationships before they understand where it came from. His wife speaks into a silence — there is no voice in the home naming what she carries, affirming who she is, or calling out what God placed in her. His wife is unprotected — whether the failure is material, emotional, or spiritual; she has learned that the perimeter is unmanned and she cannot rely on him to stand between her and what threatens the home. No one is speaking the child's design into existence before the world gets there first; their sense of self is built entirely from external mirrors — peer approval, performance, whatever fills the silence. His children are growing up inside a home with an unlocked door — exposed to whatever fills the vacuum the father has left, and no one standing watch. His children are growing up in a home with no held line — not because no one cares, but because the person designed to hold it has stopped; and what a mother holds alone is never quite the same as what a father and mother hold together. He tries to hold lines in the home but has stopped providing the covering that makes discipline feel like love rather than control — children without protection experience correction as threat. What his children are building their picture of fatherhood from is what remains — and the Discipliner they needed is one of the things they are not getting. The daughters will accept less than they deserve and not know why; the sons will drift toward the same emotional distance their father modeled and call it normal.

Scenario 159

Fractured Pillars: S (Spiritual Leader) + H1 (Husband Who Loves Sacrificially) + E1 (Encourager & Nurturer) + H2 (Heart of Integrity) + E2 (Example Who Inspires Potential)

Solid Pillars: P (Protector & Provider) + R (Reprover & Wise Mentor) + D (Discipliner)

What Happens to the Family:

Five of the eight pillars have failed. The three that remain — Protector & Provider + Reprover & Wise Mentor +

Discipliner — are real. But three pillars doing the work of eight is not a framework — it is survival, and his children are being raised inside that gap. His wife carries the spiritual weight of the home alone — praying over children her husband will not lead to the altar, covering in faith a family designed to move under his authority. At the same time, his wife is not being pursued — she is being maintained; the covenant runs on autopilot, and she carries the relational weight of the marriage alone, managing rather than being led. His children are inheriting both deficits simultaneously. His children grow up with a picture of God as ceremonially present and practically irrelevant — faith is what their mother did, not what their father modeled. His children are absorbing a picture of marriage as coexistence — two people occupying the same house — and they will bring that picture into their own relationships before they understand where it came from. His wife speaks into a silence — there is no voice in the home naming what she carries, affirming who she is, or calling out what God placed in her. His wife is married to two men — the one the world sees and the one she lives with; she has learned that the gap between his public commitments and his private behavior is real, and she carries that knowledge alone. No one is speaking the child's design into existence before the world gets there first; their sense of self is built entirely from external mirrors — peer approval, performance, whatever fills the silence. His children will find the gap — they always do — and when they do, they will not merely lose respect for their father; they will lose their capacity to trust authority, and sometimes God, for years. His children have no picture of what a man who carries his God-given design actually looks like in daily life; the father's own unlived potential becomes the ceiling the children cannot see past. He leads spiritually in appearance but not in private — the vertical commitment he performs on Sunday is contradicted by the man his family sees Monday through Saturday, and a life not fully lived becomes the only picture of purpose his children have. What his children are building their picture of fatherhood from is what remains — and the Example Who Inspires Potential they needed is one of the things they are not getting. The fracture integrity creates is not loud — it is quiet and cumulative; the children do not announce the day they stopped believing him. They simply stop, and he rarely sees it coming.

Scenario 160

Fractured Pillars: S (Spiritual Leader) + H1 (Husband Who Loves Sacrificially) + E1 (Encourager & Nurturer) + H2 (Heart of Integrity) + R (Reprover & Wise Mentor)

Solid Pillars: P (Protector & Provider) + E2 (Example Who Inspires Potential) + D (Discipliner)

What Happens to the Family:

Five pillars have fractured. What remains — Protector & Provider + Example Who Inspires Potential + Discipliner — is what this family now calls fatherhood. His wife carries the spiritual weight of the home alone — praying over children her husband will not lead to the altar, covering in faith a family designed to move under his authority. At the same time, his wife is not being pursued — she is being maintained; the covenant runs on autopilot, and she carries the relational weight of the marriage alone, managing rather than being led. His children are inheriting both deficits simultaneously. His children grow up with a picture of God as ceremonially present and practically irrelevant — faith is what their mother did, not what their father modeled. His children are absorbing a picture of marriage as coexistence — two people occupying the same house — and they will bring that picture into their own relationships before they understand where it came from. His wife speaks into a silence — there is no voice in the home naming what she carries, affirming who she is, or calling out what God placed in her. His wife is married to two men — the one the world sees and the one she lives with; she has learned that the gap between his public commitments and his private behavior is real, and she carries that knowledge alone. No one is speaking the child's design into existence before the world gets there first; their sense of self is built entirely from external mirrors — peer approval, performance, whatever fills the silence. His children will find the gap — they always do — and when they do, they will not merely lose respect for their father; they will lose their capacity to trust authority, and sometimes God, for years. His children are drifting without calibration — no trusted voice that both knows them and tells them the true thing about where they are heading before the consequences arrive. He disciplines his children but offers neither naming nor wisdom with it — correction without encouragement or mentorship teaches a child what the line is, but not who they are or why the line matters. What his children are building their picture of fatherhood from is what remains — and the Reprover & Wise Mentor they needed is one of the things they are not getting. The fracture integrity creates is not loud — it is quiet and cumulative; the children do not announce the day they stopped believing him. They simply stop, and he rarely sees it coming.

Scenario 161

Fractured Pillars: S (Spiritual Leader) + H1 (Husband Who Loves Sacrificially) + E1 (Encourager & Nurturer) + H2 (Heart of Integrity) + D (Discipliner)

Solid Pillars: P (Protector & Provider) + E2 (Example Who Inspires Potential) + R (Reprover & Wise Mentor)

What Happens to the Family:

Five pillars are fractured. The three still standing — Protector & Provider + Example Who Inspires Potential + Reprover & Wise Mentor — have become the entire definition of fatherhood in this home. His children will grow up believing this is what fathers do, because it is what their father did. His wife carries the spiritual weight of the home alone — praying over children her husband will not lead to the altar, covering in faith a family designed to move under his authority. At the same time, his wife is not being pursued — she is being maintained; the covenant runs on autopilot, and she carries the relational weight of the marriage alone, managing rather than being led. His children are inheriting both deficits simultaneously. His children grow up with a picture of God as ceremonially present and practically irrelevant — faith is what their mother did, not what their father modeled. His children are absorbing a picture of marriage as coexistence — two people occupying the same house — and they will bring that picture into their own relationships before they understand where it came from. His wife speaks into a silence — there is no voice in the home naming what she carries, affirming who she is, or calling out what God placed in her. His wife is married to two men — the one the world sees and the one she lives with; she has learned that the gap between his public commitments and his private behavior is real, and she carries that knowledge alone. No one is speaking the child's design into existence before the world gets there first; their sense of self is built entirely from external mirrors — peer approval, performance, whatever fills the silence. His children will find the gap — they always do — and when they do, they will not merely lose respect for their father; they will lose their capacity to trust authority, and sometimes God, for years. His children are growing up in a home with no held line — not because no one cares, but because the person designed to hold it has stopped; and what a mother holds alone is never quite the same as what a father and mother hold together. He corrects his children but never names them — reproof without encouragement produces a child who knows what they did wrong and has no idea who they are. What his children are building their picture of fatherhood from is what remains — and the Discipliner they needed is one of the things they are not getting. The daughters will accept less than they deserve and not know why; the sons will drift toward the same emotional distance their father modeled and call it normal.

Fractured Pillars: S (Spiritual Leader) + H1 (Husband Who Loves Sacrificially) + E1 (Encourager & Nurturer) + E2 (Example Who Inspires Potential) + R (Reprover & Wise Mentor)

Solid Pillars: P (Protector & Provider) + H2 (Heart of Integrity) + D (Discipliner)

What Happens to the Family:

Five of the eight pillars have failed. What remains — Protector & Provider + Heart of Integrity + Discipliner — has become the whole picture of fatherhood for this family. His children will grow up believing this is what fathers do. His wife carries the spiritual weight of the home alone — praying over children her husband will not lead to the altar, covering in faith a family designed to move under his authority. At the same time, his wife is not being pursued — she is being maintained; the covenant runs on autopilot, and she carries the relational weight of the marriage alone, managing rather than being led. His children are inheriting both deficits simultaneously. His children grow up with a picture of God as ceremonially present and practically irrelevant — faith is what their mother did, not what their father modeled. His children are absorbing a picture of marriage as coexistence — two people occupying the same house — and they will bring that picture into their own relationships before they understand where it came from. His wife speaks into a silence — there is no voice in the home naming what she carries, affirming who she is, or calling out what God placed in her. His wife sees a man going through the motions of his own life — never fully alive to his design, never modeling what it looks like to pursue the thing God placed in him. No one is speaking the child's design into existence before the world gets there first; their sense of self is built entirely from external mirrors — peer approval, performance, whatever fills the silence. His children have no picture of what a man who carries his God-given design actually looks like in daily life; the father's own unlived potential becomes the ceiling the children cannot see past. His children are drifting without calibration — no trusted voice that both knows them and tells them the true thing about where they are heading before the consequences arrive. He speaks into his children but has nothing to point them toward — encouragement without example produces children who feel seen but have no picture of what they are being built for, and without spiritual grounding behind it, even that purpose has no foundation. What his children are building their picture of fatherhood from is what remains — and the Reprover & Wise Mentor they needed is one of the things they are not getting. Adults who were never named by their father spend their lives either achieving to fill the silence or collapsing when achievement fails to do it — and they rarely trace it back to the right source.

Scenario 163

Fractured Pillars: S (Spiritual Leader) + H1 (Husband Who Loves Sacrificially) + E1 (Encourager & Nurturer) + E2 (Example Who Inspires Potential) + D (Discipliner)

Solid Pillars: P (Protector & Provider) + H2 (Heart of Integrity) + R (Reprover & Wise Mentor)

What Happens to the Family:

Five pillars have failed. Three remain — Protector & Provider + Heart of Integrity + Reprover & Wise Mentor. Those three are not simply holding; they have become everything the children know about what a father is. His wife carries the spiritual weight of the home alone — praying over children her husband will not lead to the altar, covering in faith a family designed to move under his authority. At the same time, his wife is not being pursued — she is being maintained; the covenant runs on autopilot, and she carries the relational weight of the marriage alone, managing rather than being led. His children are inheriting both deficits simultaneously. His children grow up with a picture of God as ceremonially present and practically irrelevant — faith is what their mother did, not what their father modeled. His children are absorbing a picture of marriage as coexistence — two people occupying the same house — and they will bring that picture into their own relationships before they understand where it came from. His wife speaks into a silence — there is no voice in the home naming what she carries, affirming who she is, or calling out what God placed in her. His wife sees a man going through the motions of his own life — never fully alive to his design, never modeling what it looks like to pursue the thing God placed in him. No one is speaking the child's design into existence before the world gets there first; their sense of self is built entirely from external mirrors — peer approval, performance, whatever fills the silence. His children have no picture of what a man who carries his God-given design actually looks like in daily life; the father's own unlived potential becomes the ceiling the children cannot see past. His children are growing up in a home with no held line — not because no one cares, but because the person designed to hold it has stopped; and what a mother holds alone is never quite the same as what a father and mother hold together. He speaks into his children but has nothing to point them toward — encouragement without example produces children who feel seen but have no picture of what they are being built for, and without spiritual grounding behind it, even that purpose has no foundation. What his children are building their picture of fatherhood from is what remains — and the.Discipliner they needed is one of the things they are not getting. The daughters will accept less than they deserve and not know why; the sons will drift toward the same emotional distance their father modeled and call it normal.

Scenario 164

Fractured Pillars: S (Spiritual Leader) + H1 (Husband Who Loves Sacrificially) + E1 (Encourager & Nurturer) + R (Reprover & Wise Mentor) + D (Discipliner)

Solid Pillars: P (Protector & Provider) + H2 (Heart of Integrity) + E2 (Example Who Inspires Potential)

What Happens to the Family:

Five pillars are down. Three are standing: Protector & Provider + Heart of Integrity + Example Who Inspires Potential. And those three have become the entire definition of fatherhood in this home. His wife carries the spiritual weight of the home alone — praying over children her husband will not lead to the altar, covering in faith a family designed to move under his authority. At the same time, his wife is not being pursued — she is being maintained; the covenant runs on autopilot, and she carries the relational weight of the marriage alone, managing rather than being led. His children are inheriting both deficits simultaneously. His children grow up with a picture of God as ceremonially present and practically irrelevant — faith is what their mother did, not what their father modeled. His children are absorbing a picture of marriage as coexistence — two people occupying the same house — and they will bring that picture into their own relationships before they understand where it came from. His wife speaks into a silence — there is no voice in the home naming what she carries, affirming who she is, or calling out what God placed in her. His wife has no one in the home willing to tell her the true thing — not in cruelty, but in love; she navigates without the steady voice of a man who knows her and speaks honestly into her life. No one is speaking the child's design into existence before the world gets there first; their sense of self is built entirely from external mirrors — peer approval, performance, whatever fills the silence. His children are drifting without calibration — no trusted voice that both knows them and tells them the true thing about where they are heading before the consequences arrive. His children are growing up in a home with no held line — not because no one cares, but because the person designed to hold it has stopped; and what a mother holds alone is never quite the same as what a father and mother hold together. He disciplines his children but offers neither naming nor wisdom with it — correction without encouragement or mentorship teaches a child what the line is, but not who they are or why the line matters. What his children are building their picture of fatherhood from is what remains — and the Discipliner they needed is one of the things they are not getting. The daughters will accept less than they deserve and not know why; the sons will drift toward the same emotional distance their father modeled and call it normal.

Scenario 165

Fractured Pillars: S (Spiritual Leader) + H1 (Husband Who Loves Sacrificially) + P (Protector & Provider) + H2 (Heart of Integrity) + E2 (Example Who Inspires Potential)

Solid Pillars: E1 (Encourager & Nurturer) + R (Reprover & Wise Mentor) + D (Discipliner)

What Happens to the Family:

Five of the eight pillars have failed. The three that remain — Encourager & Nurturer + Reprover & Wise Mentor + Discipliner — are real. But three pillars doing the work of eight is not a framework — it is survival, and his children are being raised inside that gap. His wife carries the spiritual weight of the home alone — praying over children her husband will not lead to the altar, covering in faith a family designed to move under his authority. At the same time, his wife is not being pursued — she is being maintained; the covenant runs on autopilot, and she carries the relational weight of the marriage alone, managing rather than being led. His children are inheriting both deficits simultaneously. His children grow up with a picture of God as ceremonially present and practically irrelevant — faith is what their mother did, not what their father modeled. His children are absorbing a picture of marriage as coexistence — two people occupying the same house — and they will bring that picture into their own relationships before they understand where it came from. His wife is unprotected — whether the failure is material, emotional, or spiritual; she has learned that the perimeter is unmanned and she cannot rely on him to stand between her and what threatens the home. His wife is married to two men — the one the world sees and the one she lives with; she has learned that the gap between his public commitments and his private behavior is real, and she carries that knowledge alone. His children are growing up inside a home with an unlocked door — exposed to whatever fills the vacuum the father has left, and no one standing watch. His children will find the gap — they always do — and when they do, they will not merely lose respect for their father; they will lose their capacity to trust authority, and sometimes God, for years. His children have no picture of what a man who carries his God-given design actually looks like in daily life; the father's own unlived potential becomes the ceiling the children cannot see past. He leads spiritually in appearance but not in private — the vertical commitment he performs on Sunday is contradicted by the man his family sees Monday through Saturday, and a life not fully lived becomes the only picture of purpose his children have. What his children are building their picture of fatherhood from is what remains — and the Example Who Inspires Potential they needed is one of the things they are not getting. The fracture integrity creates is not loud — it is quiet and cumulative; the children do not announce the day they stopped believing him. They simply stop, and he rarely sees it coming.

Scenario 166

Fractured Pillars: S (Spiritual Leader) + H1 (Husband Who Loves Sacrificially) + P (Protector & Provider) + H2 (Heart of Integrity) + R (Reprover & Wise Mentor)

Solid Pillars: E1 (Encourager & Nurturer) + E2 (Example Who Inspires Potential) + D (Discipliner)

What Happens to the Family:

Five pillars have fractured. What remains — Encourager & Nurturer + Example Who Inspires Potential + Discipliner — is what this family now calls fatherhood. His wife carries the spiritual weight of the home alone — praying over children her husband will not lead to the altar, covering in faith a family designed to move under his authority. At the same time, his wife is not being pursued — she is being maintained; the covenant runs on autopilot, and she carries the relational weight of the marriage alone, managing rather than being led. His children are inheriting both deficits simultaneously. His children grow up with a picture of God as ceremonially present and practically irrelevant — faith is what their mother did, not what their father modeled. His children are absorbing a picture of marriage as coexistence — two people occupying the same house — and they will bring that picture into their own relationships before they understand where it came from. His wife is unprotected — whether the failure is material, emotional, or spiritual; she has learned that the perimeter is unmanned and she cannot rely on him to stand between her and what threatens the home. His wife is married to two men — the one the world sees and the one she lives with; she has learned that the gap between his public commitments and his private behavior is real, and she carries that knowledge alone. His children are growing up inside a home with an unlocked door — exposed to whatever fills the vacuum the father has left, and no one standing watch. His children will find the gap — they always do — and when they do, they will not merely lose respect for their father; they will lose their capacity to trust authority, and sometimes God, for years. His children are drifting without calibration — no trusted voice that both knows them and tells them the true thing about where they are heading before the consequences arrive. He provides for the family materially but has stopped investing in the marriage — provision without pursuit leaves his wife feeling like a dependent, not a covenant partner. What his children are building their picture of fatherhood from is what remains — and the Reprover & Wise Mentor they needed is one of the things they are not getting. The fracture integrity creates is not loud — it is quiet and cumulative; the children do not announce the day they stopped believing him. They simply stop, and he rarely sees it coming.

Scenario 167

Fractured Pillars: S (Spiritual Leader) + H1 (Husband Who Loves Sacrificially) + P (Protector & Provider) + H2 (Heart of Integrity) + D (Discipliner)

Solid Pillars: E1 (Encourager & Nurturer) + E2 (Example Who Inspires Potential) + R (Reprover & Wise Mentor)

What Happens to the Family:

Five pillars are fractured. The three still standing — Encourager & Nurturer + Example Who Inspires Potential +

Reprover & Wise Mentor — have become the entire definition of fatherhood in this home. His children will grow up believing this is what fathers do, because it is what their father did. His wife carries the spiritual weight of the home alone — praying over children her husband will not lead to the altar, covering in faith a family designed to move under his authority. At the same time, his wife is not being pursued — she is being maintained; the covenant runs on autopilot, and she carries the relational weight of the marriage alone, managing rather than being led. His children are inheriting both deficits simultaneously. His children grow up with a picture of God as ceremonially present and practically irrelevant — faith is what their mother did, not what their father modeled. His children are absorbing a picture of marriage as coexistence — two people occupying the same house — and they will bring that picture into their own relationships before they understand where it came from. His wife is unprotected — whether the failure is material, emotional, or spiritual; she has learned that the perimeter is unmanned and she cannot rely on him to stand between her and what threatens the home. His wife is married to two men — the one the world sees and the one she lives with; she has learned that the gap between his public commitments and his private behavior is real, and she carries that knowledge alone. His children are growing up inside a home with an unlocked door — exposed to whatever fills the vacuum the father has left, and no one standing watch. His children will find the gap — they always do — and when they do, they will not merely lose respect for their father; they will lose their capacity to trust authority, and sometimes God, for years. His children are growing up in a home with no held line — not because no one cares, but because the person designed to hold it has stopped; and what a mother holds alone is never quite the same as what a father and mother hold together. He tries to hold lines in the home but has stopped providing the covering that makes discipline feel like love rather than control — children without protection experience correction as threat. What his children are building their picture of fatherhood from is what remains — and the Discipliner they needed is one of the things they are not getting. The daughters will accept less than they deserve and not know why; the sons will drift toward the same emotional distance their father modeled and call it normal.

Scenario 168

Fractured Pillars: S (Spiritual Leader) + H1 (Husband Who Loves Sacrificially) + P (Protector & Provider) + E2 (Example Who Inspires Potential) + R (Reprover & Wise Mentor)

Solid Pillars: E1 (Encourager & Nurturer) + H2 (Heart of Integrity) + D (Discipliner)

What Happens to the Family:

Five of the eight pillars have failed. What remains — Encourager & Nurturer + Heart of Integrity + Discipliner — has become the whole picture of fatherhood for this family. His children will grow up believing this is what fathers do. His wife carries the spiritual weight of the home alone — praying over children her husband will not lead to the altar, covering in faith a family designed to move under his authority. At the same time, his wife is not being pursued — she is being maintained; the covenant runs on autopilot, and she carries the relational weight of the marriage alone, managing rather than being led. His children are inheriting both deficits simultaneously. His children grow up with a picture of God as ceremonially present and practically irrelevant — faith is what their mother did, not what their father modeled. His children are absorbing a picture of marriage as coexistence — two people occupying the same house — and they will bring that picture into their own relationships before they understand where it came from. His wife is unprotected — whether the failure is material, emotional, or spiritual; she has learned that the perimeter is unmanned and she cannot rely on him to stand between her and what threatens the home. His wife sees a man going through the motions of his own life — never fully alive to his design, never modeling what it looks like to pursue the thing God placed in him. His children are growing up inside a home with an unlocked door — exposed to whatever fills the vacuum the father has left, and no one standing watch. His children have no picture of what a man who carries his God-given design actually looks like in daily life; the father's own unlived potential becomes the ceiling the children cannot see past. His children are drifting without calibration — no trusted voice that both knows them and tells them the true thing about where they are heading before the consequences arrive. He speaks into his children but has nothing to point them toward — encouragement without example produces children who feel seen but have no picture of what they are being built for, and without spiritual grounding behind it, even that purpose has no foundation. What his children are building their picture of fatherhood from is what remains — and the Reprover & Wise Mentor they needed is one of the things they are not getting. They will reach adulthood without a template for what a man surrendered to something greater than himself actually looks like, and they will not know what they are missing until they are trying to build something themselves.

Scenario 169

Fractured Pillars: S (Spiritual Leader) + H1 (Husband Who Loves Sacrificially) + P (Protector & Provider) + E2 (Example Who Inspires Potential) + D (Discipliner)

Solid Pillars: E1 (Encourager & Nurturer) + H2 (Heart of Integrity) + R (Reprover & Wise Mentor)

What Happens to the Family:

Five pillars have failed. Three remain — Encourager & Nurturer + Heart of Integrity + Reprover & Wise Mentor. Those three are not simply holding; they have become everything the children know about what a father is. His wife carries the spiritual weight of the home alone — praying over children her husband will not lead to the altar, covering in faith a family designed to move under his authority. At the same time, his wife is not being pursued — she is being maintained; the covenant runs on autopilot, and she carries the relational weight of the marriage alone, managing rather than being led. His children are inheriting both deficits simultaneously. His children grow up with a picture of God as ceremonially present and practically irrelevant — faith is what their mother did, not what their father modeled. His children are absorbing a picture of marriage as coexistence — two people occupying the same house — and they will bring that picture into their own relationships before they understand where it came from. His wife is unprotected — whether the failure is material, emotional, or spiritual; she has learned that the perimeter is unmanned and she cannot rely on him to stand between her and what threatens the home. His wife sees a man going through the motions of his own life — never fully alive to his design, never modeling what it looks like to pursue the thing God placed in him. His children are growing up inside a home with an unlocked door — exposed to whatever fills the vacuum the father has left, and no one standing watch. His children have no picture of what a man who carries his God-given design actually looks like in daily life; the father's own unlived potential becomes the ceiling the children cannot see past. His children are growing up in a home with no held line — not because no one cares, but because the person designed to hold it has stopped; and what a mother holds alone is never quite the same as what a father and mother hold together. He speaks into his children but has nothing to point them toward — encouragement without example produces children who feel seen but have no picture of what they are being built for, and without spiritual grounding behind it, even that purpose has no foundation. What his children are building their picture of fatherhood from is what remains — and the Discipliner they needed is one of the things they are not getting. The daughters will accept less than they deserve and not know why; the sons will drift toward the same emotional distance their father modeled and call it normal.

Scenario 170

Fractured Pillars: S (Spiritual Leader) + H1 (Husband Who Loves Sacrificially) + P (Protector & Provider) + R (Reprover & Wise Mentor) + D (Discipliner)

Solid Pillars: E1 (Encourager & Nurturer) + H2 (Heart of Integrity) + E2 (Example Who Inspires Potential)

What Happens to the Family:

Five pillars are down. Three are standing: Encourager & Nurturer + Heart of Integrity + Example Who Inspires Potential. And those three have become the entire definition of fatherhood in this home. His wife carries the spiritual weight of the home alone — praying over children her husband will not lead to the altar, covering in faith a family designed to move under his authority. At the same time, his wife is not being pursued — she is being maintained; the covenant runs on autopilot, and she carries the relational weight of the marriage alone, managing rather than being led. His children are inheriting both deficits simultaneously. His children grow up with a picture of God as ceremonially present and practically irrelevant — faith is what their mother did, not what their father modeled. His children are absorbing a picture of marriage as coexistence — two people occupying the same house — and they will bring that picture into their own relationships before they understand where it came from. His wife is unprotected — whether the failure is material, emotional, or spiritual; she has learned that the perimeter is unmanned and she cannot rely on him to stand between her and what threatens the home. His wife has no one in the home willing to tell her the true thing — not in cruelty, but in love; she navigates without the steady voice of a man who knows her and speaks honestly into her life. His children are growing up inside a home with an unlocked door — exposed to whatever fills the vacuum the father has left, and no one standing watch. His children are drifting without calibration — no trusted voice that both knows them and tells them the true thing about where they are heading before the consequences arrive. His children are growing up in a home with no held line — not because no one cares, but because the person designed to hold it has stopped; and what a mother holds alone is never quite the same as what a father and mother hold together. He tries to hold lines in the home but has stopped providing the covering that makes discipline feel like love rather than control — children without protection experience correction as threat. What his children are building their picture of fatherhood from is what remains — and the Discipliner they needed is one of the things they are not getting. The daughters will accept less than they deserve and not know why; the sons will drift toward the same emotional distance their father modeled and call it normal.

Scenario 171

Fractured Pillars: S (Spiritual Leader) + H1 (Husband Who Loves Sacrificially) + H2 (Heart of Integrity) + E2 (Example Who Inspires Potential) + R (Reprover & Wise Mentor)

Solid Pillars: E1 (Encourager & Nurturer) + P (Protector & Provider) + D (Discipliner)

What Happens to the Family:

Five of the eight pillars have failed. The three that remain — Encourager & Nurturer + Protector & Provider + Discipliner — are real. But three pillars doing the work of eight is not a framework — it is survival, and his children are being raised inside that gap. His wife carries the spiritual weight of the home alone — praying over children her husband will not lead to the altar, covering in faith a family designed to move under his authority. At the same time, his wife is not being pursued — she is being maintained; the covenant runs on autopilot, and she carries the relational weight of the marriage alone, managing rather than being led. His children are inheriting both deficits simultaneously. His children grow up with a picture of God as ceremonially present and practically irrelevant — faith is what their mother did, not what their father modeled. His children are absorbing a picture of marriage as coexistence — two people occupying the same house — and they will bring that picture into their own relationships before they understand where it came from. His wife is married to two men — the one the world sees and the one she lives with; she has learned that the gap between his public commitments and his private behavior is real, and she carries that knowledge alone. His wife sees a man going through the motions of his own life — never fully alive to his design, never modeling what it looks like to pursue the thing God placed in him. His children will find the gap — they always do — and when they do, they will not merely lose respect for their father; they will lose their capacity to trust authority, and sometimes God, for years. His children have no picture of what a man who carries his God-given design actually looks like in daily life; the father's own unlived potential becomes the ceiling the children cannot see past. His children are drifting without calibration — no trusted voice that both knows them and tells them the true thing about where they are heading before the consequences arrive. He leads spiritually in appearance but not in private — the vertical commitment he performs on Sunday is contradicted by the man his family sees Monday through Saturday, and a life not fully lived becomes the only picture of purpose his children have. What his children are building their picture of fatherhood from is what remains — and the Reprover & Wise Mentor they needed is one of the things they are not getting. The fracture integrity creates is not loud — it is quiet and cumulative; the children do not announce the day they stopped believing him. They simply stop, and he rarely sees it coming.

Scenario 172

Fractured Pillars: S (Spiritual Leader) + H1 (Husband Who Loves Sacrificially) + H2 (Heart of Integrity) + E2 (Example Who Inspires Potential) + D (Discipliner)

Solid Pillars: E1 (Encourager & Nurturer) + P (Protector & Provider) + R (Reprover & Wise Mentor)

What Happens to the Family:

Five pillars have fractured. What remains — Encourager & Nurturer + Protector & Provider + Reprover & Wise Mentor — is what this family now calls fatherhood. His wife carries the spiritual weight of the home alone — praying over children her husband will not lead to the altar, covering in faith a family designed to move under his authority. At the same time, his wife is not being pursued — she is being maintained; the covenant runs on autopilot, and she carries the relational weight of the marriage alone, managing rather than being led. His children are inheriting both deficits simultaneously. His children grow up with a picture of God as ceremonially present and practically irrelevant — faith is what their mother did, not what their father modeled. His children are absorbing a picture of marriage as coexistence — two people occupying the same house — and they will bring that picture into their own relationships before they understand where it came from. His wife is married to two men — the one the world sees and the one she lives with; she has learned that the gap between his public commitments and his private behavior is real, and she carries that knowledge alone. His wife sees a man going through the motions of his own life — never fully alive to his design, never modeling what it looks like to pursue the thing God placed in him. His children will find the gap — they always do — and when they do, they will not merely lose respect for their father; they will lose their capacity to trust authority, and sometimes God, for years. His children have no picture of what a man who carries his God-given design actually looks like in daily life; the father's own unlived potential becomes the ceiling the children cannot see past. His children are growing up in a home with no held line — not because no one cares, but because the person designed to hold it has stopped; and what a mother holds alone is never quite the same as what a father and mother hold together. He leads spiritually in appearance but not in private — the vertical commitment he performs on Sunday is contradicted by the man his family sees Monday through Saturday, and a life not fully lived becomes the only picture of purpose his children have. What his children are building their picture of fatherhood from is what remains — and the Discipliner they needed is one of the things they are not getting. The daughters will accept less than they deserve and not know why; the sons will drift toward the same emotional distance their father modeled and call it normal.

Scenario 173

Fractured Pillars: S (Spiritual Leader) + H1 (Husband Who Loves Sacrificially) + H2 (Heart of Integrity) + R (Reprover & Wise Mentor) + D (Discipliner)

Solid Pillars: E1 (Encourager & Nurturer) + P (Protector & Provider) + E2 (Example Who Inspires Potential)

What Happens to the Family:

Five pillars are fractured. The three still standing — Encourager & Nurturer + Protector & Provider + Example Who Inspires Potential — have become the entire definition of fatherhood in this home. His children will grow up believing this is what fathers do, because it is what their father did. His wife carries the spiritual weight of the home alone — praying over children her husband will not lead to the altar, covering in faith a family designed to move under his authority. At the same time, his wife is not being pursued — she is being maintained; the covenant runs on autopilot, and she carries the relational weight of the marriage alone, managing rather than being led. His children are inheriting both deficits simultaneously. His children grow up with a picture of God as ceremonially present and practically irrelevant — faith is what their mother did, not what their father modeled. His children are absorbing a picture of marriage as coexistence — two people occupying the same house — and they will bring that picture into their own relationships before they understand where it came from. His wife is married to two men — the one the world sees and the one she lives with; she has learned that the gap between his public commitments and his private behavior is real, and she carries that knowledge alone. His wife has no one in the home willing to tell her the true thing — not in cruelty, but in love; she navigates without the steady voice of a man who knows her and speaks honestly into her life. His children will find the gap — they always do — and when they do, they will not merely lose respect for their father; they will lose their capacity to trust authority, and sometimes God, for years. His children are drifting without calibration — no trusted voice that both knows them and tells them the true thing about where they are heading before the consequences arrive. His children are growing up in a home with no held line — not because no one cares, but because the person designed to hold it has stopped; and what a mother holds alone is never quite the same as what a father and mother hold together. He speaks wisdom into his children but enforces nothing — mentorship without discipline produces a child who knows what is right and has learned they do not have to do it. What his children are building their picture of fatherhood from is what remains — and the Discipliner they needed is one of the things they are not getting. The daughters will accept less than they deserve and not know why; the sons will drift toward the same emotional distance their father modeled and call it normal.

Scenario 174

Fractured Pillars: S (Spiritual Leader) + H1 (Husband Who Loves Sacrificially) + E2 (Example Who Inspires Potential) + R (Reprover & Wise Mentor) + D (Discipliner)

Solid Pillars: E1 (Encourager & Nurturer) + P (Protector & Provider) + H2 (Heart of Integrity)

What Happens to the Family:

Five of the eight pillars have failed. What remains — Encourager & Nurturer + Protector & Provider + Heart of Integrity — has become the whole picture of fatherhood for this family. His children will grow up believing this is what fathers do. His wife carries the spiritual weight of the home alone — praying over children her husband will not lead to the altar, covering in faith a family designed to move under his authority. At the same time, his wife is not being pursued — she is being maintained; the covenant runs on autopilot, and she carries the relational weight of the marriage alone, managing rather than being led. His children are inheriting both deficits simultaneously. His children grow up with a picture of God as ceremonially present and practically irrelevant — faith is what their mother did, not what their father modeled. His children are absorbing a picture of marriage as coexistence — two people occupying the same house — and they will bring that picture into their own relationships before they understand where it came from. His wife sees a man going through the motions of his own life — never fully alive to his design, never modeling what it looks like to pursue the thing God placed in him. His wife has no one in the home willing to tell her the true thing — not in cruelty, but in love; she navigates without the steady voice of a man who knows her and speaks honestly into her life. His children have no picture of what a man who carries his God-given design actually looks like in daily life; the father's own unlived potential becomes the ceiling the children cannot see past. His children are drifting without calibration — no trusted voice that both knows them and tells them the true thing about where they are heading before the consequences arrive. His children are growing up in a home with no held line — not because no one cares, but because the person designed to hold it has stopped; and what a mother holds alone is never quite the same as what a father and mother hold together. He speaks into his children but has nothing to point them toward — encouragement without example produces children who feel seen but have no picture of what they are being built for, and without spiritual grounding behind it, even that purpose has no foundation. What his children are building their picture of fatherhood from is what remains — and the Discipliner they needed is one of the things they are not getting. The daughters will accept less than they deserve and not know why; the sons will drift toward the same emotional distance their father modeled and call it normal.

Scenario 175

Fractured Pillars: S (Spiritual Leader) + E1 (Encourager & Nurturer) + P (Protector & Provider) + H2 (Heart of Integrity) + E2 (Example Who Inspires Potential)

Solid Pillars: H1 (Husband Who Loves Sacrificially) + R (Reprover & Wise Mentor) + D (Discipliner)

What Happens to the Family:

Five pillars have failed. Three remain — Husband Who Loves Sacrificially + Reprover & Wise Mentor + Discipliner. Those three are not simply holding; they have become everything the children know about what a father is. His wife carries the spiritual weight of the home alone — praying over children her husband will not lead to the altar, covering in faith a family designed to move under his authority. At the same time, his wife speaks into a silence — there is no voice in the home naming what she carries, affirming who she is, or calling out what God placed in her. His children are inheriting both deficits simultaneously. His children grow up with a picture of God as ceremonially present and practically irrelevant — faith is what their mother did, not what their father modeled. No one is speaking the child's design into existence before the world gets there first; their sense of self is built entirely from external mirrors — peer approval, performance, whatever fills the silence. His wife is unprotected — whether the failure is material, emotional, or spiritual; she has learned that the perimeter is unmanned and she cannot rely on him to stand between her and what threatens the home. His wife is married to two men — the one the world sees and the one she lives with; she has learned that the gap between his public commitments and his private behavior is real, and she carries that knowledge alone. His children are growing up inside a home with an unlocked door — exposed to whatever fills the vacuum the father has left, and no one standing watch. His children will find the gap — they always do — and when they do, they will not merely lose respect for their father; they will lose their capacity to trust authority, and sometimes God, for years. His children have no picture of what a man who carries his God-given design actually looks like in daily life; the father's own unlived potential becomes the ceiling the children cannot see past. He leads spiritually in appearance but not in private — the vertical commitment he performs on Sunday is contradicted by the man his family sees Monday through Saturday, and a life not fully lived becomes the only picture of purpose his children have. What his children are building their picture of fatherhood from is what remains — and the Example Who Inspires Potential they needed is one of the things they are not getting. The fracture integrity creates is not loud — it is quiet and cumulative; the children do not announce the day they stopped believing him. They simply stop, and he rarely sees it coming.

Fractured Pillars: S (Spiritual Leader) + E1 (Encourager & Nurturer) + P (Protector & Provider) + H2 (Heart of Integrity) + R (Reprover & Wise Mentor)

Solid Pillars: H1 (Husband Who Loves Sacrificially) + E2 (Example Who Inspires Potential) + D (Discipliner)

What Happens to the Family:

Five pillars are down. Three are standing: Husband Who Loves Sacrificially + Example Who Inspires Potential + Discipliner. And those three have become the entire definition of fatherhood in this home. His wife carries the spiritual weight of the home alone — praying over children her husband will not lead to the altar, covering in faith a family designed to move under his authority. At the same time, his wife speaks into a silence — there is no voice in the home naming what she carries, affirming who she is, or calling out what God placed in her. His children are inheriting both deficits simultaneously. His children grow up with a picture of God as ceremonially present and practically irrelevant — faith is what their mother did, not what their father modeled. No one is speaking the child's design into existence before the world gets there first; their sense of self is built entirely from external mirrors — peer approval, performance, whatever fills the silence. His wife is unprotected — whether the failure is material, emotional, or spiritual; she has learned that the perimeter is unmanned and she cannot rely on him to stand between her and what threatens the home. His wife is married to two men — the one the world sees and the one she lives with; she has learned that the gap between his public commitments and his private behavior is real, and she carries that knowledge alone. His children are growing up inside a home with an unlocked door — exposed to whatever fills the vacuum the father has left, and no one standing watch. His children will find the gap — they always do — and when they do, they will not merely lose respect for their father; they will lose their capacity to trust authority, and sometimes God, for years. His children are drifting without calibration — no trusted voice that both knows them and tells them the true thing about where they are heading before the consequences arrive. He disciplines his children but offers neither naming nor wisdom with it — correction without encouragement or mentorship teaches a child what the line is, but not who they are or why the line matters. What his children are building their picture of fatherhood from is what remains — and the Reprover & Wise Mentor they needed is one of the things they are not getting. The fracture integrity creates is not loud — it is quiet and cumulative; the children do not announce the day they stopped believing him. They simply stop, and he rarely sees it coming.

Scenario 177

Fractured Pillars: S (Spiritual Leader) + E1 (Encourager & Nurturer) + P (Protector & Provider) + H2 (Heart of Integrity) + D (Discipliner)

Solid Pillars: H1 (Husband Who Loves Sacrificially) + E2 (Example Who Inspires Potential) + R (Reprover & Wise Mentor)

What Happens to the Family:

Five of the eight pillars have failed. The three that

remain — Husband Who Loves Sacrificially + Example Who Inspires Potential + Reprover & Wise Mentor — are real. But three pillars doing the work of eight is not a framework — it is survival, and his children are being raised inside that gap. His wife carries the spiritual weight of the home alone — praying over children her husband will not lead to the altar, covering in faith a family designed to move under his authority. At the same time, his wife speaks into a silence — there is no voice in the home naming what she carries, affirming who she is, or calling out what God placed in her. His children are inheriting both deficits simultaneously. His children grow up with a picture of God as ceremonially present and practically irrelevant — faith is what their mother did, not what their father modeled. No one is speaking the child's design into existence before the world gets there first; their sense of self is built entirely from external mirrors — peer approval, performance, whatever fills the silence. His wife is unprotected — whether the failure is material, emotional, or spiritual; she has learned that the perimeter is unmanned and she cannot rely on him to stand between her and what threatens the home. His wife is married to two men — the one the world sees and the one she lives with; she has learned that the gap between his public commitments and his private behavior is real, and she carries that knowledge alone. His children are growing up inside a home with an unlocked door — exposed to whatever fills the vacuum the father has left, and no one standing watch. His children will find the gap — they always do — and when they do, they will not merely lose respect for their father; they will lose their capacity to trust authority, and sometimes God, for years. His children are growing up in a home with no held line — not because no one cares, but because the person designed to hold it has stopped; and what a mother holds alone is never quite the same as what a father and mother hold together. He tries to hold lines in the home but has stopped providing the covering that makes discipline feel like love rather than control — children without protection experience correction as threat. What his children are building their picture of fatherhood from is what remains — and the Discipliner they needed is one of the things they are not getting. The fracture integrity creates is not loud — it is quiet and cumulative; the children do not announce the day they stopped believing him. They simply stop, and he rarely sees it coming.

Scenario 178

Fractured Pillars: S (Spiritual Leader) + E1 (Encourager & Nurturer) + P (Protector & Provider) + E2 (Example Who Inspires Potential) + R (Reprover & Wise Mentor)

Solid Pillars: H1 (Husband Who Loves Sacrificially) + H2 (Heart of Integrity) + D (Discipliner)

What Happens to the Family:

Five pillars have fractured. What remains — Husband Who Loves Sacrificially + Heart of Integrity + Discipliner — is what this family now calls fatherhood. His wife carries the spiritual weight of the home alone — praying over children her husband will not lead to the altar, covering in faith a family designed to move under his authority. At the same time, his wife speaks into a silence — there is no voice in the home naming what she carries, affirming who she is, or calling out what God placed in her. His children are inheriting both deficits simultaneously. His children grow up with a picture of God as ceremonially present and practically irrelevant — faith is what their mother did, not what their father modeled. No one is speaking the child's design into existence before the world gets there first; their sense of self is built entirely from external mirrors — peer approval, performance, whatever fills the silence. His wife is unprotected — whether the failure is material, emotional, or spiritual; she has learned that the perimeter is unmanned and she cannot rely on him to stand between her and what threatens the home. His wife sees a man going through the motions of his own life — never fully alive to his design, never modeling what it looks like to pursue the thing God placed in him. His children are growing up inside a home with an unlocked door — exposed to whatever fills the vacuum the father has left, and no one standing watch. His children have no picture of what a man who carries his God-given design actually looks like in daily life; the father's own unlived potential becomes the ceiling the children cannot see past. His children are drifting without calibration — no trusted voice that both knows them and tells them the true thing about where they are heading before the consequences arrive. He speaks into his children but has nothing to point them toward — encouragement without example produces children who feel seen but have no picture of what they are being built for, and without spiritual grounding behind it, even that purpose has no foundation. What his children are building their picture of fatherhood from is what remains — and the Reprover & Wise Mentor they needed is one of the things they are not getting. Adults who were never named by their father spend their lives either achieving to fill the silence or collapsing when achievement fails to do it — and they rarely trace it back to the right source.

Scenario 179

Fractured Pillars: S (Spiritual Leader) + E1 (Encourager & Nurturer) + P (Protector & Provider) + E2 (Example Who Inspires Potential) + D (Discipliner)

Solid Pillars: H1 (Husband Who Loves Sacrificially) + H2 (Heart of Integrity) + R (Reprover & Wise Mentor)

What Happens to the Family:

Five pillars are fractured. The three still standing — Husband Who Loves Sacrificially + Heart of Integrity + Reprover & Wise Mentor — have become the entire definition of fatherhood in this home. His children will grow up believing this is what fathers do, because it is what their father did. His wife carries the spiritual weight of the home alone — praying over children her husband will not lead to the altar, covering in faith a family designed to move under his authority. At the same time, his wife speaks into a silence — there is no voice in the home naming what she carries, affirming who she is, or calling out what God placed in her. His children are inheriting both deficits simultaneously. His children grow up with a picture of God as ceremonially present and practically irrelevant — faith is what their mother did, not what their father modeled. No one is speaking the child's design into existence before the world gets there first; their sense of self is built entirely from external mirrors — peer approval, performance, whatever fills the silence. His wife is unprotected — whether the failure is material, emotional, or spiritual; she has learned that the perimeter is unmanned and she cannot rely on him to stand between her and what threatens the home. His wife sees a man going through the motions of his own life — never fully alive to his design, never modeling what it looks like to pursue the thing God placed in him. His children are growing up inside a home with an unlocked door — exposed to whatever fills the vacuum the father has left, and no one standing watch. His children have no picture of what a man who carries his God-given design actually looks like in daily life; the father's own unlived potential becomes the ceiling the children cannot see past. His children are growing up in a home with no held line — not because no one cares, but because the person designed to hold it has stopped; and what a mother holds alone is never quite the same as what a father and mother hold together. He speaks into his children but has nothing to point them toward — encouragement without example produces children who feel seen but have no picture of what they are being built for, and without spiritual grounding behind it, even that purpose has no foundation. What his children are building their picture of fatherhood from is what remains — and the Discipliner they needed is one of the things they are not getting. Adults who were never named by their father spend their lives either achieving to fill the silence or collapsing when achievement fails to do it — and they rarely trace it back to the right source.

Scenario 180

Fractured Pillars: S (Spiritual Leader) + E1 (Encourager & Nurturer) + P (Protector & Provider) + R (Reprover & Wise Mentor) + D (Discipliner)

Solid Pillars: H1 (Husband Who Loves Sacrificially) + H2 (Heart of Integrity) + E2 (Example Who Inspires Potential)

What Happens to the Family:

Five of the eight pillars have failed. What remains — Husband Who Loves Sacrificially + Heart of Integrity + Example Who Inspires Potential — has become the whole picture of fatherhood for this family. His children will grow up believing this is what fathers do. His wife carries the spiritual weight of the home alone — praying over children her husband will not lead to the altar, covering in faith a family designed to move under his authority. At the same time, his wife speaks into a silence — there is no voice in the home naming what she carries, affirming who she is, or calling out what God placed in her. His children are inheriting both deficits simultaneously. His children grow up with a picture of God as ceremonially present and practically irrelevant — faith is what their mother did, not what their father modeled. No one is speaking the child's design into existence before the world gets there first; their sense of self is built entirely from external mirrors — peer approval, performance, whatever fills the silence. His wife is unprotected — whether the failure is material, emotional, or spiritual; she has learned that the perimeter is unmanned and she cannot rely on him to stand between her and what threatens the home. His wife has no one in the home willing to tell her the true thing — not in cruelty, but in love; she navigates without the steady voice of a man who knows her and speaks honestly into her life. His children are growing up inside a home with an unlocked door — exposed to whatever fills the vacuum the father has left, and no one standing watch. His children are drifting without calibration — no trusted voice that both knows them and tells them the true thing about where they are heading before the consequences arrive. His children are growing up in a home with no held line — not because no one cares, but because the person designed to hold it has stopped; and what a mother holds alone is never quite the same as what a father and mother hold together. He disciplines his children but offers neither naming nor wisdom with it — correction without encouragement or mentorship teaches a child what the line is, but not who they are or why the line matters. What his children are building their picture of fatherhood from is what remains — and the Discipliner they needed is one of the things they are not getting. Adults who were never named by their father spend their lives either achieving to fill the silence or collapsing when achievement fails to do it — and they rarely trace it back to the right source.

Scenario **181**

Fractured Pillars: S (Spiritual Leader) + E1 (Encourager & Nurturer) + H2 (Heart of Integrity) + E2 (Example Who Inspires Potential) + R (Reprover & Wise Mentor)

Solid Pillars: H1 (Husband Who Loves Sacrificially) + P (Protector & Provider) + D (Discipliner)

What Happens to the Family:

Five pillars have failed. Three remain — Husband Who Loves Sacrificially + Protector & Provider + Discipliner. Those three are not simply holding; they have become everything the children know about what a father is. His wife carries the spiritual weight of the home alone — praying over children her husband will not lead to the altar, covering in faith a family designed to move under his authority. At the same time, his wife speaks into a silence — there is no voice in the home naming what she carries, affirming who she is, or calling out what God placed in her. His children are inheriting both deficits simultaneously. His children grow up with a picture of God as ceremonially present and practically irrelevant — faith is what their mother did, not what their father modeled. No one is speaking the child's design into existence before the world gets there first; their sense of self is built entirely from external mirrors — peer approval, performance, whatever fills the silence. His wife is married to two men — the one the world sees and the one she lives with; she has learned that the gap between his public commitments and his private behavior is real, and she carries that knowledge alone. His wife sees a man going through the motions of his own life — never fully alive to his design, never modeling what it looks like to pursue the thing God placed in him. His children will find the gap — they always do — and when they do, they will not merely lose respect for their father; they will lose their capacity to trust authority, and sometimes God, for years. His children have no picture of what a man who carries his God-given design actually looks like in daily life; the father's own unlived potential becomes the ceiling the children cannot see past. His children are drifting without calibration — no trusted voice that both knows them and tells them the true thing about where they are heading before the consequences arrive. He leads spiritually in appearance but not in private — the vertical commitment he performs on Sunday is contradicted by the man his family sees Monday through Saturday, and a life not fully lived becomes the only picture of purpose his children have. What his children are building their picture of fatherhood from is what remains — and the Reprover & Wise Mentor they needed is one of the things they are not getting. The fracture integrity creates is not loud — it is quiet and cumulative; the children do not announce the day they stopped believing him. They simply stop, and he rarely sees it coming.

Scenario 182

Fractured Pillars: S (Spiritual Leader) + E1 (Encourager & Nurturer) + H2 (Heart of Integrity) + E2 (Example Who Inspires Potential) + D (Discipliner)

Solid Pillars: H1 (Husband Who Loves Sacrificially) + P (Protector & Provider) + R (Reprover & Wise Mentor)

What Happens to the Family:

Five pillars are down. Three are standing: Husband Who Loves Sacrificially + Protector & Provider + Reprover & Wise Mentor. And those three have become the entire definition of fatherhood in this home. His wife carries the spiritual weight of the home alone — praying over children her husband will not lead to the altar, covering in faith a family designed to move under his authority. At the same time, his wife speaks into a silence — there is no voice in the home naming what she carries, affirming who she is, or calling out what God placed in her. His children are inheriting both deficits simultaneously. His children grow up with a picture of God as ceremonially present and practically irrelevant — faith is what their mother did, not what their father modeled. No one is speaking the child's design into existence before the world gets there first; their sense of self is built entirely from external mirrors — peer approval, performance, whatever fills the silence. His wife is married to two men — the one the world sees and the one she lives with; she has learned that the gap between his public commitments and his private behavior is real, and she carries that knowledge alone. His wife sees a man going through the motions of his own life — never fully alive to his design, never modeling what it looks like to pursue the thing God placed in him. His children will find the gap —

they always do — and when they do, they will not merely lose respect for their father; they will lose their capacity to trust authority, and sometimes God, for years. His children have no picture of what a man who carries his God-given design actually looks like in daily life; the father's own unlived potential becomes the ceiling the children cannot see past. His children are growing up in a home with no held line — not because no one cares, but because the person designed to hold it has stopped; and what a mother holds alone is never quite the same as what a father and mother hold together. He leads spiritually in appearance but not in private — the vertical commitment he performs on Sunday is contradicted by the man his family sees Monday through Saturday, and a life not fully lived becomes the only picture of purpose his children have. What his children are building their picture of fatherhood from is what remains — and the Discipliner they needed is one of the things they are not getting. The fracture integrity creates is not loud — it is quiet and cumulative; the children do not announce the day they stopped believing him. They simply stop, and he rarely sees it coming.

Scenario 183

Fractured Pillars: S (Spiritual Leader) + E1 (Encourager & Nurturer) + H2 (Heart of Integrity) + R (Reprover & Wise Mentor) + D (Discipliner)

Solid Pillars: H1 (Husband Who Loves Sacrificially) + P (Protector & Provider) + E2 (Example Who Inspires Potential)

What Happens to the Family:

Five of the eight pillars have failed. The three that remain — Husband Who Loves Sacrificially + Protector & Provider + Example Who Inspires Potential — are real. But three pillars doing the work of eight is not a framework — it is survival, and his children are being raised inside that gap. His wife carries the spiritual weight of the home alone — praying over children her husband will not lead to the altar, covering in faith a family designed to move under his authority. At the same time, his wife speaks into a silence — there is no voice in the home naming what she carries, affirming who she is, or calling out what God placed in her. His children are inheriting both deficits simultaneously. His children grow up with a picture of God as ceremonially present and practically irrelevant — faith is what their mother did, not what their father modeled. No one is speaking the child's design into existence before the world gets there first; their sense of self is built entirely from external mirrors — peer approval, performance, whatever fills the silence. His wife is married to two men — the one the world sees and the one she lives with; she has learned that the gap between his public commitments and his private behavior is real, and she carries that knowledge alone. His wife has no one in the home willing to tell her the true thing — not in cruelty, but in love; she navigates without the steady voice of a man who knows her and speaks honestly into her life. His children will find the gap — they always do — and when they do, they will not merely lose respect for their father; they will lose their capacity to trust authority, and sometimes God, for years. His children are drifting without calibration — no trusted voice that both knows them and tells them the true thing about where they are heading before the consequences arrive. His children are growing up in a home with no held line — not because no one cares, but because the person designed to hold it has stopped; and what a mother holds alone is never quite the same as what a father and mother hold together. He disciplines his children but offers neither naming nor wisdom with it — correction without encouragement or mentorship teaches a child what the line is, but not who they are or why the line matters. What his children are building their picture of fatherhood from is what remains — and the Discipliner they needed is one of the things they are not getting. The fracture integrity creates is not loud — it is quiet and cumulative; the children do not announce the day they stopped believing him. They simply stop, and he rarely sees it coming.

Scenario 184

Fractured Pillars: S (Spiritual Leader) + E1 (Encourager & Nurturer) + E2 (Example Who Inspires Potential) + R (Reprover & Wise Mentor) + D (Discipliner)

Solid Pillars: H1 (Husband Who Loves Sacrificially) + P (Protector & Provider) + H2 (Heart of Integrity)

What Happens to the Family:

Five pillars have fractured. What remains — Husband Who Loves Sacrificially + Protector & Provider + Heart of Integrity — is what this family now calls fatherhood. His wife carries the spiritual weight of the home alone — praying over children her husband will not lead to the altar, covering in faith a family designed to move under his authority. At the same time, his wife speaks into a silence — there is no voice in the home naming what she carries, affirming who she is, or calling out what God placed in her. His children are inheriting both deficits simultaneously. His children grow up with a picture of God as ceremonially present and practically irrelevant — faith is what their mother did, not what their father modeled. No one is speaking the child's design into existence before the world gets there first; their sense of self is built entirely from external mirrors — peer approval, performance, whatever fills the silence. His wife sees a man going through the motions of his own life — never fully alive to his design, never modeling what it looks like to pursue the thing God placed in him. His wife has no one in the home willing to tell her the true thing — not in cruelty, but in love; she navigates without the steady voice of a man who knows her and speaks honestly into her life. His children have no picture of what a man who carries his God-given design actually looks like in daily life; the father's own unlived potential becomes the ceiling the children cannot see past. His children are drifting without calibration — no trusted voice that both knows them and tells them the true thing about where they are heading before the consequences arrive. His children are growing up in a home with no held line — not because no one cares, but because the person designed to hold it has stopped; and what a mother holds alone is never quite the same as what a father and mother hold together. He speaks into his children but has nothing to point them toward — encouragement without example produces children who feel seen but have no picture of what they are being built for, and without spiritual grounding behind it, even that purpose has no foundation. What his children are building their picture of fatherhood from is what remains — and the Discipliner they needed is one of the things they are not getting. Adults who were never named by their father spend their lives either achieving to fill the silence or collapsing when achievement fails to do it — and they rarely trace it back to the right source.

Scenario 185

Fractured Pillars: S (Spiritual Leader) + P (Protector & Provider) + H2 (Heart of Integrity) + E2 (Example Who Inspires Potential) + R (Reprover & Wise Mentor)

Solid Pillars: H1 (Husband Who Loves Sacrificially) + E1 (Encourager & Nurturer) + D (Discipliner)

What Happens to the Family:

Five pillars are fractured. The three still standing — Husband Who Loves Sacrificially + Encourager & Nurturer + Discipliner — have become the entire definition of fatherhood in this home. His children will grow up believing this is what fathers do, because it is what their father did. His wife carries the spiritual weight of the home alone — praying over children her husband will not lead to the altar, covering in faith a family designed to move under his authority. At the same time, his wife is unprotected — whether the failure is material, emotional, or spiritual; she has learned that the perimeter is unmanned and she cannot rely on him to stand between her and what threatens the home. His children are inheriting both deficits simultaneously. His children grow up with a picture of God as ceremonially present and practically irrelevant — faith is what their mother did, not what their father modeled. His children are growing up inside a home with an unlocked door — exposed to whatever fills the vacuum the father has left, and no one standing watch. His wife is married to two men — the one the world sees and the one she lives with; she has learned that the gap between his public commitments and his private behavior is real, and she carries that knowledge alone. His wife sees a man going through the motions of his own life — never fully alive to his design, never modeling what it looks like to pursue the thing God placed in him. His children will find the gap — they always do — and when they do, they will not merely lose respect for their father; they will lose their capacity to trust authority, and sometimes God, for years. His children have no picture of what a man who carries his God-given design actually looks like in daily life; the father's own unlived potential becomes the ceiling the children cannot see past. His children are drifting without calibration — no trusted voice that both knows them and tells them the true thing about where they are heading before the consequences arrive. He leads spiritually in appearance but not in private — the vertical commitment he performs on Sunday is contradicted by the man his family sees Monday through Saturday, and a life not fully lived becomes the only picture of purpose his children have. What his children are building their picture of fatherhood from is what remains — and the Reprover & Wise Mentor they needed is one of the things they are not getting. The fracture integrity creates is not loud — it is quiet and cumulative; the children do not announce the day they stopped believing him. They simply stop, and he rarely sees it coming.

Scenario 186

Fractured Pillars: S (Spiritual Leader) + P (Protector & Provider) + H2 (Heart of Integrity) + E2 (Example Who Inspires Potential) + D (Discipliner)

Solid Pillars: H1 (Husband Who Loves Sacrificially) + E1 (Encourager & Nurturer) + R (Reprover & Wise Mentor)

What Happens to the Family:

Five of the eight pillars have failed. What remains — Husband Who Loves Sacrificially + Encourager & Nurturer + Reprover & Wise Mentor — has become the whole picture of fatherhood for this family. His children will grow up believing this is what fathers do. His wife carries the spiritual weight of the home alone — praying over children her husband will not lead to the altar, covering in faith a family designed to move under his authority. At the same time, his wife is unprotected — whether the failure is material, emotional, or spiritual; she has learned that the perimeter is unmanned and she cannot rely on him to stand between her and what threatens the home. His children are inheriting both deficits simultaneously. His children grow up with a picture of God as ceremonially present and practically irrelevant — faith is what their mother did, not what their father modeled. His children are growing up inside a home with an unlocked door — exposed to whatever fills the vacuum the father has left, and no one standing watch. His wife is married to two men — the one the world sees and the one she lives with; she has learned that the gap between his public commitments and his private behavior is real, and she carries that knowledge alone. His wife sees a man going through the motions of his own life — never fully alive to his design, never modeling what it looks like to pursue the thing God placed in him. His children will find the gap — they always do — and when they do, they will not merely lose respect for their father; they will lose their capacity to trust authority, and sometimes God, for years. His children have no picture of what a man who carries his God-given design actually looks like in daily life; the father's own unlived potential becomes the ceiling the children cannot see past. His children are growing up in a home with no held line — not because no one cares, but because the person designed to hold it has stopped; and what a mother holds alone is never quite the same as what a father and mother hold together. He leads spiritually in appearance but not in private — the vertical commitment he performs on Sunday is contradicted by the man his family sees Monday through Saturday, and a life not fully lived becomes the only picture of purpose his children have. What his children are building their picture of fatherhood from is what remains — and the Discipliner they needed is one of the things they are not getting. The fracture integrity creates is not loud — it is quiet and cumulative; the children do not announce the day they stopped believing him. They simply stop, and he rarely sees it coming.

Fractured Pillars: S (Spiritual Leader) + P (Protector & Provider) + H2 (Heart of Integrity) + R (Reprover & Wise Mentor) + D (Discipliner)

Solid Pillars: H1 (Husband Who Loves Sacrificially) + E1 (Encourager & Nurturer) + E2 (Example Who Inspires Potential)

What Happens to the Family:

Five pillars have failed. Three remain — Husband Who Loves Sacrificially + Encourager & Nurturer + Example Who Inspires Potential. Those three are not simply holding; they have become everything the children know about what a father is. His wife carries the spiritual weight of the home alone — praying over children her husband will not lead to the altar, covering in faith a family designed to move under his authority. At the same time, his wife is unprotected — whether the failure is material, emotional, or spiritual; she has learned that the perimeter is unmanned and she cannot rely on him to stand between her and what threatens the home. His children are inheriting both deficits simultaneously. His children grow up with a picture of God as ceremonially present and practically irrelevant — faith is what their mother did, not what their father modeled. His children are growing up inside a home with an unlocked door — exposed to whatever fills the vacuum the father has left, and no one standing watch. His wife is married to two men — the one the world sees and the one she lives with; she has learned that the gap between his public commitments and his private behavior is real, and she carries that knowledge alone. His wife has no one in the home willing to tell her the true thing — not in cruelty, but in love; she navigates without the steady voice of a man who knows her and speaks honestly into her life. His children will find the gap — they always do — and when they do, they will not merely lose respect for their father; they will lose their capacity to trust authority, and sometimes God, for years. His children are drifting without calibration — no trusted voice that both knows them and tells them the true thing about where they are heading before the consequences arrive. His children are growing up in a home with no held line — not because no one cares, but because the person designed to hold it has stopped; and what a mother holds alone is never quite the same as what a father and mother hold together. He tries to hold lines in the home but has stopped providing the covering that makes discipline feel like love rather than control — children without protection experience correction as threat. What his children are building their picture of fatherhood from is what remains — and the Discipliner they needed is one of the things they are not getting. The fracture integrity creates is not loud — it is quiet and cumulative; the children do not announce the day they stopped believing him. They simply stop, and he rarely sees it coming.

Scenario **188**

Fractured Pillars: S (Spiritual Leader) + P (Protector & Provider) + E2 (Example Who Inspires Potential) + R (Reprover & Wise Mentor) + D (Discipliner)

Solid Pillars: H1 (Husband Who Loves Sacrificially) + E1 (Encourager & Nurturer) + H2 (Heart of Integrity)

What Happens to the Family:

Five pillars are down. Three are standing: Husband Who Loves Sacrificially + Encourager & Nurturer + Heart of Integrity. And those three have become the entire definition of fatherhood in this home. His wife carries the spiritual weight of the home alone — praying over children her husband will not lead to the altar, covering in faith a family designed to move under his authority. At the same time, his wife is unprotected — whether the failure is material, emotional, or spiritual; she has learned that the perimeter is unmanned and she cannot rely on him to stand between her and what threatens the home. His children are inheriting both deficits simultaneously. His children grow up with a picture of God as ceremonially present and practically irrelevant — faith is what their mother did, not what their father modeled. His children are growing up inside a home with an unlocked door — exposed to whatever fills the vacuum the father has left, and no one standing watch. His wife sees a man going through the motions of his own life — never fully alive to his design, never modeling what it looks like to pursue the thing God placed in him. His wife has no one in the home willing to tell her the true thing — not in cruelty, but in love; she navigates without the steady voice of a man who knows her and speaks honestly into her life.

His children have no picture of what a man who carries his God-given design actually looks like in daily life; the father's own unlived potential becomes the ceiling the children cannot see past. His children are drifting without calibration — no trusted voice that both knows them and tells them the true thing about where they are heading before the consequences arrive. His children are growing up in a home with no held line — not because no one cares, but because the person designed to hold it has stopped; and what a mother holds alone is never quite the same as what a father and mother hold together. He speaks into his children but has nothing to point them toward — encouragement without example produces children who feel seen but have no picture of what they are being built for, and without spiritual grounding behind it, even that purpose has no foundation. What his children are building their picture of fatherhood from is what remains — and the Discipliner they needed is one of the things they are not getting. They will reach adulthood without a template for what a man surrendered to something greater than himself actually looks like, and they will not know what they are missing until they are trying to build something themselves.

Fractured Pillars: S (Spiritual Leader) + H2 (Heart of Integrity) + E2 (Example Who Inspires Potential) + R (Reprover & Wise Mentor) + D (Discipliner)

Solid Pillars: H1 (Husband Who Loves Sacrificially) + E1 (Encourager & Nurturer) + P (Protector & Provider)

What Happens to the Family:

Five of the eight pillars have failed. The three that remain — Husband Who Loves Sacrificially + Encourager & Nurturer + Protector & Provider — are real. But three pillars doing the work of eight is not a framework — it is survival, and his children are being raised inside that gap. His wife carries the spiritual weight of the home alone — praying over children her husband will not lead to the altar, covering in faith a family designed to move under his authority. At the same time, his wife is married to two men — the one the world sees and the one she lives with; she has learned that the gap between his public commitments and his private behavior is real, and she carries that knowledge alone. His children are inheriting both deficits simultaneously. His children grow up with a picture of God as ceremonially present and practically irrelevant — faith is what their mother did, not what their father modeled. His children will find the gap — they always do — and when they do, they will not merely lose respect for their father; they will lose their capacity to trust authority, and sometimes God, for years. His wife sees a man going through the motions of his own life — never fully alive to his design, never modeling what it looks like to pursue the thing God placed in him. His wife has no one in the home willing to tell her the true thing — not in cruelty, but in love; she navigates without the steady voice of a man who knows her and speaks honestly into her life. His children have no picture of what a man who carries his God-given design actually looks like in daily life; the father's own unlived potential becomes the ceiling the children cannot see past. His children are drifting without calibration — no trusted voice that both knows them and tells them the true thing about where they are heading before the consequences arrive. His children are growing up in a home with no held line — not because no one cares, but because the person designed to hold it has stopped; and what a mother holds alone is never quite the same as what a father and mother hold together. He leads spiritually in appearance but not in private — the vertical commitment he performs on Sunday is contradicted by the man his family sees Monday through Saturday, and a life not fully lived becomes the only picture of purpose his children have. What his children are building their picture of fatherhood from is what remains — and the Discipliner they needed is one of the things they are not getting. The fracture integrity creates is not loud — it is quiet and cumulative; the children do not announce the day they stopped believing him. They simply stop, and he rarely sees it coming.

Fractured Pillars: H1 (Husband Who Loves Sacrificially) + E1 (Encourager & Nurturer) + P (Protector & Provider) + H2 (Heart of Integrity) + E2 (Example Who Inspires Potential)

Solid Pillars: S (Spiritual Leader) + R (Reprover & Wise Mentor) + D (Discipliner)

What Happens to the Family:

Five pillars have fractured. What remains — Spiritual Leader + Reprover & Wise Mentor + Discipliner — is what this family now calls fatherhood. His wife is not being pursued — she is being maintained; the covenant runs on autopilot, and she carries the relational weight of the marriage alone, managing rather than being led. At the same time, his wife speaks into a silence — there is no voice in the home naming what she carries, affirming who she is, or calling out what God placed in her. His children are inheriting both deficits simultaneously. His children are absorbing a picture of marriage as coexistence — two people occupying the same house — and they will bring that picture into their own relationships before they understand where it came from. No one is speaking the child's design into existence before the world gets there first; their sense of self is built entirely from external mirrors — peer approval, performance, whatever fills the silence. His wife is unprotected — whether the failure is material, emotional, or spiritual; she has learned that the perimeter is unmanned and she cannot rely on him to stand between her and what threatens the home. His wife is married to two men — the one the world sees and the one she lives with; she has learned that the gap between his public commitments and his private behavior is real, and she carries that knowledge alone. His children are growing up inside a home with an unlocked door — exposed to whatever fills the vacuum the father has left, and no one standing watch. His children will find the gap — they always do — and when they do, they will not merely lose respect for their father; they will lose their capacity to trust authority, and sometimes God, for years. His children have no picture of what a man who carries his God-given design actually looks like in daily life; the father's own unlived potential becomes the ceiling the children cannot see past. He provides for the home materially but has stopped investing in either the marriage or the people inside it — provision without pursuit, correction without naming, leaves his family feeling managed rather than known. What his children are building their picture of fatherhood from is what remains — and the Example Who Inspires Potential they needed is one of the things they are not getting. The fracture integrity creates is not loud — it is quiet and cumulative; the children do not announce the day they stopped believing him. They simply stop, and he rarely sees it coming.

Scenario **191**

Fractured Pillars: H1 (Husband Who Loves Sacrificially) + E1 (Encourager & Nurturer) + P (Protector & Provider) + H2 (Heart of Integrity) + R (Reprover & Wise Mentor)

Solid Pillars: S (Spiritual Leader) + E2 (Example Who Inspires Potential) + D (Discipliner)

What Happens to the Family:

Five pillars are fractured. The three still standing — Spiritual Leader + Example Who Inspires Potential + Discipliner — have become the entire definition of fatherhood in this home. His children will grow up believing this is what fathers do, because it is what their father did. His wife is not being pursued — she is being maintained; the covenant runs on autopilot, and she carries the relational weight of the marriage alone, managing rather than being led. At the same time, his wife speaks into a silence — there is no voice in the home naming what she carries, affirming who she is, or calling out what God placed in her. His children are inheriting both deficits simultaneously. His children are absorbing a picture of marriage as coexistence — two people occupying the same house — and they will bring that picture into their own relationships before they understand where it came from. No one is speaking the child's design into existence before the world gets there first; their sense of self is built entirely from external mirrors — peer approval, performance, whatever fills the silence. His wife is unprotected — whether the failure is material, emotional, or spiritual; she has learned that the perimeter is unmanned and she cannot rely on him to stand between her and what threatens the home. His wife is married to two men — the one the world sees and the one she lives with; she has learned that the gap between his public commitments and his private behavior is real, and she carries that knowledge alone. His children are growing up inside a home with an unlocked door — exposed to whatever fills the vacuum the father has left, and no one standing watch. His children will find the gap — they always do — and when they do, they will not merely lose respect for their father; they will lose their capacity to trust authority, and sometimes God, for years. His children are drifting without calibration — no trusted voice that both knows them and tells them the true thing about where they are heading before the consequences arrive. He provides for the home materially but has stopped investing in either the marriage or the people inside it — provision without pursuit, correction without naming, leaves his family feeling managed rather than known. What his children are building their picture of fatherhood from is what remains — and the Reprover & Wise Mentor they needed is one of the things they are not getting. The fracture integrity creates is not loud — it is quiet and cumulative; the children do not announce the day they stopped believing him. They simply stop, and he rarely sees it coming.

Scenario 192

Fractured Pillars: H1 (Husband Who Loves Sacrificially) + E1 (Encourager & Nurturer) + P (Protector & Provider) + H2 (Heart of Integrity) + D (Discipliner)

Solid Pillars: S (Spiritual Leader) + E2 (Example Who Inspires Potential) + R (Reprover & Wise Mentor)

What Happens to the Family:

Five of the eight pillars have failed. What remains — Spiritual Leader + Example Who Inspires Potential + Reprover & Wise Mentor — has become the whole picture of fatherhood for this family. His children will grow up believing this is what fathers do. His wife is not being pursued — she is being maintained; the covenant runs on autopilot, and she carries the relational weight of the marriage alone, managing rather than being led. At the same time, his wife speaks into a silence — there is no voice in the home naming what she carries, affirming who she is, or calling out what God placed in her. His children are inheriting both deficits simultaneously. His children are absorbing a picture of marriage as coexistence — two people occupying the same house — and they will bring that picture into their own relationships before they understand where it came from. No one is speaking the child's design into existence before the world gets there first; their sense of self is built entirely from external mirrors — peer approval, performance, whatever fills the silence. His wife is unprotected — whether the failure is material, emotional, or spiritual; she has learned that the perimeter is unmanned and she cannot rely on him to stand between her and what threatens the home. His wife is married to two men — the one the world sees and the one she lives with; she has learned that the gap between his public commitments and his private behavior is real, and she carries that knowledge alone. His children are growing up inside a home with an unlocked door — exposed to whatever fills the vacuum the father has left, and no one standing watch. His children will find the gap — they always do — and when they do, they will not merely lose respect for their father; they will lose their capacity to trust authority, and sometimes God, for years. His children are growing up in a home with no held line — not because no one cares, but because the person designed to hold it has stopped; and what a mother holds alone is never quite the same as what a father and mother hold together. He provides for the home materially but has stopped investing in either the marriage or the people inside it — provision without pursuit, correction without naming, leaves his family feeling managed rather than known. What his children are building their picture of fatherhood from is what remains — and the Discipliner they needed is one of the things they are not getting. The daughters will accept less than they deserve and not know why; the sons will drift toward the same emotional distance their father modeled and call it normal.

Scenario 193

Fractured Pillars: H1 (Husband Who Loves Sacrificially) + E1 (Encourager & Nurturer) + P (Protector & Provider) + E2 (Example Who Inspires Potential) + R (Reprover & Wise Mentor)

Solid Pillars: S (Spiritual Leader) + H2 (Heart of Integrity) + D (Discipliner)

What Happens to the Family:

Five pillars have failed. Three remain — Spiritual Leader + Heart of Integrity + Discipliner. Those three are not simply holding; they have become everything the children know about what a father is. His wife is not being pursued — she is being maintained; the covenant runs on autopilot, and she carries the relational weight of the marriage alone, managing rather than being led. At the same time, his wife speaks into a silence — there is no voice in the home naming what she carries, affirming who she is, or calling out what God placed in her. His children are inheriting both deficits simultaneously. His children are absorbing a picture of marriage as coexistence — two people occupying the same house — and they will bring that picture into their own relationships before they understand where it came from. No one is speaking the child's design into existence before the world gets there first; their sense of self is built entirely from external mirrors — peer approval, performance, whatever fills the silence. His wife is unprotected — whether the failure is material, emotional, or spiritual; she has learned that the perimeter is unmanned and she cannot rely on him to stand between her and what threatens the home. His wife sees a man going through the motions of his own life — never fully alive to his design, never modeling what it looks like to pursue the thing God placed in him. His children are growing up inside a home with an unlocked door — exposed to whatever fills the vacuum the father has left, and no one standing watch. His children have no picture of what a man who carries his God-given design actually looks like in daily life; the father's own unlived potential becomes the ceiling the children cannot see past. His children are drifting without calibration — no trusted voice that both knows them and tells them the true thing about where they are heading before the consequences arrive. He provides for the home materially but has stopped investing in either the marriage or the people inside it — provision without pursuit, correction without naming, leaves his family feeling managed rather than known. What his children are building their picture of fatherhood from is what remains — and the Reprover & Wise Mentor they needed is one of the things they are not getting. Adults who were never named by their father spend their lives either achieving to fill the silence or collapsing when achievement fails to do it — and they rarely trace it back to the right source.

Scenario 194

Fractured Pillars: H1 (Husband Who Loves Sacrificially) + E1 (Encourager & Nurturer) + P (Protector & Provider) + E2 (Example Who Inspires Potential) + D (Discipliner)

Solid Pillars: S (Spiritual Leader) + H2 (Heart of Integrity) + R (Reprover & Wise Mentor)

What Happens to the Family:

Five pillars are down. Three are standing: Spiritual

Leader + Heart of Integrity + Reprover & Wise Mentor. And those three have become the entire definition of fatherhood in this home. His wife is not being pursued — she is being maintained; the covenant runs on autopilot, and she carries the relational weight of the marriage alone, managing rather than being led. At the same time, his wife speaks into a silence — there is no voice in the home naming what she carries, affirming who she is, or calling out what God placed in her. His children are inheriting both deficits simultaneously. His children are absorbing a picture of marriage as coexistence — two people occupying the same house — and they will bring that picture into their own relationships before they understand where it came from. No one is speaking the child's design into existence before the world gets there first; their sense of self is built entirely from external mirrors — peer approval, performance, whatever fills the silence. His wife is unprotected — whether the failure is material, emotional, or spiritual; she has learned that the perimeter is unmanned and she cannot rely on him to stand between her and what threatens the home. His wife sees a man going through the motions of his own life — never fully alive to his design, never modeling what it looks like to pursue the thing God placed in him. His children are growing up inside a home with an unlocked door — exposed to whatever fills the vacuum the father has left, and no one standing watch. His children have no picture of what a man who carries his God-given design actually looks like in daily life; the father's own unlived potential becomes the ceiling the children cannot see past. His children are growing up in a home with no held line —

not because no one cares, but because the person designed to hold it has stopped; and what a mother holds alone is never quite the same as what a father and mother hold together. He provides for the home materially but has stopped investing in either the marriage or the people inside it — provision without pursuit, correction without naming, leaves his family feeling managed rather than known. What his children are building their picture of fatherhood from is what remains — and the Discipliner they needed is one of the things they are not getting. The daughters will accept less than they deserve and not know why; the sons will drift toward the same emotional distance their father modeled and call it normal.

Scenario 195

Fractured Pillars: H1 (Husband Who Loves Sacrificially) + E1 (Encourager & Nurturer) + P (Protector & Provider) + R (Reprover & Wise Mentor) + D (Discipliner)

Solid Pillars: S (Spiritual Leader) + H2 (Heart of Integrity) + E2 (Example Who Inspires Potential)

What Happens to the Family:

Five of the eight pillars have failed. The three that remain — Spiritual Leader + Heart of Integrity + Example Who Inspires Potential — are real. But three pillars doing the work of eight is not a framework — it is survival, and his children are being raised inside that gap. His wife is not being pursued — she is being maintained; the covenant runs on autopilot, and she carries the relational weight of the marriage alone, managing rather than being led. At the same time, his wife speaks into a silence — there is no voice in the home naming what she carries, affirming who she is, or calling out what God placed in her. His children are inheriting both deficits simultaneously. His children are absorbing a picture of marriage as coexistence — two people occupying the same house — and they will bring that picture into their own relationships before they understand where it came from. No one is speaking the child's design into existence before the world gets there first; their sense of self is built entirely from external mirrors — peer approval, performance, whatever fills the silence. His wife is unprotected — whether the failure is material, emotional, or spiritual; she has learned that the perimeter is unmanned and she cannot rely on him to stand between her and what threatens the home. His wife has no one in the home willing to tell her the true thing — not in cruelty, but in love; she navigates without the steady voice of a man who knows her and speaks honestly into her life. His children are growing up inside a home with an unlocked door — exposed to whatever fills the vacuum the father has left, and no one standing watch. His children are drifting without calibration — no trusted voice that both knows them and tells them the true thing about where they are heading before the consequences arrive. His children are growing up in a home with no held line — not because no one cares, but because the person designed to hold it has stopped; and what a mother holds alone is never quite the same as what a father and mother hold together. He provides for the home materially but has stopped investing in either the marriage or the people inside it — provision without pursuit, correction without naming, leaves his family feeling managed rather than known. What his children are building their picture of fatherhood from is what remains — and the Discipliner they needed is one of the things they are not getting. The daughters will accept less than they deserve and not know why; the sons will drift toward the same emotional distance their father modeled and call it normal.

Scenario 196

Fractured Pillars: H1 (Husband Who Loves Sacrificially) + E1 (Encourager & Nurturer) + H2 (Heart of Integrity) + E2 (Example Who Inspires Potential) + R (Reprover & Wise Mentor)

Solid Pillars: S (Spiritual Leader) + P (Protector & Provider) + D (Discipliner)

What Happens to the Family:

Five pillars have fractured. What remains — Spiritual Leader + Protector & Provider + Discipliner — is what this family now calls fatherhood. His wife is not being pursued — she is being maintained; the covenant runs on autopilot, and she carries the relational weight of the marriage alone, managing rather than being led. At the same time, his wife speaks into a silence — there is no voice in the home naming what she carries, affirming who she is, or calling out what God placed in her. His children are inheriting both deficits simultaneously. His children are absorbing a picture of marriage as coexistence — two people occupying the same house — and they will bring that picture into their own relationships before they understand where it came from. No one is speaking the child's design into existence before the world gets there first; their sense of self is built entirely from external mirrors — peer approval, performance, whatever fills the silence. His wife is married to two men — the one the world sees and the one she lives with; she has learned that the gap between his public commitments and his private behavior is real, and she carries that knowledge alone. His wife sees a man going through the motions of his own life — never fully alive to his design, never modeling what it looks like to pursue the thing God placed in him. His children will find the gap — they always do — and when they do, they will not merely lose respect for their father; they will lose their capacity to trust authority, and sometimes God, for years. His children have no picture of what a man who carries his God-given design actually looks like in daily life; the father's own unlived potential becomes the ceiling the children cannot see past. His children are drifting without calibration — no trusted voice that both knows them and tells them the true thing about where they are heading before the consequences arrive. He provides for the home materially but has stopped investing in either the marriage or the people inside it — provision without pursuit, correction without naming, leaves his family feeling managed rather than known. What his children are building their picture of fatherhood from is what remains — and the Reprover & Wise Mentor they needed is one of the things they are not getting. The fracture integrity creates is not loud — it is quiet and cumulative; the children do not announce the day they stopped believing him. They simply stop, and he rarely sees it coming.

Scenario 197

Fractured Pillars: H1 (Husband Who Loves Sacrificially) + E1 (Encourager & Nurturer) + H2 (Heart of Integrity) + E2 (Example Who Inspires Potential) + D (Discipliner)

Solid Pillars: S (Spiritual Leader) + P (Protector & Provider) + R (Reprover & Wise Mentor)

What Happens to the Family:

Five pillars are fractured. The three still standing — Spiritual Leader + Protector & Provider + Reprover & Wise Mentor — have become the entire definition of fatherhood in this home. His children will grow up believing this is what fathers do, because it is what their father did. His wife is not being pursued — she is being maintained; the covenant runs on autopilot, and she carries the relational weight of the marriage alone, managing rather than being led. At the same time, his wife speaks into a silence — there is no voice in the home naming what she carries, affirming who she is, or calling out what God placed in her. His children are inheriting both deficits simultaneously. His children are absorbing a picture of marriage as coexistence — two people occupying the same house — and they will bring that picture into their own relationships before they understand where it came from. No one is speaking the child's design into existence before the world gets there first; their sense of self is built entirely from external mirrors — peer approval, performance, whatever fills the silence. His wife is married to two men — the one the world sees and the one she lives with; she has learned that the gap between his public commitments and his private behavior is real, and she carries that knowledge alone. His wife sees a man going through the motions of his own life — never fully alive to his design, never modeling what it looks like to pursue the thing God placed in him. His children will find the gap — they always do — and when they do, they will not merely lose respect for their father; they will lose their capacity to trust authority, and sometimes God, for years. His children have no picture of what a man who carries his God-given design actually looks like in daily life; the father's own unlived potential becomes the ceiling the children cannot see past. His children are growing up in a home with no held line — not because no one cares, but because the person designed to hold it has stopped; and what a mother holds alone is never quite the same as what a father and mother hold together. He provides for the home materially but has stopped investing in either the marriage or the people inside it — provision without pursuit, correction without naming, leaves his family feeling managed rather than known. What his children are building their picture of fatherhood from is what remains — and the Discipliner they needed is one of the things they are not getting. The daughters will accept less than they deserve and not know why; the sons will drift toward the same emotional distance their father modeled and call it normal.

Scenario **198**

Fractured Pillars: H1 (Husband Who Loves Sacrificially) + E1 (Encourager & Nurturer) + H2 (Heart of Integrity) + R (Reprover & Wise Mentor) + D (Discipliner)

Solid Pillars: S (Spiritual Leader) + P (Protector & Provider) + E2 (Example Who Inspires Potential)

What Happens to the Family:

Five of the eight pillars have failed. What remains — Spiritual Leader + Protector & Provider + Example Who Inspires Potential — has become the whole picture of fatherhood for this family. His children will grow up believing this is what fathers do. His wife is not being pursued — she is being maintained; the covenant runs on autopilot, and she carries the relational weight of the marriage alone, managing rather than being led. At the same time, his wife speaks into a silence — there is no voice in the home naming what she carries, affirming who she is, or calling out what God placed in her. His children are inheriting both deficits simultaneously. His children are absorbing a picture of marriage as coexistence — two people occupying the same house — and they will bring that picture into their own relationships before they understand where it came from. No one is speaking the child's design into existence before the world gets there first; their sense of self is built entirely from external mirrors — peer approval, performance, whatever fills the silence. His wife is married to two men — the one the world sees and the one she lives with; she has learned that the gap between his public commitments and his private behavior is real, and she carries that knowledge alone. His wife has no one in the home willing to tell her the true thing — not in cruelty, but in love; she navigates without the steady voice of a man who knows her and speaks honestly into her life. His children will find the gap — they always do — and when they do, they will not merely lose respect for their father; they will lose their capacity to trust authority, and sometimes God, for years. His children are drifting without calibration — no trusted voice that both knows them and tells them the true thing about where they are heading before the consequences arrive. His children are growing up in a home with no held line — not because no one cares, but because the person designed to hold it has stopped; and what a mother holds alone is never quite the same as what a father and mother hold together. He provides for the home materially but has stopped investing in either the marriage or the people inside it — provision without pursuit, correction without naming, leaves his family feeling managed rather than known. What his children are building their picture of fatherhood from is what remains — and the Discipliner they needed is one of the things they are not getting. The daughters will accept less than they deserve and not know why; the sons will drift toward the same emotional distance their father modeled and call it normal.

Scenario 199

Fractured Pillars: H1 (Husband Who Loves Sacrificially) + E1 (Encourager & Nurturer) + E2 (Example Who Inspires Potential) + R (Reprover & Wise Mentor) + D (Discipliner)

Solid Pillars: S (Spiritual Leader) + P (Protector & Provider) + H2 (Heart of Integrity)

What Happens to the Family:

Five pillars have failed. Three remain — Spiritual Leader + Protector & Provider + Heart of Integrity. Those three are not simply holding; they have become everything the children know about what a father is. His wife is not being pursued — she is being maintained; the covenant runs on autopilot, and she carries the relational weight of the marriage alone, managing rather than being led. At the same time, his wife speaks into a silence — there is no voice in the home naming what she carries, affirming who she is, or calling out what God placed in her. His children are inheriting both deficits simultaneously. His children are absorbing a picture of marriage as coexistence — two people occupying the same house — and they will bring that picture into their own relationships before they understand where it came from. No one is speaking the child's design into existence before the world gets there first; their sense of self is built entirely from external mirrors — peer approval, performance, whatever fills the silence. His wife sees a man going through the motions of his own life — never fully alive to his design, never modeling what it looks like to pursue the thing God placed in him. His wife has no one in the home willing to tell her the true thing — not in cruelty, but in love; she navigates without the steady voice of a man who knows her and speaks honestly into her life. His children have no picture of what a man who carries his God-given design actually looks like in daily life; the father's own unlived potential becomes the ceiling the children cannot see past. His children are drifting without calibration — no trusted voice that both knows them and tells them the true thing about where they are heading before the consequences arrive. His children are growing up in a home with no held line — not because no one cares, but because the person designed to hold it has stopped; and what a mother holds alone is never quite the same as what a father and mother hold together. He provides for the home materially but has stopped investing in either the marriage or the people inside it — provision without pursuit, correction without naming, leaves his family feeling managed rather than known. What his children are building their picture of fatherhood from is what remains — and the Discipliner they needed is one of the things they are not getting. The daughters will accept less than they deserve and not know why; the sons will drift toward the same emotional distance their father modeled and call it normal.

Scenario 200

Fractured Pillars: H1 (Husband Who Loves Sacrificially) + P (Protector & Provider) + H2 (Heart of Integrity) + E2 (Example Who Inspires Potential) + R (Reprover & Wise Mentor)

Solid Pillars: S (Spiritual Leader) + E1 (Encourager & Nurturer) + D (Discipliner)

What Happens to the Family:

Five pillars are down. Three are standing: Spiritual Leader + Encourager & Nurturer + Discipliner. And those three have become the entire definition of fatherhood in this home. His wife is not being pursued — she is being maintained; the covenant runs on autopilot, and she carries the relational weight of the marriage alone, managing rather than being led. At the same time, his wife is unprotected — whether the failure is material, emotional, or spiritual; she has learned that the perimeter is unmanned and she cannot rely on him to stand between her and what threatens the home. His children are inheriting both deficits simultaneously. His children are absorbing a picture of marriage as coexistence — two people occupying the same house — and they will bring that picture into their own relationships before they understand where it came from. His children are growing up inside a home with an unlocked door — exposed to whatever fills the vacuum the father has left, and no one standing watch. His wife is married to two men — the one the world sees and the one she lives with; she has learned that the gap between his public commitments and his private behavior is real, and she carries that knowledge alone. His wife sees a man going through the motions of his own life — never fully alive to his design, never modeling what it looks like to pursue the thing God placed in him. His children will find the gap — they always do — and when they do, they will not merely lose respect for their father; they will lose their capacity to trust authority, and sometimes God, for years. His children have no picture of what a man who carries his God-given design actually looks like in daily life; the father's own unlived potential becomes the ceiling the children cannot see past. His children are drifting without calibration — no trusted voice that both knows them and tells them the true thing about where they are heading before the consequences arrive. He leads spiritually in appearance but not in private — the vertical commitment he performs on Sunday is contradicted by the man his family sees Monday through Saturday, and a life not fully lived becomes the only picture of purpose his children have. What his children are building their picture of fatherhood from is what remains — and the Reprover & Wise Mentor they needed is one of the things they are not getting. The fracture integrity creates is not loud — it is quiet and cumulative; the children do not announce the day they stopped believing him. They simply stop, and he rarely sees it coming.

Scenario 201

Fractured Pillars: H1 (Husband Who Loves Sacrificially) + P (Protector & Provider) + H2 (Heart of Integrity) + E2 (Example Who Inspires Potential) + D (Discipliner)

Solid Pillars: S (Spiritual Leader) + E1 (Encourager & Nurturer) + R (Reprover & Wise Mentor)

What Happens to the Family:

Five of the eight pillars have failed. The three that remain — Spiritual Leader + Encourager & Nurturer + Reprover & Wise Mentor — are real. But three pillars doing the work of eight is not a framework — it is survival, and his children are being raised inside that gap. His wife is not being pursued — she is being maintained; the covenant runs on autopilot, and she carries the relational weight of the marriage alone, managing rather than being led. At the same time, his wife is unprotected — whether the failure is material, emotional, or spiritual; she has learned that the perimeter is unmanned and she cannot rely on him to stand between her and what threatens the home. His children are inheriting both deficits simultaneously. His children are absorbing a picture of marriage as coexistence — two people occupying the same house — and they will bring that picture into their own relationships before they understand where it came from. His children are growing up inside a home with an unlocked door — exposed to whatever fills the vacuum the father has left, and no one standing watch. His wife is married to two men — the one the world sees and the one she lives with; she has learned that the gap between his public commitments and his private behavior is real, and she carries that knowledge alone. His wife sees a man going through the motions of his own life — never fully alive to his design, never modeling what it looks like to pursue the thing God placed in him. His children will find the gap — they always do — and when they do, they will not merely lose respect for their father; they will lose their capacity to trust authority, and sometimes God, for years. His children have no picture of what a man who carries his God-given design actually looks like in daily life; the father's own unlived potential becomes the ceiling the children cannot see past. His children are growing up in a home with no held line — not because no one cares, but because the person designed to hold it has stopped; and what a mother holds alone is never quite the same as what a father and mother hold together. He leads spiritually in appearance but not in private — the vertical commitment he performs on Sunday is contradicted by the man his family sees Monday through Saturday, and a life not fully lived becomes the only picture of purpose his children have. What his children are building their picture of fatherhood from is what remains — and the Discipliner they needed is one of the things they are not getting. The daughters will accept less than they deserve and not know why; the sons will drift toward the same emotional distance their father modeled and call it normal.

Scenario 202

Fractured Pillars: H1 (Husband Who Loves Sacrificially) + P (Protector & Provider) + H2 (Heart of Integrity) + R (Reprover & Wise Mentor) + D (Discipliner)

Solid Pillars: S (Spiritual Leader) + E1 (Encourager & Nurturer) + E2 (Example Who Inspires Potential)

What Happens to the Family:

Five pillars have fractured. What remains — Spiritual Leader + Encourager & Nurturer + Example Who Inspires Potential — is what this family now calls fatherhood. His wife is not being pursued — she is being maintained; the covenant runs on autopilot, and she carries the relational weight of the marriage alone, managing rather than being led. At the same time, his wife is unprotected — whether the failure is material, emotional, or spiritual; she has learned that the perimeter is unmanned and she cannot rely on him to stand between her and what threatens the home. His children are inheriting both deficits simultaneously. His children are absorbing a picture of marriage as coexistence — two people occupying the same house — and they will bring that picture into their own relationships before they understand where it came from. His children are growing up inside a home with an unlocked door — exposed to whatever fills the vacuum the father has left, and no one standing watch. His wife is married to two men — the one the world sees and the one she lives with; she has learned that the gap between his public commitments and his private behavior is real, and she carries that knowledge alone. His wife has no one in the home willing to tell her the true thing — not in cruelty, but in love; she navigates without the steady voice of a man who knows her and speaks honestly into her life. His children will find the gap — they always do — and when they do, they will not merely lose respect for their father; they will lose their capacity to trust authority, and sometimes God, for years. His children are drifting without calibration — no trusted voice that both knows them and tells them the true thing about where they are heading before the consequences arrive. His children are growing up in a home with no held line — not because no one cares, but because the person designed to hold it has stopped; and what a mother holds alone is never quite the same as what a father and mother hold together. He leads spiritually in appearance but not in private — the vertical commitment he performs on Sunday is contradicted by the man his family sees Monday through Saturday. What his children are building their picture of fatherhood from is what remains — and the Discipliner they needed is one of the things they are not getting. The daughters will accept less than they deserve and not know why; the sons will drift toward the same emotional distance their father modeled and call it normal.

Fractured Pillars: H1 (Husband Who Loves Sacrificially) + P (Protector & Provider) + E2 (Example Who Inspires Potential) + R (Reprover & Wise Mentor) + D (Discipliner)

Solid Pillars: S (Spiritual Leader) + E1 (Encourager & Nurturer) + H2 (Heart of Integrity)

What Happens to the Family:

Five pillars are fractured. The three still standing — Spiritual Leader + Encourager & Nurturer + Heart of Integrity — have become the entire definition of fatherhood in this home. His children will grow up believing this is what fathers do, because it is what their father did. His wife is not being pursued — she is being maintained; the covenant runs on autopilot, and she carries the relational weight of the marriage alone, managing rather than being led. At the same time, his wife is unprotected — whether the failure is material, emotional, or spiritual; she has learned that the perimeter is unmanned and she cannot rely on him to stand between her and what threatens the home. His children are inheriting both deficits simultaneously. His children are absorbing a picture of marriage as coexistence — two people occupying the same house — and they will bring that picture into their own relationships before they understand where it came from. His children are growing up inside a home with an unlocked door — exposed to whatever fills the vacuum the father has left, and no one standing watch. His wife sees a man going through the motions of his own life — never fully alive to his design, never modeling what it looks like to pursue the thing God placed in him. His wife has no one in the home willing to tell her the true thing — not in cruelty, but in love; she navigates without the steady voice of a man who knows her and speaks honestly into her life. His children have no picture of what a man who carries his God-given design actually looks like in daily life; the father's own unlived potential becomes the ceiling the children cannot see past. His children are drifting without calibration — no trusted voice that both knows them and tells them the true thing about where they are heading before the consequences arrive. His children are growing up in a home with no held line — not because no one cares, but because the person designed to hold it has stopped; and what a mother holds alone is never quite the same as what a father and mother hold together. He tries to hold lines in the home but has stopped providing the covering that makes discipline feel like love rather than control — children without protection experience correction as threat. What his children are building their picture of fatherhood from is what remains — and the Discipliner they needed is one of the things they are not getting. The daughters will accept less than they deserve and not know why; the sons will drift toward the same emotional distance their father modeled and call it normal.

Scenario 204

Fractured Pillars: H1 (Husband Who Loves Sacrificially) + H2 (Heart of Integrity) + E2 (Example Who Inspires Potential) + R (Reprover & Wise Mentor) + D (Discipliner)

Solid Pillars: S (Spiritual Leader) + E1 (Encourager & Nurturer) + P (Protector & Provider)

What Happens to the Family:

Five of the eight pillars have failed. What remains — Spiritual Leader + Encourager & Nurturer + Protector & Provider — has become the whole picture of fatherhood for this family. His children will grow up believing this is what fathers do. His wife is not being pursued — she is being maintained; the covenant runs on autopilot, and she carries the relational weight of the marriage alone, managing rather than being led. At the same time, his wife is married to two men — the one the world sees and the one she lives with; she has learned that the gap between his public commitments and his private behavior is real, and she carries that knowledge alone. His children are inheriting both deficits simultaneously. His children are absorbing a picture of marriage as coexistence — two people occupying the same house — and they will bring that picture into their own relationships before they understand where it came from. His children will find the gap — they always do — and when they do, they will not merely lose respect for their father; they will lose their capacity to trust authority, and sometimes God, for years. His wife sees a man going through the motions of his own life — never fully alive to his design, never modeling what it looks like to pursue the thing God placed in him. His wife has no one in the home willing to tell her the true thing — not in cruelty, but in love; she navigates without the steady voice of a man who knows her and speaks honestly into her life. His children have no picture of what a man who carries his God-given design actually looks like in daily life; the father's own unlived potential becomes the ceiling the children cannot see past. His children are drifting without calibration — no trusted voice that both knows them and tells them the true thing about where they are heading before the consequences arrive. His children are growing up in a home with no held line — not because no one cares, but because the person designed to hold it has stopped; and what a mother holds alone is never quite the same as what a father and mother hold together. He leads spiritually in appearance but not in private — the vertical commitment he performs on Sunday is contradicted by the man his family sees Monday through Saturday, and a life not fully lived becomes the only picture of purpose his children have. What his children are building their picture of fatherhood from is what remains — and the Discipliner they needed is one of the things they are not getting. The daughters will accept less than they deserve and not know why; the sons will drift toward the same emotional distance their father modeled and call it normal.

Scenario 205

Fractured Pillars: E1 (Encourager & Nurturer) + P (Protector & Provider) + H2 (Heart of Integrity) + E2 (Example Who Inspires Potential) + R (Reprover & Wise Mentor)

Solid Pillars: S (Spiritual Leader) + H1 (Husband Who Loves Sacrificially) + D (Discipliner)

What Happens to the Family:

Five pillars have failed. Three remain — Spiritual Leader + Husband Who Loves Sacrificially + Discipliner. Those three are not simply holding; they have become everything the children know about what a father is. His wife speaks into a silence — there is no voice in the home naming what she carries, affirming who she is, or calling out what God placed in her. At the same time, his wife is unprotected — whether the failure is material, emotional, or spiritual; she has learned that the perimeter is unmanned and she cannot rely on him to stand between her and what threatens the home. His children are inheriting both deficits simultaneously. No one is speaking the child's design into existence before the world gets there first; their sense of self is built entirely from external mirrors — peer approval, performance, whatever fills the silence. His children are growing up inside a home with an unlocked door — exposed to whatever fills the vacuum the father has left, and no one standing watch. His wife is married to two men — the one the world sees and the one she lives with; she has learned that the gap between his public commitments and his private behavior is real, and she carries that knowledge alone. His wife sees a man going through the motions of his own life — never fully alive to his design, never modeling what it looks like to pursue the thing God placed in him. His children will find the gap — they always do — and when they do, they will not merely lose respect for their father; they will lose their capacity to trust authority, and sometimes God, for years. His children have no picture of what a man who carries his God-given design actually looks like in daily life; the father's own unlived potential becomes the ceiling the children cannot see past. His children are drifting without calibration — no trusted voice that both knows them and tells them the true thing about where they are heading before the consequences arrive. He leads spiritually in appearance but not in private — the vertical commitment he performs on Sunday is contradicted by the man his family sees Monday through Saturday, and a life not fully lived becomes the only picture of purpose his children have. What his children are building their picture of fatherhood from is what remains — and the Reprover & Wise Mentor they needed is one of the things they are not getting. The fracture integrity creates is not loud — it is quiet and cumulative; the children do not announce the day they stopped believing him. They simply stop, and he rarely sees it coming.

Scenario 206

Fractured Pillars: E1 (Encourager & Nurturer) + P (Protector & Provider) + H2 (Heart of Integrity) + E2 (Example Who Inspires Potential) + D (Discipliner)

Solid Pillars: S (Spiritual Leader) + H1 (Husband Who Loves Sacrificially) + R (Reprover & Wise Mentor)

What Happens to the Family:

Five pillars are down. Three are standing: Spiritual Leader + Husband Who Loves Sacrificially + Reprover & Wise Mentor. And those three have become the entire definition of fatherhood in this home. His wife speaks into a silence — there is no voice in the home naming what she carries, affirming who she is, or calling out what God placed in her. At the same time, his wife is unprotected — whether the failure is material, emotional, or spiritual; she has learned that the perimeter is unmanned and she cannot rely on him to stand between her and what threatens the home. His children are inheriting both deficits simultaneously. No one is speaking the child's design into existence before the world gets there first; their sense of self is built entirely from external mirrors — peer approval, performance, whatever fills the silence. His children are growing up inside a home with an unlocked door — exposed to whatever fills the vacuum the father has left, and no one standing watch. His wife is married to two men — the one the world sees and the one she lives with; she has learned that the gap between his public commitments and his private behavior is real, and she carries that knowledge alone. His wife sees a man going through the motions of his own life — never fully alive to his design, never modeling what it looks like to pursue the thing God placed in him. His children will find the gap — they always do — and when they do, they will not merely lose respect for their father; they will lose their capacity to trust authority, and sometimes God, for years. His children have no picture of what a man who carries his God-given design actually looks like in daily life; the father's own unlived potential becomes the ceiling the children cannot see past. His children are growing up in a home with no held line — not because no one cares, but because the person designed to hold it has stopped; and what a mother holds alone is never quite the same as what a father and mother hold together. He leads spiritually in appearance but not in private — the vertical commitment he performs on Sunday is contradicted by the man his family sees Monday through Saturday, and a life not fully lived becomes the only picture of purpose his children have. What his children are building their picture of fatherhood from is what remains — and the Discipliner they needed is one of the things they are not getting. The fracture integrity creates is not loud — it is quiet and cumulative; the children do not announce the day they stopped believing him. They simply stop, and he rarely sees it coming.

Scenario 207

Fractured Pillars: E1 (Encourager & Nurturer) + P (Protector & Provider) + H2 (Heart of Integrity) + R (Reprover & Wise Mentor) + D (Discipliner)

Solid Pillars: S (Spiritual Leader) + H1 (Husband Who Loves Sacrificially) + E2 (Example Who Inspires Potential)

What Happens to the Family:

Five of the eight pillars have failed. The three that remain — Spiritual Leader + Husband Who Loves Sacrificially + Example Who Inspires Potential — are real. But three pillars doing the work of eight is not a framework — it is survival, and his children are being raised inside that gap. His wife speaks into a silence — there is no voice in the home naming what she carries, affirming who she is, or calling out what God placed in her. At the same time, his wife is unprotected — whether the failure is material, emotional, or spiritual; she has learned that the perimeter is unmanned and she cannot rely on him to stand between her and what threatens the home. His children are inheriting both deficits simultaneously. No one is speaking the child's design into existence before the world gets there first; their sense of self is built entirely from external mirrors — peer approval, performance, whatever fills the silence. His children are growing up inside a home with an unlocked door — exposed to whatever fills the vacuum the father has left, and no one standing watch. His wife is married to two men — the one the world sees and the one she lives with; she has learned that the gap between his public commitments and his private behavior is real, and she carries that knowledge alone. His wife has no one in the home willing to tell her the true thing — not in cruelty, but in love; she navigates without the steady voice of a man who knows her and speaks honestly into her life. His children will find the gap — they always do — and when they do, they will not merely lose respect for their father; they will lose their capacity to trust authority, and sometimes God, for years. His children are drifting without calibration — no trusted voice that both knows them and tells them the true thing about where they are heading before the consequences arrive. His children are growing up in a home with no held line — not because no one cares, but because the person designed to hold it has stopped; and what a mother holds alone is never quite the same as what a father and mother hold together. He leads spiritually in appearance but not in private — the vertical commitment he performs on Sunday is contradicted by the man his family sees Monday through Saturday. What his children are building their picture of fatherhood from is what remains — and the Discipliner they needed is one of the things they are not getting. The fracture integrity creates is not loud — it is quiet and cumulative; the children do not announce the day they stopped believing him. They simply stop, and he rarely sees it coming.

Scenario 208

Fractured Pillars: E1 (Encourager & Nurturer) + P (Protector & Provider) + E2 (Example Who Inspires Potential) + R (Reprover & Wise Mentor) + D (Discipliner)

Solid Pillars: S (Spiritual Leader) + H1 (Husband Who Loves Sacrificially) + H2 (Heart of Integrity)

What Happens to the Family:

Five pillars have fractured. What remains — Spiritual Leader + Husband Who Loves Sacrificially + Heart of Integrity — is what this family now calls fatherhood. His wife speaks into a silence — there is no voice in the home naming what she carries, affirming who she is, or calling out what God placed in her. At the same time, his wife is unprotected — whether the failure is material, emotional, or spiritual; she has learned that the perimeter is unmanned and she cannot rely on him to stand between her and what threatens the home. His children are inheriting both deficits simultaneously. No one is speaking the child's design into existence before the world gets there first; their sense of self is built entirely from external mirrors — peer approval, performance, whatever fills the silence. His children are growing up inside a home with an unlocked door — exposed to whatever fills the vacuum the father has left, and no one standing watch. His wife sees a man going through the motions of his own life — never fully alive to his design, never modeling what it looks like to pursue the thing God placed in him. His wife has no one in the home willing to tell her the true thing — not in cruelty, but in love; she navigates without the steady voice of a man who knows her and speaks honestly into her life. His children have no picture of what a man who carries his God-given design actually looks like in daily life; the father's own unlived potential becomes the ceiling the children cannot see past. His children are drifting without calibration — no trusted voice that both knows them and tells them the true thing about where they are heading before the consequences arrive. His children are growing up in a home with no held line — not because no one cares, but because the person designed to hold it has stopped; and what a mother holds alone is never quite the same as what a father and mother hold together. He disciplines his children but offers neither naming nor wisdom with it — correction without encouragement or mentorship teaches a child what the line is, but not who they are or why the line matters. What his children are building their picture of fatherhood from is what remains — and the Discipliner they needed is one of the things they are not getting. Adults who were never named by their father spend their lives either achieving to fill the silence or collapsing when achievement fails to do it — and they rarely trace it back to the right source.

Scenario 209

Fractured Pillars: E1 (Encourager & Nurturer) + H2 (Heart of Integrity) + E2 (Example Who Inspires Potential) + R (Reprover & Wise Mentor) + D (Discipliner)

Solid Pillars: S (Spiritual Leader) + H1 (Husband Who Loves Sacrificially) + P (Protector & Provider)

What Happens to the Family:

Five pillars are fractured. The three still standing — Spiritual Leader + Husband Who Loves Sacrificially + Protector & Provider — have become the entire definition of fatherhood in this home. His children will grow up believing this is what fathers do, because it is what their father did. His wife speaks into a silence — there is no voice in the home naming what she carries, affirming who she is, or calling out what God placed in her. At the same time, his wife is married to two men — the one the world sees and the one she lives with; she has learned that the gap between his public commitments and his private behavior is real, and she carries that knowledge alone. His children are inheriting both deficits simultaneously. No one is speaking the child's design into existence before the world gets there first; their sense of self is built entirely from external mirrors — peer approval, performance, whatever fills the silence. His children will find the gap — they always do — and when they do, they will not merely lose respect for their father; they will lose their capacity to trust authority, and sometimes God, for years. His wife sees a man going through the motions of his own life — never fully alive to his design, never modeling what it looks like to pursue the thing God placed in him. His wife has no one in the home willing to tell her the true thing — not in cruelty, but in love; she navigates without the steady voice of a man who knows her and speaks honestly into her life. His children have no picture of what a man who carries his God-given design actually looks like in daily life; the father's own unlived potential becomes the ceiling the children cannot see past. His children are drifting without calibration — no trusted voice that both knows them and tells them the true thing about where they are heading before the consequences arrive. His children are growing up in a home with no held line — not because no one cares, but because the person designed to hold it has stopped; and what a mother holds alone is never quite the same as what a father and mother hold together. He leads spiritually in appearance but not in private — the vertical commitment he performs on Sunday is contradicted by the man his family sees Monday through Saturday, and a life not fully lived becomes the only picture of purpose his children have. What his children are building their picture of fatherhood from is what remains — and the Discipliner they needed is one of the things they are not getting. The fracture integrity creates is not loud — it is quiet and cumulative; the children do not announce the day they stopped believing him. They simply stop, and he rarely sees it coming.

Scenario 210

Fractured Pillars: P (Protector & Provider) + H2 (Heart of Integrity) + E2 (Example Who Inspires Potential) + R (Reprover & Wise Mentor) + D (Discipliner)

Solid Pillars: S (Spiritual Leader) + H1 (Husband Who Loves Sacrificially) + E1 (Encourager & Nurturer)

What Happens to the Family:

Five of the eight pillars have failed. What remains — Spiritual Leader + Husband Who Loves Sacrificially + Encourager & Nurturer — has become the whole picture of fatherhood for this family. His children will grow up believing this is what fathers do. His wife is unprotected — whether the failure is material, emotional, or spiritual; she has learned that the perimeter is unmanned and she cannot rely on him to stand between her and what threatens the home. At the same time, his wife is married to two men — the one the world sees and the one she lives with; she has learned that the gap between his public commitments and his private behavior is real, and she carries that knowledge alone. His children are inheriting both deficits simultaneously. His children are growing up inside a home with an unlocked door — exposed to whatever fills the vacuum the father has left, and no one standing watch. His children will find the gap — they always do — and when they do, they will not merely lose respect for their father; they will lose their capacity to trust authority, and sometimes God, for years. His wife sees a man going through the motions of his own life — never fully alive to his design, never modeling what it looks like to pursue the thing God placed in him. His wife has no one in the home willing to tell her the true thing — not in cruelty, but in love; she navigates without the steady voice of a man who knows her and speaks honestly into her life. His children have no picture of what a man who carries his God-given design actually looks like in daily life; the father's own unlived potential becomes the ceiling the children cannot see past. His children are drifting without calibration — no trusted voice that both knows them and tells them the true thing about where they are heading before the consequences arrive. His children are growing up in a home with no held line — not because no one cares, but because the person designed to hold it has stopped; and what a mother holds alone is never quite the same as what a father and mother hold together. He leads spiritually in appearance but not in private — the vertical commitment he performs on Sunday is contradicted by the man his family sees Monday through Saturday, and a life not fully lived becomes the only picture of purpose his children have. What his children are building their picture of fatherhood from is what remains — and the Discipliner they needed is one of the things they are not getting. The fracture integrity creates is not loud — it is quiet and cumulative; the children do not announce the day they stopped believing him. They simply stop, and he rarely sees it coming.

Six Pillars Failing

28 scenarios

Near-total collapse. Two pillars remain. The father can be identified by two things he still does — and his children will know him by those two things, and by the profound absence of everything else. The two remaining pillars are real. They are not enough to substitute for the whole. At this level, the family is absorbing six simultaneous deficits while the father may not understand why nothing seems to be working.

Scenario 211

Fractured Pillars: S (Spiritual Leader) + H1 (Husband Who Loves Sacrificially) + E1 (Encourager & Nurturer) + P (Protector & Provider) + H2 (Heart of Integrity) + E2 (Example Who Inspires Potential)

Solid Pillars: R (Reprover & Wise Mentor) + D (Discipliner)

What Happens to the Family:

Six of eight pillars have failed. What remains — Reprover & Wise Mentor + Discipliner — are two load-bearing points in a structure designed for eight. The family feels the weight of what is missing far more than the presence of what is left. His wife carries the spiritual weight of the home alone — praying over children her husband will not lead to the altar, covering in faith a family designed to move under his authority. His wife is not being pursued — she is being maintained; the covenant runs on autopilot, and she carries the relational weight of the marriage alone, managing rather than being led. The remaining fractures compound what she is already carrying. His children are absorbing six simultaneous deficits: His children grow up with a picture of God as ceremonially present and practically irrelevant — faith is what their mother did, not what their father modeled. His children are absorbing a picture of marriage as coexistence — two people occupying the same house — and they will bring that picture into their own relationships before they understand where it came from. No one is speaking the child's design into existence before the world gets there first; their sense of self is built entirely from external mirrors — peer approval, performance, whatever fills the silence. His children are growing up inside a home with an unlocked door — exposed to whatever fills the vacuum the father has left, and no one standing watch. They do not experience these as separate failures. They experience them as the texture of their home. He leads spiritually in appearance but not in private — the vertical commitment he performs on Sunday is contradicted by the man his family sees Monday through Saturday, and a life not fully lived becomes the only picture of purpose his children have. The two things he still does are real. But they cannot carry six absences. His children will know him by what he gave — and be shaped far more by what he withheld.

Scenario 212

Fractured Pillars: S (Spiritual Leader) + H1 (Husband Who Loves Sacrificially) + E1 (Encourager & Nurturer) + P (Protector & Provider) + H2 (Heart of Integrity) + R (Reprover & Wise Mentor)

Solid Pillars: E2 (Example Who Inspires Potential) + D (Discipliner)

What Happens to the Family:

Six pillars have failed. Two remain — Example Who Inspires Potential + Discipliner. The family does not experience those two remaining pillars as sufficient; they experience the six that are absent as the texture of their home. His wife carries the spiritual weight of the home alone — praying over children her husband will not lead to the altar, covering in faith a family designed to move under his authority. His wife is not being pursued — she is being maintained; the covenant runs on autopilot, and she carries the relational weight of the marriage alone, managing rather than being led. The remaining fractures compound what she is already carrying. His children are absorbing six simultaneous deficits: His children grow up with a picture of God as ceremonially present and practically irrelevant — faith is what their mother did, not what their father modeled. His children are absorbing a picture of marriage as coexistence — two people occupying the same house — and they will bring that picture into their own relationships before they understand where it came from. No one is speaking the child's design into existence before the world gets there first; their sense of self is built entirely from external mirrors — peer approval, performance, whatever fills the silence. His children are growing up inside a home with an unlocked door — exposed to whatever fills the vacuum the father has left, and no one standing watch. They do not experience these as separate failures. They experience them as the texture of their home. He disciplines his children but offers neither naming nor wisdom with it — correction without encouragement or mentorship teaches a child what the line is, but not who they are or why the line matters. The two things he still does are real. But they cannot carry six absences. His children will know him by what he gave — and be shaped far more by what he withheld.

Scenario 213

Fractured Pillars: S (Spiritual Leader) + H1 (Husband Who Loves Sacrificially) + E1 (Encourager & Nurturer) + P (Protector & Provider) + H2 (Heart of Integrity) + D (Discipliner)

Solid Pillars: E2 (Example Who Inspires Potential) + R (Reprover & Wise Mentor)

What Happens to the Family:

Six of the eight pillars have failed. What remains — Example Who Inspires Potential + Reprover & Wise Mentor — is two structural commitments in a structure that required eight. The family feels the weight of what is missing far more than the presence of what is left. His wife carries the spiritual weight of the home alone — praying over children her husband will not lead to the altar, covering in faith a family designed to move under his authority. His wife is not being pursued — she is being maintained; the covenant runs on autopilot, and she carries the relational weight of the marriage alone, managing rather than being led. The remaining fractures compound what she is already carrying. His children are absorbing six simultaneous deficits: His children grow up with a picture of God as ceremonially present and practically irrelevant — faith is what their mother did, not what their father modeled. His children are absorbing a picture of marriage as coexistence — two people occupying the same house — and they will bring that picture into their own relationships before they understand where it came from. No one is speaking the child's design into existence before the world gets there first; their sense of self is built entirely from external mirrors — peer approval, performance, whatever fills the silence. His children are growing up inside a home with an unlocked door — exposed to whatever fills the vacuum the father has left, and no one standing watch. They do not experience these as separate failures. They experience them as the texture of their home. He tries to hold lines in the home but has stopped providing the covering that makes discipline feel like love rather than control — children without protection experience correction as threat. The two things he still does are real. But they cannot carry six absences. His children will know him by what he gave — and be shaped far more by what he withheld.

Scenario 214

Fractured Pillars: S (Spiritual Leader) + H1 (Husband Who Loves Sacrificially) + E1 (Encourager & Nurturer) + P (Protector & Provider) + E2 (Example Who Inspires Potential) + R (Reprover & Wise Mentor)

Solid Pillars: H2 (Heart of Integrity) + D (Discipliner)

What Happens to the Family:

Six pillars down. Two remaining: Heart of Integrity + Discipliner. At this level, the father can be identified by two things he still does — and his children know him by those two things and by the profound absence of everything else. His wife carries the spiritual weight of the home alone — praying over children her husband will not lead to the altar, covering in faith a family designed to move under his authority. His wife is not being pursued — she is being maintained; the covenant runs on autopilot, and she carries the relational weight of the marriage alone, managing rather than being led. The remaining fractures compound what she is already carrying. His children are absorbing six simultaneous deficits: His children grow up with a picture of God as ceremonially present and practically irrelevant — faith is what their mother did, not what their father modeled. His children are absorbing a picture of marriage as coexistence — two people occupying the same house — and they will bring that picture into their own relationships before they understand where it came from. No one is speaking the child's design into existence before the world gets there first; their sense of self is built entirely from external mirrors — peer approval, performance, whatever fills the silence. His children are growing up inside a home with an unlocked door — exposed to whatever fills the vacuum the father has left, and no one standing watch. They do not experience these as separate failures. They experience them as the texture of their home. He speaks into his children but has nothing to point them toward — encouragement without example produces children who feel seen but have no picture of what they are being built for, and without spiritual grounding behind it, even that purpose has no foundation. The two things he still does are real. But they cannot carry six absences. His children will know him by what he gave — and be shaped far more by what he withheld.

Scenario 215

Fractured Pillars: S (Spiritual Leader) + H1 (Husband Who Loves Sacrificially) + E1 (Encourager & Nurturer) + P (Protector & Provider) + E2 (Example Who Inspires Potential) + D (Discipliner)

Solid Pillars: H2 (Heart of Integrity) + R (Reprover & Wise Mentor)

What Happens to the Family:

Six of eight pillars have failed. Two remain — Heart of Integrity + Reprover & Wise Mentor — and they are real. But they were not designed to carry the home alone, and the family is being shaped far more by what is missing than by what is left. His wife carries the spiritual weight of the home alone — praying over children her husband will not lead to the altar, covering in faith a family designed to move under his authority. His wife is not being pursued — she is being maintained; the covenant runs on autopilot, and she carries the relational weight of the marriage alone, managing rather than being led. The remaining fractures compound what she is already carrying. His children are absorbing six simultaneous deficits: His children grow up with a picture of God as ceremonially present and practically irrelevant — faith is what their mother did, not what their father modeled. His children are absorbing a picture of marriage as coexistence — two people occupying the same house — and they will bring that picture into their own relationships before they understand where it came from. No one is speaking the child's design into existence before the world gets there first; their sense of self is built entirely from external mirrors — peer approval, performance, whatever fills the silence. His children are growing up inside a home with an unlocked door — exposed to whatever fills the vacuum the father has left, and no one standing watch. They do not experience these as separate failures. They experience them as the texture of their home. He speaks into his children but has nothing to point them toward — encouragement without example produces children who feel seen but have no picture of what they are being built for, and without spiritual grounding behind it, even that purpose has no foundation. The two things he still does are real. But they cannot carry six absences. His children will know him by what he gave — and be shaped far more by what he withheld.

Scenario 216

Fractured Pillars: S (Spiritual Leader) + H1 (Husband Who Loves Sacrificially) + E1 (Encourager & Nurturer) + P (Protector & Provider) + R (Reprover & Wise Mentor) + D (Discipliner)

Solid Pillars: H2 (Heart of Integrity) + E2 (Example Who Inspires Potential)

What Happens to the Family:

Six pillars have failed. What remains is Heart of Integrity + Example Who Inspires Potential — two points of contact in a framework designed for eight. His wife carries the spiritual weight of the home alone — praying over children her husband will not lead to the altar, covering in faith a family designed to move under his authority. His wife is not being pursued — she is being maintained; the covenant runs on autopilot, and she carries the relational weight of the marriage alone, managing rather than being led. The remaining fractures compound what she is already carrying. His children are absorbing six simultaneous deficits: His children grow up with a picture of God as ceremonially present and practically irrelevant — faith is what their mother did, not what their father modeled. His children are absorbing a picture of marriage as coexistence — two people occupying the same house — and they will bring that picture into their own relationships before they understand where it came from. No one is speaking the child's design into existence before the world gets there first; their sense of self is built entirely from external mirrors — peer approval, performance, whatever fills the silence. His children are growing up inside a home with an unlocked door — exposed to whatever fills the vacuum the father has left, and no one standing watch. They do not experience these as separate failures. They experience them as the texture of their home. He disciplines his children but offers neither naming nor wisdom with it — correction without encouragement or mentorship teaches a child what the line is, but not who they are or why the line matters. The two things he still does are real. But they cannot carry six absences. His children will know him by what he gave — and be shaped far more by what he withheld.

Scenario 217

Fractured Pillars: S (Spiritual Leader) + H1 (Husband Who Loves Sacrificially) + E1 (Encourager & Nurturer) + H2 (Heart of Integrity) + E2 (Example Who Inspires Potential) + R (Reprover & Wise Mentor)

Solid Pillars: P (Protector & Provider) + D (Discipliner)

What Happens to the Family:

Six of eight pillars have failed. What remains — Protector & Provider + Discipliner — are two load-bearing points in a structure designed for eight. The family feels the weight of what is missing far more than the presence of what is left. His wife carries the spiritual weight of the home alone — praying over children her husband will not lead to the altar, covering in faith a family designed to move under his authority. His wife is not being pursued — she is being maintained; the covenant runs on autopilot, and she carries the relational weight of the marriage alone, managing rather than being led. The remaining fractures compound what she is already carrying. His children are absorbing six simultaneous deficits: His children grow up with a picture of God as ceremonially present and practically irrelevant — faith is what their mother did, not what their father modeled. His children are absorbing a picture of marriage as coexistence — two people occupying the same house — and they will bring that picture into their own relationships before they understand where it came from. No one is speaking the child's design into existence before the world gets there first; their sense of self is built entirely from external mirrors — peer approval, performance, whatever fills the silence. His children will find the gap — they always do — and when they do, they will not merely lose respect for their father; they will lose their capacity to trust authority, and sometimes God, for years. They do not experience these as separate failures. They experience them as the texture of their home. He leads spiritually in appearance but not in private — the vertical commitment he performs on Sunday is contradicted by the man his family sees Monday through Saturday, and a life not fully lived becomes the only picture of purpose his children have. The two things he still does are real. But they cannot carry six absences. His children will know him by what he gave — and be shaped far more by what he withheld.

Scenario 218

Fractured Pillars: S (Spiritual Leader) + H1 (Husband Who Loves Sacrificially) + E1 (Encourager & Nurturer) + H2 (Heart of Integrity) + E2 (Example Who Inspires Potential) + D (Discipliner)

Solid Pillars: P (Protector & Provider) + R (Reprover & Wise Mentor)

What Happens to the Family:

Six pillars have failed. Two remain — Protector & Provider + Reprover & Wise Mentor. The family does not experience those two remaining pillars as sufficient; they experience the six that are absent as the texture of their home. His wife carries the spiritual weight of the home alone — praying over children her husband will not lead to the altar, covering in faith a family designed to move under his authority. His wife is not being pursued — she is being maintained; the covenant runs on autopilot, and she carries the relational weight of the marriage alone, managing rather than being led. The remaining fractures compound what she is already carrying. His children are absorbing six simultaneous deficits: His children grow up with a picture of God as ceremonially present and practically irrelevant — faith is what their mother did, not what their father modeled. His children are absorbing a picture of marriage as coexistence — two people occupying the same house — and they will bring that picture into their own relationships before they understand where it came from. No one is speaking the child's design into existence before the world gets there first; their sense of self is built entirely from external mirrors — peer approval, performance, whatever fills the silence. His children will find the gap — they always do — and when they do, they will not merely lose respect for their father; they will lose their capacity to trust authority, and sometimes God, for years. They do not experience these as separate failures. They experience them as the texture of their home. He leads spiritually in appearance but not in private — the vertical commitment he performs on Sunday is contradicted by the man his family sees Monday through Saturday, and a life not fully lived becomes the only picture of purpose his children have. The two things he still does are real. But they cannot carry six absences. His children will know him by what he gave — and be shaped far more by what he withheld.

Scenario 219

Fractured Pillars: S (Spiritual Leader) + H1 (Husband Who Loves Sacrificially) + E1 (Encourager & Nurturer) + H2 (Heart of Integrity) + R (Reprover & Wise Mentor) + D (Discipliner)

Solid Pillars: P (Protector & Provider) + E2 (Example Who Inspires Potential)

What Happens to the Family:

Six of the eight pillars have failed. What remains — Protector & Provider + Example Who Inspires Potential — is two structural commitments in a structure that required eight. The family feels the weight of what is missing far more than the presence of what is left. His wife carries the spiritual weight of the home alone — praying over children her husband will not lead to the altar, covering in faith a family designed to move under his authority. His wife is not being pursued — she is being maintained; the covenant runs on autopilot, and she carries the relational weight of the marriage alone, managing rather than being led. The remaining fractures compound what she is already carrying. His children are absorbing six simultaneous deficits: His children grow up with a picture of God as ceremonially present and practically irrelevant — faith is what their mother did, not what their father modeled. His children are absorbing a picture of marriage as coexistence — two people occupying the same house — and they will bring that picture into their own relationships before they understand where it came from. No one is speaking the child's design into existence before the world gets there first; their sense of self is built entirely from external mirrors — peer approval, performance, whatever fills the silence. His children will find the gap — they always do — and when they do, they will not merely lose respect for their father; they will lose their capacity to trust authority, and sometimes God, for years. They do not experience these as separate failures. They experience them as the texture of their home. He disciplines his children but offers neither naming nor wisdom with it — correction without encouragement or mentorship teaches a child what the line is, but not who they are or why the line matters. The two things he still does are real. But they cannot carry six absences. His children will know him by what he gave — and be shaped far more by what he withheld.

Scenario 220

Fractured Pillars: S (Spiritual Leader) + H1 (Husband Who Loves Sacrificially) + E1 (Encourager & Nurturer) + E2 (Example Who Inspires Potential) + R (Reprover & Wise Mentor) + D (Discipliner)

Solid Pillars: P (Protector & Provider) + H2 (Heart of Integrity)

What Happens to the Family:

Six pillars down. Two remaining: Protector & Provider + Heart of Integrity. At this level, the father can be identified by two things he still does — and his children know him by those two things and by the profound absence of everything else. His wife carries the spiritual weight of the home alone — praying over children her husband will not lead to the altar, covering in faith a family designed to move under his authority. His wife is not being pursued — she is being maintained; the covenant runs on autopilot, and she carries the relational weight of the marriage alone, managing rather than being led. The remaining fractures compound what she is already carrying. His children are absorbing six simultaneous deficits: His children grow up with a picture of God as ceremonially present and practically irrelevant — faith is what their mother did, not what their father modeled. His children are absorbing a picture of marriage as coexistence — two people occupying the same house — and they will bring that picture into their own relationships before they understand where it came from. No one is speaking the child's design into existence before the world gets there first; their sense of self is built entirely from external mirrors — peer approval, performance, whatever fills the silence. His children have no picture of what a man who carries his God-given design actually looks like in daily life; the father's own unlived potential becomes the ceiling the children cannot see past. They do not experience these as separate failures. They experience them as the texture of their home. He speaks into his children but has nothing to point them toward — encouragement without example produces children who feel seen but have no picture of what they are being built for, and without spiritual grounding behind it, even that purpose has no foundation. The two things he still does are real. But they cannot carry six absences. His children will know him by what he gave — and be shaped far more by what he withheld.

Scenario 221

Fractured Pillars: S (Spiritual Leader) + H1 (Husband Who Loves Sacrificially) + P (Protector & Provider) + H2 (Heart of Integrity)

+ E2 (Example Who Inspires Potential) + R (Reprover & Wise Mentor)
Solid Pillars: E1 (Encourager & Nurturer) + D (Discipliner)

What Happens to the Family:

Six of eight pillars have failed. Two remain — Encourager & Nurturer + Discipliner — and they are real. But they were not designed to carry the home alone, and the family is being shaped far more by what is missing than by what is left. His wife carries the spiritual weight of the home alone — praying over children her husband will not lead to the altar, covering in faith a family designed to move under his authority. His wife is not being pursued — she is being maintained; the covenant runs on autopilot, and she carries the relational weight of the marriage alone, managing rather than being led. The remaining fractures compound what she is already carrying. His children are absorbing six simultaneous deficits: His children grow up with a picture of God as ceremonially present and practically irrelevant — faith is what their mother did, not what their father modeled. His children are absorbing a picture of marriage as coexistence — two people occupying the same house — and they will bring that picture into their own relationships before they understand where it came from. His children are growing up inside a home with an unlocked door — exposed to whatever fills the vacuum the father has left, and no one standing watch. His children will find the gap — they always do — and when they do, they will not merely lose respect for their father; they will lose their capacity to trust authority, and sometimes God, for years. They do not experience these as separate failures. They experience them as the texture of their home. He leads spiritually in appearance but not in private — the vertical commitment he performs on Sunday is contradicted by the man his family sees Monday through Saturday, and a life not fully lived becomes the only picture of purpose his children have. The two things he still does are real. But they cannot carry six absences. His children will know him by what he gave — and be shaped far more by what he withheld.

Scenario 222

Fractured Pillars: S (Spiritual Leader) + H1 (Husband Who Loves Sacrificially) + P (Protector & Provider) + H2 (Heart of Integrity) + E2 (Example Who Inspires Potential) + D (Discipliner)

Solid Pillars: E1 (Encourager & Nurturer) + R (Reprover & Wise Mentor)

What Happens to the Family:

Six pillars have failed. What remains is Encourager & Nurturer + Reprover & Wise Mentor — two points of contact in a framework designed for eight. His wife carries the spiritual weight of the home alone — praying over children her husband will not lead to the altar, covering in faith a family designed to move under his authority. His wife is not being pursued — she is being maintained; the covenant runs on autopilot, and she carries the relational weight of the marriage alone, managing rather than being led. The remaining fractures compound what she is already carrying. His children are absorbing six simultaneous deficits: His children grow up with a picture of God as ceremonially present and practically irrelevant — faith is what their mother did, not what their father modeled. His children are absorbing a picture of marriage as coexistence — two people occupying the same house — and they will bring that picture into their own relationships before they understand where it came from. His children are growing up inside a home with an unlocked door — exposed to whatever fills the vacuum the father has left, and no one standing watch. His children will find the gap — they always do — and when they do, they will not merely lose respect for their father; they will lose their capacity to trust authority, and sometimes God, for years. They do not experience these as separate failures. They experience them as the texture of their home. He leads spiritually in appearance but not in private — the vertical commitment he performs on Sunday is contradicted by the man his family sees Monday through Saturday, and a life not fully lived becomes the only picture of purpose his children have. The two things he still does are real. But they cannot carry six absences. His children will know him by what he gave — and be shaped far more by what he withheld.

Scenario 223

Fractured Pillars: S (Spiritual Leader) + H1 (Husband Who Loves Sacrificially) + P (Protector & Provider) + H2 (Heart of Integrity) + R (Reprover & Wise Mentor) + D (Discipliner)

Solid Pillars: E1 (Encourager & Nurturer) + E2 (Example Who Inspires Potential)

What Happens to the Family:

Six of eight pillars have failed. What remains — Encourager & Nurturer + Example Who Inspires Potential — are two load-bearing points in a structure designed for eight. The family feels the weight of what is missing far more than the presence of what is left. His wife carries the spiritual weight of the home alone — praying over children her husband will not lead to the altar, covering in faith a family designed to move under his authority. His wife is not being pursued — she is being maintained; the covenant runs on autopilot, and she carries the relational weight of the marriage alone, managing rather than being led. The remaining fractures compound what she is already carrying. His children are absorbing six simultaneous deficits: His children grow up with a picture of God as ceremonially present and practically irrelevant — faith is what their mother did, not what their father modeled. His children are absorbing a picture of marriage as coexistence — two people occupying the same house — and they will bring that picture into their own relationships before they understand where it came from. His children are growing up inside a home with an unlocked door — exposed to whatever fills the vacuum the father has left, and no one standing watch. His children will find the gap — they always do — and when they do, they will not merely lose respect for their father; they will lose their capacity to trust authority, and sometimes God, for years. They do not experience these as separate failures. They experience them as the texture of their home. He tries to hold lines in the home but has stopped providing the covering that makes discipline feel like love rather than control — children without protection experience correction as threat. The two things he still does are real. But they cannot carry six absences. His children will know him by what he gave — and be shaped far more by what he withheld.

Scenario 224

Fractured Pillars: S (Spiritual Leader) + H1 (Husband Who Loves Sacrificially) + P (Protector & Provider) + E2 (Example Who Inspires Potential) + R (Reprover & Wise Mentor) + D (Discipliner)

Solid Pillars: E1 (Encourager & Nurturer) + H2 (Heart of Integrity)

What Happens to the Family:

Six pillars have failed. Two remain — Encourager & Nurturer + Heart of Integrity. The family does not experience those two remaining pillars as sufficient; they experience the six that are absent as the texture of their home. His wife carries the spiritual weight of the home alone — praying over children her husband will not lead to the altar, covering in faith a family designed to move under his authority. His wife is not being pursued — she is being maintained; the covenant runs on autopilot, and she carries the relational weight of the marriage alone, managing rather than being led. The remaining fractures compound what she is already carrying. His children are absorbing six simultaneous deficits: His children grow up with a picture of God as ceremonially present and practically irrelevant — faith is what their mother did, not what their father modeled. His children are absorbing a picture of marriage as coexistence — two people occupying the same house — and they will bring that picture into their own relationships before they understand where it came from. His children are growing up inside a home with an unlocked door — exposed to whatever fills the vacuum the father has left, and no one standing watch. His children have no picture of what a man who carries his God-given design actually looks like in daily life; the father's own unlived potential becomes the ceiling the children cannot see past. They do not experience these as separate failures. They experience them as the texture of their home. He speaks into his children but has nothing to point them toward — encouragement without example produces children who feel seen but have no picture of what they are being built for, and without spiritual grounding behind it, even that purpose has no foundation. The two things he still does are real. But they cannot carry six absences. His children will know him by what he gave — and be shaped far more by what he withheld.

Fractured Pillars: S (Spiritual Leader) + H1 (Husband Who Loves Sacrificially) + H2 (Heart of Integrity) + E2 (Example Who Inspires Potential) + R (Reprover & Wise Mentor) + D (Discipliner)

Solid Pillars: E1 (Encourager & Nurturer) + P (Protector & Provider)

What Happens to the Family:

Six of the eight pillars have failed. What remains — Encourager & Nurturer + Protector & Provider — is two structural commitments in a structure that required eight. The family feels the weight of what is missing far more than the presence of what is left. His wife carries the spiritual weight of the home alone — praying over children her husband will not lead to the altar, covering in faith a family designed to move under his authority. His wife is not being pursued — she is being maintained; the covenant runs on autopilot, and she carries the relational weight of the marriage alone, managing rather than being led. The remaining fractures compound what she is already carrying. His children are absorbing six simultaneous deficits: His children grow up with a picture of God as ceremonially present and practically irrelevant — faith is what their mother did, not what their father modeled. His children are absorbing a picture of marriage as coexistence — two people occupying the same house — and they will bring that picture into their own relationships before they understand where it came from. His children will find the gap — they always do — and when they do, they will not merely lose respect for their father; they will lose their capacity to trust authority, and sometimes God, for years. His children have no picture of what a man who carries his God-given design actually looks like in daily life; the father's own unlived potential becomes the ceiling the children cannot see past. They do not experience these as separate failures. They experience them as the texture of their home. He leads spiritually in appearance but not in private — the vertical commitment he performs on Sunday is contradicted by the man his family sees Monday through Saturday, and a life not fully lived becomes the only picture of purpose his children have. The two things he still does are real. But they cannot carry six absences. His children will know him by what he gave — and be shaped far more by what he withheld.

Fractured Pillars: S (Spiritual Leader) + E1 (Encourager & Nurturer) + P (Protector & Provider) + H2 (Heart of Integrity) + E2 (Example Who Inspires Potential) + R (Reprover & Wise Mentor)

Solid Pillars: H1 (Husband Who Loves Sacrificially) + D (Discipliner)

What Happens to the Family:

Six pillars down. Two remaining: Husband Who Loves Sacrificially + Discipliner. At this level, the father can be identified by two things he still does — and his children know him by those two things and by the profound absence of everything else. His wife carries the spiritual weight of the home alone — praying over children her husband will not lead to the altar, covering in faith a family designed to move under his authority. His wife speaks into a silence — there is no voice in the home naming what she carries, affirming who she is, or calling out what God placed in her. The remaining fractures compound what she is already carrying. His children are absorbing six simultaneous deficits: His children grow up with a picture of God as ceremonially present and practically irrelevant — faith is what their mother did, not what their father modeled. No one is speaking the child's design into existence before the world gets there first; their sense of self is built entirely from external mirrors — peer approval, performance, whatever fills the silence. His children are growing up inside a home with an unlocked door — exposed to whatever fills the vacuum the father has left, and no one standing watch. His children will find the gap — they always do — and when they do, they will not merely lose respect for their father; they will lose their capacity to trust authority, and sometimes God, for years. They do not experience these as separate failures. They experience them as the texture of their home. He leads spiritually in appearance but not in private — the vertical commitment he performs on Sunday is contradicted by the man his family sees Monday through Saturday, and a life not fully lived becomes the only picture of purpose his children have. The two things he still does are real. But they cannot carry six absences. His children will know him by what he gave — and be shaped far more by what he withheld.

Scenario 227

Fractured Pillars: S (Spiritual Leader) + E1 (Encourager & Nurturer) + P (Protector & Provider) + H2 (Heart of Integrity) + E2 (Example Who Inspires Potential) + D (Discipliner)

Solid Pillars: H1 (Husband Who Loves Sacrificially) + R (Reprover & Wise Mentor)

What Happens to the Family:

Six of eight pillars have failed. Two remain — Husband Who Loves Sacrificially + Reprover & Wise Mentor — and they are real. But they were not designed to carry the home alone, and the family is being shaped far more by what is missing than by what is left. His wife carries the spiritual weight of the home alone — praying over children her husband will not lead to the altar, covering in faith a family designed to move under his authority. His wife speaks into a silence — there is no voice in the home naming what she carries, affirming who she is, or calling out what God placed in her. The remaining fractures compound what she is already carrying. His children are absorbing six simultaneous deficits: His children grow up with a picture of God as ceremonially present and practically irrelevant — faith is what their mother did, not what their father modeled. No one is speaking the child's design into existence before the world gets there first; their sense of self is built entirely from external mirrors — peer approval, performance, whatever fills the silence. His children are growing up inside a home with an unlocked door — exposed to whatever fills the vacuum the father has left, and no one standing watch. His children will find the gap — they always do — and when they do, they will not merely lose respect for their father; they will lose their capacity to trust authority, and sometimes God, for years. They do not experience these as separate failures. They experience them as the texture of their home. He leads spiritually in appearance but not in private — the vertical commitment he performs on Sunday is contradicted by the man his family sees Monday through Saturday, and a life not fully lived becomes the only picture of purpose his children have. The two things he still does are real. But they cannot carry six absences. His children will know him by what he gave — and be shaped far more by what he withheld.

Scenario 228

Fractured Pillars: S (Spiritual Leader) + E1 (Encourager & Nurturer) + P (Protector & Provider) + H2 (Heart of Integrity) + R (Reprover & Wise Mentor) + D (Discipliner)

Solid Pillars: H1 (Husband Who Loves Sacrificially) + E2 (Example Who Inspires Potential)

What Happens to the Family:

Six pillars have failed. What remains is Husband Who Loves Sacrificially + Example Who Inspires Potential — two points of contact in a framework designed for eight. His wife carries the spiritual weight of the home alone — praying over children her husband will not lead to the altar, covering in faith a family designed to move under his authority. His wife speaks into a silence — there is no voice in the home naming what she carries, affirming who she is, or calling out what God placed in her. The remaining fractures compound what she is already carrying. His children are absorbing six simultaneous deficits: His children grow up with a picture of God as ceremonially present and practically irrelevant — faith is what their mother did, not what their father modeled. No one is speaking the child's design into existence before the world gets there first; their sense of self is built entirely from external mirrors — peer approval, performance, whatever fills the silence. His children are growing up inside a home with an unlocked door — exposed to whatever fills the vacuum the father has left, and no one standing watch. His children will find the gap — they always do — and when they do, they will not merely lose respect for their father; they will lose their capacity to trust authority, and sometimes

God, for years. They do not experience these as separate failures. They experience them as the texture of their home. He disciplines his children but offers neither naming nor wisdom with it — correction without encouragement or mentorship teaches a child what the line is, but not who they are or why the line matters. The two things he still does are real. But they cannot carry six absences. His children will know him by what he gave — and be shaped far more by what he withheld.

Scenario 229

Fractured Pillars: S (Spiritual Leader) + E1 (Encourager & Nurturer) + P (Protector & Provider) + E2 (Example Who Inspires Potential) + R (Reprover & Wise Mentor) + D (Discipliner)

Solid Pillars: H1 (Husband Who Loves Sacrificially) + H2 (Heart of Integrity)

What Happens to the Family:

Six of eight pillars have failed. What remains — Husband Who Loves Sacrificially + Heart of Integrity — are two load-bearing points in a structure designed for eight. The family feels the weight of what is missing far more than the presence of what is left. His wife carries the spiritual weight of the home alone — praying over children her husband will not lead to the altar, covering in faith a family designed to move under his authority. His wife speaks into a silence — there is no voice in the home naming what she carries, affirming who she is, or calling out what God placed in her. The remaining fractures compound what she is already carrying. His children are absorbing six simultaneous deficits: His children grow up with a picture of God as ceremonially present and practically irrelevant — faith is what their mother did, not what their father modeled. No one is speaking the child's design into existence before the world gets there first; their sense of self is built entirely from external mirrors — peer approval, performance, whatever fills the silence. His children are growing up inside a home with an unlocked door — exposed to whatever fills the vacuum the father has left, and no one standing watch. His children have no picture of what a man who carries his God-given design actually looks like in daily life; the father's own unlived potential becomes the ceiling the children cannot see past. They do not experience these as separate failures. They experience them as the texture of their home. He speaks into his children but has nothing to point them toward — encouragement without example produces children who feel seen but have no picture of what they are being built for, and without spiritual grounding behind it, even that purpose has no foundation. The two things he still does are real. But they cannot carry six absences. His children will know him by what he gave — and be shaped far more by what he withheld.

Scenario 230

Fractured Pillars: S (Spiritual Leader) + E1 (Encourager & Nurturer) + H2 (Heart of Integrity) + E2 (Example Who Inspires Potential) + R (Reprover & Wise Mentor) + D (Discipliner)

Solid Pillars: H1 (Husband Who Loves Sacrificially) + P (Protector & Provider)

What Happens to the Family:

Six pillars have failed. Two remain — Husband Who Loves Sacrificially + Protector & Provider. The family does not experience those two remaining pillars as sufficient; they experience the six that are absent as the texture of their home. His wife carries the spiritual weight of the home alone — praying over children her husband will not lead to the altar, covering in faith a family designed to move under his authority. His wife speaks into a silence — there is no voice in the home naming what she carries, affirming who she is, or calling out what God placed in her. The remaining fractures compound what she is already carrying. His children are absorbing six simultaneous deficits: His children grow up with a picture of God as ceremonially present and practically irrelevant — faith is what their mother did, not what their father modeled. No one is speaking the child's design into existence before the world gets there first; their sense of self is built entirely from external mirrors — peer approval, performance, whatever fills the silence. His children will find the gap — they always do — and when they do, they will not merely lose respect for their father; they will lose their capacity to trust authority, and sometimes God, for years. His children have no picture of what a man who carries his God-given design actually looks like in daily life; the father's own unlived potential becomes the ceiling the children cannot see past. They do not experience these as separate failures. They experience them as the texture of their home. He leads spiritually in appearance but not in private — the vertical commitment he performs on Sunday is contradicted by the man his family sees Monday through Saturday, and a life not fully lived becomes the only picture of purpose his children have. The two things he still does are real. But they cannot carry six absences. His children will know him by what he gave — and be shaped far more by what he withheld.

Scenario 231

Fractured Pillars: S (Spiritual Leader) + P (Protector & Provider) + H2 (Heart of Integrity) + E2 (Example Who Inspires Potential) + R (Reprover & Wise Mentor) + D (Discipliner)

Solid Pillars: H1 (Husband Who Loves Sacrificially) + E1 (Encourager & Nurturer)

What Happens to the Family:

Six of the eight pillars have failed. What remains — Husband Who Loves Sacrificially + Encourager & Nurturer — is two structural commitments in a structure that required eight. The family feels the weight of what is missing far more than the presence of what is left. His wife carries the spiritual weight of the home alone — praying over children her husband will not lead to the altar, covering in faith a family designed to move under his authority. His wife is unprotected — whether the failure is

370

material, emotional, or spiritual; she has learned that the perimeter is unmanned and she cannot rely on him to stand between her and what threatens the home. The remaining fractures compound what she is already carrying. His children are absorbing six simultaneous deficits: His children grow up with a picture of God as ceremonially present and practically irrelevant — faith is what their mother did, not what their father modeled. His children are growing up inside a home with an unlocked door — exposed to whatever fills the vacuum the father has left, and no one standing watch. His children will find the gap — they always do — and when they do, they will not merely lose respect for their father; they will lose their capacity to trust authority, and sometimes God, for years. His children have no picture of what a man who carries his God-given design actually looks like in daily life; the father's own unlived potential becomes the ceiling the children cannot see past. They do not experience these as separate failures. They experience them as the texture of their home. He leads spiritually in appearance but not in private — the vertical commitment he performs on Sunday is contradicted by the man his family sees Monday through Saturday, and a life not fully lived becomes the only picture of purpose his children have. The two things he still does are real. But they cannot carry six absences. His children will know him by what he gave — and be shaped far more by what he withheld.

Fractured Pillars: H1 (Husband Who Loves Sacrificially) + E1 (Encourager & Nurturer) + P (Protector & Provider) + H2 (Heart of Integrity) + E2 (Example Who Inspires Potential) + R (Reprover & Wise Mentor)

Solid Pillars: S (Spiritual Leader) + D (Discipliner)

What Happens to the Family:

Six pillars down. Two remaining: Spiritual Leader + Discipliner. At this level, the father can be identified by two things he still does — and his children know him by those two things and by the profound absence of everything else. His wife is not being pursued — she is being maintained; the covenant runs on autopilot, and she carries the relational weight of the marriage alone, managing rather than being led. His wife speaks into a silence — there is no voice in the home naming what she carries, affirming who she is, or calling out what God placed in her. The remaining fractures compound what she is already carrying. His children are absorbing six simultaneous deficits: His children are absorbing a picture of marriage as coexistence — two people occupying the same house — and they will bring that picture into their own relationships before they understand where it came from. No one is speaking the child's design into existence before the world gets there first; their sense of self is built entirely from external mirrors — peer approval, performance, whatever fills the silence. His children are growing up inside a home with an unlocked door — exposed to whatever fills the vacuum the father has left, and no one standing watch. His children will find the gap — they always do — and when they do, they will not merely lose respect for their father; they will lose their capacity to trust authority, and sometimes God, for years. They do not experience these as separate failures. They experience them as the texture of their home. He provides for the home materially but has stopped investing in either the marriage or the people inside it — provision without pursuit, correction without naming, leaves his family feeling managed rather than known. The two things he still does are real. But they cannot carry six absences. His children will know him by what he gave — and be shaped far more by what he withheld.

Scenario 233

Fractured Pillars: H1 (Husband Who Loves Sacrificially) + E1 (Encourager & Nurturer) + P (Protector & Provider) + H2 (Heart of Integrity) + E2 (Example Who Inspires Potential) + D (Discipliner)

Solid Pillars: S (Spiritual Leader) + R (Reprover & Wise Mentor)

What Happens to the Family:

Six of eight pillars have failed. Two remain — Spiritual Leader + Reprover & Wise Mentor — and they are real. But they were not designed to carry the home alone, and the family is being shaped far more by what is missing than by what is left. His wife is not being pursued — she is being maintained; the covenant runs on autopilot, and she carries the relational weight of the marriage alone, managing rather than being led. His wife speaks into a silence — there is no voice in the home naming what she carries, affirming who she is, or calling out what God placed in her. The remaining fractures compound what she is already carrying. His children are absorbing six simultaneous deficits: His children are absorbing a picture of marriage as coexistence — two people occupying the same house — and they will bring that picture into their own relationships before they understand where it came from. No one is speaking the child's design into existence before the world gets there first; their sense of self is built entirely from external mirrors — peer approval, performance, whatever fills the silence. His children are growing up inside a home with an unlocked door — exposed to whatever fills the vacuum the father has left, and no one standing watch. His children will find the gap — they always do — and when they do, they will not merely lose respect for their father; they will lose their capacity to trust authority, and sometimes God, for years. They do not experience these as separate failures. They experience them as the texture of their home. He provides for the home materially but has stopped investing in either the marriage or the people inside it — provision without pursuit, correction without naming, leaves his family feeling managed rather than known. The two things he still does are real. But they cannot carry six absences. His children will know him by what he gave — and be shaped far more by what he withheld.

Scenario 234

Fractured Pillars: H1 (Husband Who Loves Sacrificially) + E1 (Encourager & Nurturer) + P (Protector & Provider) + H2 (Heart of Integrity) + R (Reprover & Wise Mentor) + D (Discipliner)

Solid Pillars: S (Spiritual Leader) + E2 (Example Who Inspires Potential)

What Happens to the Family:

Six pillars have failed. What remains is Spiritual Leader + Example Who Inspires Potential — two points of contact in a framework designed for eight. His wife is not being pursued — she is being maintained; the covenant runs on autopilot, and she carries the relational weight of the marriage alone, managing rather than being led. His wife speaks into a silence — there is no voice in the home naming what she carries, affirming who she is, or calling out what God placed in her. The remaining fractures compound what she is already carrying. His children are absorbing six simultaneous deficits: His children are absorbing a picture of marriage as coexistence — two people occupying the same house — and they will bring that picture into their own relationships before they understand where it came from. No one is speaking the child's design into existence before the world gets there first; their sense of self is built entirely from external mirrors — peer approval, performance, whatever fills the silence. His children are growing up inside a home with an unlocked door — exposed to whatever fills the vacuum the father has left, and no one standing watch. His children will find the gap — they always do — and when they do, they will not merely lose respect for their father; they will lose their capacity to trust authority, and sometimes God, for years. They do not experience these as separate failures. They experience them as the texture of their home. He provides for the home materially but has stopped investing in either the marriage or the people inside it — provision without pursuit, correction without naming, leaves his family feeling managed rather than known. The two things he still does are real. But they cannot carry six absences. His children will know him by what he gave — and be shaped far more by what he withheld.

Scenario 235

Fractured Pillars: H1 (Husband Who Loves Sacrificially) + E1 (Encourager & Nurturer) + P (Protector & Provider) + E2 (Example Who Inspires Potential) + R (Reprover & Wise Mentor) + D (Discipliner)

Solid Pillars: S (Spiritual Leader) + H2 (Heart of Integrity)

What Happens to the Family:

Six of eight pillars have failed. What remains — Spiritual Leader + Heart of Integrity — are two load-bearing points in a structure designed for eight. The family feels the weight of what is missing far more than the presence of what is left. His wife is not being pursued — she is being maintained; the covenant runs on autopilot, and she carries the relational weight of the marriage alone, managing rather than being led. His wife speaks into a silence — there is no voice in the home naming what she carries, affirming who she is, or calling out what God placed in her. The remaining fractures compound what she is already carrying. His children are absorbing six simultaneous deficits: His children are absorbing a picture of marriage as coexistence — two people occupying the same house — and they will bring that picture into their own relationships before they understand where it came from. No one is speaking the child's design into existence before the world gets there first; their sense of self is built entirely from external mirrors — peer approval, performance, whatever fills the silence. His children are growing up inside a home with an unlocked door — exposed to whatever fills the vacuum the father has left, and no one standing watch. His children have no picture of what a man who carries his God-given design actually looks like in daily life; the father's own unlived potential becomes the ceiling the children cannot see past. They do not experience these as separate failures. They experience them as the texture of their home. He provides for the home materially but has stopped investing in either the marriage or the people inside it — provision without pursuit, correction without naming, leaves his family feeling managed rather than known. The two things he still does are real. But they cannot carry six absences. His children will know him by what he gave — and be shaped far more by what he withheld.

Scenario 236

Fractured Pillars: H1 (Husband Who Loves Sacrificially) + E1 (Encourager & Nurturer) + H2 (Heart of Integrity) + E2 (Example Who Inspires Potential) + R (Reprover & Wise Mentor) + D (Discipliner)

Solid Pillars: S (Spiritual Leader) + P (Protector & Provider)

What Happens to the Family:

Six pillars have failed. Two remain — Spiritual Leader + Protector & Provider. The family does not experience those two remaining pillars as sufficient; they experience the six that are absent as the texture of their home. His wife is not being pursued — she is being maintained; the covenant runs on autopilot, and she carries the relational weight of the marriage alone, managing rather than being led. His wife speaks into a silence — there is no voice in the home naming what she carries, affirming who she is, or calling out what God placed in her. The remaining fractures compound what she is already carrying. His children are absorbing six simultaneous deficits: His children are absorbing a picture of marriage as coexistence — two people occupying the same house — and they will bring that picture into their own relationships before they understand where it came from. No one is speaking the child's design into existence before the world gets there first; their sense of self is built entirely from external mirrors — peer approval, performance, whatever fills the silence. His children will find the gap — they always do — and when they do, they will not merely lose respect for their father; they will lose their capacity to trust authority, and sometimes God, for years. His children have no picture of what a man who carries his God-given design actually looks like in daily life; the father's own unlived potential becomes the ceiling the children cannot see past. They do not experience these as separate failures. They experience them as the texture of their home. He provides for the home materially but has stopped investing in either the marriage or the people inside it — provision without pursuit, correction without naming, leaves his family feeling managed rather than known. The two things he still does are real. But they cannot carry six absences. His children will know him by what he gave — and be shaped far more by what he withheld.

Scenario 237

Fractured Pillars: H1 (Husband Who Loves Sacrificially) + P (Protector & Provider) + H2 (Heart of Integrity) + E2 (Example Who Inspires Potential) + R (Reprover & Wise Mentor) + D (Discipliner)

Solid Pillars: S (Spiritual Leader) + E1 (Encourager & Nurturer)

What Happens to the Family:

Six of the eight pillars have failed. What remains — Spiritual Leader + Encourager & Nurturer — is two structural commitments in a structure that required eight. The family feels the weight of what is missing far more than the presence of what is left. His wife is not being pursued — she is being maintained; the covenant runs on autopilot, and she carries the relational weight of the marriage alone, managing rather than being led. His wife is unprotected — whether the failure is material, emotional, or spiritual; she has learned that the perimeter is unmanned and she cannot rely on him to stand between her and what threatens the home. The remaining fractures compound what she is already carrying. His children are absorbing six simultaneous deficits: His children are absorbing a picture of marriage as coexistence — two people occupying the same house — and they will bring that picture into their own relationships before they understand where it came from. His children are growing up inside a home with an unlocked door — exposed to whatever fills the vacuum the father has left, and no one standing watch. His children will find the gap — they always do — and when they do, they will not merely lose respect for their father; they will lose their capacity to trust authority, and sometimes God, for years. His children have no picture of what a man who carries his God-given design actually looks like in daily life; the father's own unlived potential becomes the ceiling the children cannot see past. They do not experience these as separate failures. They experience them as the texture of their home. He leads spiritually in appearance but not in private — the vertical commitment he performs on Sunday is contradicted by the man his family sees Monday through Saturday, and a life not fully lived becomes the only picture of purpose his children have. The two things he still does are real. But they cannot carry six absences. His children will know him by what he gave — and be shaped far more by what he withheld.

Scenario 238

Fractured Pillars: E1 (Encourager & Nurturer) + P (Protector & Provider) + H2 (Heart of Integrity) + E2 (Example Who Inspires Potential) + R (Reprover & Wise Mentor) + D (Discipliner)

Solid Pillars: S (Spiritual Leader) + H1 (Husband Who Loves Sacrificially)

What Happens to the Family:

Six pillars down. Two remaining: Spiritual Leader + Husband Who Loves Sacrificially. At this level, the father can be identified by two things he still does — and his children know him by those two things and by the profound absence of everything else. His wife speaks into a silence — there is no voice in the home naming what she carries, affirming who she is, or calling out what God placed in her. His wife is unprotected — whether the failure is material, emotional, or spiritual; she has learned that the perimeter is unmanned and she cannot rely on him to stand between her and what threatens the home. The remaining fractures compound what she is already carrying. His children are absorbing six simultaneous deficits: No one is speaking the child's design into existence before the world gets there first; their sense of self is built entirely from external mirrors — peer approval, performance, whatever fills the silence. His children are growing up inside a home with an unlocked door — exposed to whatever fills the vacuum the father has left, and no one standing watch. His children will find the gap — they always do — and when they do, they will not merely lose respect for their father; they will lose their capacity to trust authority, and sometimes God, for years. His children have no picture of what a man who carries his God-given design actually looks like in daily life; the father's own unlived potential becomes the ceiling the children cannot see past. They do not experience these as separate failures. They experience them as the texture of their home. He leads spiritually in appearance but not in private — the vertical commitment he performs on Sunday is contradicted by the man his family sees Monday through Saturday, and a life not fully lived becomes the only picture of purpose his children have. The two things he still does are real. But they cannot carry six absences. His children will know him by what he gave — and be shaped far more by what he withheld.

Seven Pillars Failing

8 scenarios

One pillar remains. This is the final edge before total collapse — a father who has reduced his entire framework to a single commitment. His children will know him by that one thing. They will be shaped far more by the seven things he is no longer being. The single remaining pillar is the last recognizable act of fatherhood in the home.

Scenario 239

Fractured Pillars: S (Spiritual Leader) + H1 (Husband Who Loves Sacrificially) + E1 (Encourager & Nurturer) + P (Protector & Provider) + H2 (Heart of Integrity) + E2 (Example Who Inspires Potential) + R (Reprover & Wise Mentor)

Solid Pillars: D (Discipliner)

What Happens to the Family:

Seven pillars have failed. Only Discipliner remains — the single last structural commitment of fatherhood still functioning in this home. It is real. It is not enough. His wife carries the spiritual weight of the home alone — praying over children her husband will not lead to the altar, covering in faith a family designed to move under his authority. His wife is not being pursued — she is being maintained; the covenant runs on autopilot, and she carries the relational weight of the marriage alone, managing rather than being led. The remaining fractures compound what she is already carrying. His children are absorbing seven simultaneous deficits: His children grow up with a picture of God as ceremonially present and practically irrelevant — faith is what their mother did, not what their father modeled. His children are absorbing a picture of marriage as coexistence — two people occupying the same house — and they will bring that picture into their own relationships before they understand where it came from. No one is speaking the child's design into existence before the world gets there first; their sense of self is built entirely from external mirrors — peer approval, performance, whatever fills the silence. They do not experience these as separate failures. They experience them as the texture of their home. He leads spiritually in appearance but not in private — the vertical commitment he performs on Sunday is contradicted by the man his family sees Monday through Saturday, and a life not fully lived becomes the only picture of purpose his children have. His children will know him by Discipliner. They will be shaped far more by the seven things he stopped being. And he may never understand why the one thing he kept doing was not enough.

Scenario 240

Fractured Pillars: S (Spiritual Leader) + H1 (Husband Who Loves Sacrificially) + E1 (Encourager & Nurturer) + P (Protector & Provider) + H2 (Heart of Integrity) + E2 (Example Who Inspires Potential) + D (Discipliner)

Solid Pillars: R (Reprover & Wise Mentor)

What Happens to the Family:

Seven of the eight pillars have failed. Reprover & Wise Mentor alone remains — and a framework of one is not a framework. It is a remnant. His wife carries the spiritual weight of the home alone — praying over children her husband will not lead to the altar, covering in faith a family designed to move under his authority. His wife is not being pursued — she is being maintained; the covenant runs on autopilot, and she carries the relational weight of the marriage alone, managing rather than being led. The remaining fractures compound what she is already carrying. His children are absorbing seven simultaneous deficits: His children grow up with a picture of God as ceremonially present and practically irrelevant — faith is what their mother did, not what their father modeled. His children are absorbing a picture of marriage as coexistence — two people occupying the same house — and they will bring that picture into their own relationships before they understand where it came from. No one is speaking the child's design into existence before the world gets there first; their sense of self is built entirely from external mirrors — peer approval, performance, whatever fills the silence. They do not experience these as separate failures. They experience them as the texture of their home. He leads spiritually in appearance but not in private — the vertical commitment he performs on Sunday is contradicted by the man his family sees Monday through Saturday, and a life not fully lived becomes the only picture of purpose his children have. His children will know him by Reprover & Wise Mentor. They will be shaped far more by the seven things he stopped being. And he may never understand why the one thing he kept doing was not enough.

Scenario 241

Fractured Pillars: S (Spiritual Leader) + H1 (Husband Who Loves Sacrificially) + E1 (Encourager & Nurturer) + P (Protector & Provider) + H2 (Heart of Integrity) + R (Reprover & Wise Mentor) + D (Discipliner)

Solid Pillars: E2 (Example Who Inspires Potential)

What Happens to the Family:

Seven pillars have failed. One remains — Example Who Inspires Potential — and a single commitment, however real, cannot carry what was designed for eight. His wife carries the spiritual weight of the home alone — praying over children her husband will not lead to the altar, covering in faith a family designed to move under his authority. His wife is not being pursued — she is being maintained; the covenant runs on autopilot, and she carries the relational weight of the marriage alone, managing rather than being led. The remaining fractures compound what she is already carrying. His children are absorbing seven simultaneous deficits: His children grow up with a picture of God as ceremonially present and practically irrelevant — faith is what their mother did, not what their father modeled. His children are absorbing a picture of marriage as coexistence — two people occupying the same house — and they will bring that picture into their own relationships before they understand where it came from. No one is speaking the child's design into existence before the world gets there first; their sense of self is built entirely from external mirrors — peer approval, performance, whatever fills the silence. They do not experience these as separate failures. They experience them as the texture of their home. He disciplines his children but offers neither naming nor wisdom with it — correction without encouragement or mentorship teaches a child what the line is, but not who they are or why the line matters. His children will know him by Example Who Inspires Potential. They will be shaped far more by the seven things he stopped being. And he may never understand why the one thing he kept doing was not enough.

Scenario 242

Fractured Pillars: S (Spiritual Leader) + H1 (Husband Who Loves Sacrificially) + E1 (Encourager & Nurturer) + P (Protector & Provider) + E2 (Example Who Inspires Potential) + R (Reprover & Wise Mentor) + D (Discipliner)

Solid Pillars: H2 (Heart of Integrity)

What Happens to the Family:

Seven pillars down. One still standing — Heart of Integrity. The father is still present. But he is barely fathering. His wife carries the spiritual weight of the home alone — praying over children her husband will not lead to the altar, covering in faith a family designed to move under his authority. His wife is not being pursued — she is being maintained; the covenant runs on autopilot, and she carries the relational weight of the marriage alone, managing rather than being led. The remaining fractures compound what she is already carrying. His children are absorbing seven simultaneous deficits: His children grow up with a picture of God as ceremonially present and practically irrelevant — faith is what their mother did, not what their father modeled. His children are absorbing a picture of marriage as coexistence — two people occupying the same house — and they will bring that picture into their own relationships before they understand where it came from. No one is speaking the child's design into existence before the world gets there first; their sense of self is built entirely from external mirrors — peer approval, performance, whatever fills the silence. They do not experience these as separate failures. They experience them as the texture of their home. He speaks into his children but has nothing to point them toward — encouragement without example produces children who feel seen but have no picture of what they are being built for, and without spiritual grounding behind it, even that purpose has no foundation. His children will know him by Heart of Integrity. They will be shaped far more by the seven things he stopped being. And he may never understand why the one thing he kept doing was not enough.

Scenario 243

Fractured Pillars: S (Spiritual Leader) + H1 (Husband Who Loves Sacrificially) + E1 (Encourager & Nurturer) + H2 (Heart of Integrity) + E2 (Example Who Inspires Potential) + R (Reprover & Wise Mentor) + D (Discipliner)

Solid Pillars: P (Protector & Provider)

What Happens to the Family:

Seven of the eight pillars have failed. What remains is Protector & Provider alone — real, present, and insufficient to carry the weight of everything that has been put down. His wife carries the spiritual weight of the home alone — praying over children her husband will not lead to the altar, covering in faith a family designed to move under his authority. His wife is not being pursued — she is being maintained; the covenant runs on autopilot, and she carries the relational weight of the marriage alone, managing rather than being led. The remaining fractures compound what she is already carrying. His children are absorbing seven simultaneous deficits: His children grow up with a picture of God as ceremonially present and practically irrelevant — faith is what their mother did, not what their father modeled. His children are absorbing a picture of marriage as coexistence — two people occupying the same house — and they will bring that picture into their own relationships before they understand where it came from. No one is speaking the child's design into existence before the world gets there first; their sense of self is built entirely from external mirrors — peer approval, performance, whatever fills the silence. They do not experience these as separate failures. They experience them as the texture of their home. He leads spiritually in appearance but not in private — the vertical commitment he performs on Sunday is contradicted by the man his family sees Monday through Saturday, and a life not fully lived becomes the only picture of purpose his children have. His children will know him by Protector & Provider. They will be shaped far more by the seven things he stopped being. And he may never understand why the one thing he kept doing was not enough.

Scenario 244

Fractured Pillars: S (Spiritual Leader) + H1 (Husband Who Loves Sacrificially) + P (Protector & Provider) + H2 (Heart of Integrity) + E2 (Example Who Inspires Potential) + R (Reprover & Wise Mentor) + D (Discipliner)

Solid Pillars: E1 (Encourager & Nurturer)

What Happens to the Family:

Seven pillars have failed. Encourager & Nurturer alone remains. It is real. It is not enough. And his family is living inside the gap. His wife carries the spiritual weight of the home alone — praying over children her husband will not lead to the altar, covering in faith a family designed to move under his authority. His wife is not being pursued — she is being maintained; the covenant runs on autopilot, and she carries the relational weight of the marriage alone, managing rather than being led. The remaining fractures compound what she is already carrying. His children are absorbing seven simultaneous deficits: His children grow up with a picture of God as ceremonially present and practically irrelevant — faith is what their mother did, not what their father modeled. His children are absorbing a picture of marriage as coexistence — two people occupying the same house — and they will bring that picture into their own relationships before they understand where it came from. His children are growing up inside a home with an unlocked door — exposed to whatever fills the vacuum the father has left, and no one standing watch. They do not experience these as separate failures. They experience them as the texture of their home. He leads spiritually in appearance but not in private — the vertical commitment he performs on Sunday is contradicted by the man his family sees Monday through Saturday, and a life not fully lived becomes the only picture of purpose his children have. His children will know him by Encourager & Nurturer. They will be shaped far more by the seven things he stopped being. And he may never understand why the one thing he kept doing was not enough.

Scenario 245

Fractured Pillars: S (Spiritual Leader) + E1 (Encourager & Nurturer) + P (Protector & Provider) + H2 (Heart of Integrity) + E2 (Example Who Inspires Potential) + R (Reprover & Wise Mentor) + D (Discipliner)

Solid Pillars: H1 (Husband Who Loves Sacrificially)

What Happens to the Family:

Seven pillars have failed. Only Husband Who Loves Sacrificially remains — the last thing this father is still doing. His children will know him by it. They will be shaped by everything else. His wife carries the spiritual weight of the home alone — praying over children her husband will not lead to the altar, covering in faith a family designed to move under his authority. His wife speaks into a silence — there is no voice in the home naming what she carries, affirming who she is, or calling out what God placed in her. The remaining fractures compound what she is already carrying. His children are absorbing seven simultaneous deficits: His children grow up with a picture of God as ceremonially present and practically irrelevant — faith is what their mother did, not what their father modeled. No one is speaking the child's design into existence before the world gets there first; their sense of self is built entirely from external mirrors — peer approval, performance, whatever fills the silence. His children are growing up inside a home with an unlocked door — exposed to whatever fills the vacuum the father has left, and no one standing watch. They do not experience these as separate failures. They experience them as the texture of their home. He leads spiritually in appearance but not in private — the vertical commitment he performs on Sunday is contradicted by the man his family sees Monday through Saturday, and a life not fully lived becomes the only picture of purpose his children have. His children will know him by Husband Who Loves Sacrificially. They will be shaped far more by the seven things he stopped being. And he may never understand why the one thing he kept doing was not enough.

Scenario 246

Fractured Pillars: H1 (Husband Who Loves Sacrificially) + E1 (Encourager & Nurturer) + P (Protector & Provider) + H2 (Heart of Integrity) + E2 (Example Who Inspires Potential) + R (Reprover & Wise Mentor) + D (Discipliner)

Solid Pillars: S (Spiritual Leader)

What Happens to the Family:

Seven of the eight pillars have failed. Spiritual Leader alone still holds — the final thread in a framework that was designed for eight. His wife is not being pursued — she is being maintained; the covenant runs on autopilot, and she carries the relational weight of the marriage alone, managing rather than being led. His wife speaks into a silence — there is no voice in the home naming what she carries, affirming who she is, or calling out what God placed in her. The remaining fractures compound what she is already carrying. His children are absorbing seven simultaneous deficits: His children are absorbing a picture of marriage as coexistence — two people occupying the same house — and they will bring that picture into their own relationships before they understand where it came from. No one is speaking the child's design into existence before the world gets there first; their sense of self is built entirely from external mirrors — peer approval, performance, whatever fills the silence. His children are growing up inside a home with an unlocked door — exposed to whatever fills the vacuum the father has left, and no one standing watch. They do not experience these as separate failures. They experience them as the texture of their home. He provides for the home materially but has stopped investing in either the marriage or the people inside it —

provision without pursuit, correction without naming, leaves his family feeling managed rather than known. His children will know him by Spiritual Leader. They will be shaped far more by the seven things he stopped being. And he may never understand why the one thing he kept doing was not enough.

Total Collapse

Scenario 247

This is the final scenario — not a failure of the SHEPHERD framework but an abandonment of it. The man is in the house. The father is not.

Scenario 247

Fractured Pillars: All Eight — S + H1 + E1 + P + H2 + E2 + R + D

Solid Pillars: None

All eight pillars have failed. His wife carries the spiritual weight of the home alone — praying over children her husband will not lead to the altar, covering in faith a family designed to move under his authority. His wife is not being pursued — she is being maintained; the covenant runs on autopilot, and she carries the relational weight of the marriage alone, managing rather than being led. His children are absorbing eight simultaneous deficits: they are drifting without calibration — no trusted voice that both knows them and tells them the true thing about where they are heading before the consequences arrive, and they are growing up in a home with no held line — not because no one cares, but because the person designed to hold it has stopped; and what a mother holds alone is never quite the same as what a father and mother hold together. They do not experience these as separate failures. They experience them as the texture of their home. He is present. He is not fathering. His children will not call it absence — they will call it home. That is the most expensive kind of failure.

The purpose of this book is not to condemn. It is to name. A man who can locate himself in these pages — who can read a scenario and say that is my home, that is what I have stopped carrying — is not a man without hope. He is a man with a map.

The SHEPHERD framework was not built for men who have it together. It was built for men who are willing to.

Symptom Index

- I go to church but I am not leading my family spiritually.

  → S fractured. See Sections One–Six for any scenario containing S.

- I feel spiritually empty. I have nothing to give vertically.

  → S fractured.

- I know I am not pursuing my wife the way I should.

  → H1 fractured. See Sections One–Six for any scenario containing H1.

- My marriage is surviving, not thriving.

  → H1 fractured.

- I correct my kids but I rarely speak life into them.

  → E1 fractured. See Sections One–Six for any scenario containing E1.

- I do not know how to encourage without it feeling hollow.

  → E1 fractured.

- I am working hard but my family does not feel covered.

  → P fractured. See Sections One–Six for any scenario containing P.

- I am providing financially but not protecting in other ways.

  → P fractured.

- My private life does not match my public commitments.

  → H2 fractured. See Sections One–Six for any scenario containing H2.

- There are habits or patterns I hide from my family.

  → H2 fractured.

- I am not living toward what God built me for.

  → E2 fractured. See Sections One–Six for any scenario containing E2.

- My children have no picture of a man fully alive to his purpose.

  → E2 fractured.

- I avoid hard conversations. I stay surface-level.

  → R fractured. See Sections One–Six for any scenario containing R.

- I correct but I do not mentor. I speak but I do not know them deeply.

  → R fractured.

- I have stopped holding the lines I used to hold.

  → D fractured. See Sections One–Six for any scenario containing D.

- My standards are inconsistent. My children know it.

  → D fractured.

What You Observe in Your Wife

- She carries the spiritual weight of the home alone.

  → S fractured.

- She feels like a co-manager, not a covenant partner.

  → H1 fractured.

- She is holding lines in the home that I am not holding.

  → D fractured.

- She feels unprotected — not just physically, but emotionally.

  → P fractured.

- She has stopped trusting what I say in public.

  → H2 fractured.

- She feels invisible — not seen, not named, not pursued.

  → H1 + E1 fractured. Check Section One and above for H1 + E1 combinations.

- She seems exhausted in a way I cannot explain.

  → Multiple pillars likely fractured. Begin with the Self-Diagnostic.

What You Observe in Your Children

- They have no anchor in faith. God is not real to them.

  → S fractured.

- They do not know who they are. Identity comes from peers, not home.

  → E1 fractured.

- They do not receive correction. It bounces off or destroys them.

  → R + E1 fractured. Check Section One for R + E1 combination.

- They do not respect authority — mine or anyone else's.

  → H2 + D fractured. Check Section One for H2 + D combination.

- They are anxious. They do not feel safe.

  → P fractured.

- They have no vision for their own life or purpose.

  → E2 fractured.

- They have watched us and learned that marriage is just

coexistence.

> **→ H1 fractured.**

- They are drifting and I cannot seem to reach them.

  > **→ R fractured. Possibly E1 + R. Check Section One.**

- Multiple things on this list are true.

  > **→ Use the Self-Diagnostic. You likely have three or more pillars fractured.**

What You Observe in Your Home

- No one comes to me with the hard things.

  > **→ R fractured. Possibly H2 also fractured.**

- The home feels managed rather than led.

  > **→ S + H1 likely fractured. Check Section One for S + H1 combination.**

- There is peace on the surface and distance underneath.

  > **→ H1 + H2 fractured. Check Section One for H1 + H2 combination.**

- I am present but nothing is landing.

  > **→ E1 + E2 fractured. Check Section One for E1 + E2 combination.**

- ◼ I feel like a provider and nothing more.

  → H1 + E1 + E2 fractured. Check Section Two or Three.

- ◼ Everything feels like it's running on my wife.

  → Multiple pillars fractured. Begin with the Self-Diagnostic.

If you identified four or more fractured pillars in this index, begin with Section Three or higher in this book. The goal is not to find the worst-case scenario. The goal is to find the true one — and then to do something about it.

Pillar → Scenario Cross-Reference

The table below lists every scenario number in which each pillar appears as fractured. Use it to quickly locate all scenarios relevant to a specific pillar — whether you are working from the Self-Diagnostic results or navigating from the Symptom Index above.

Scenario numbers are listed in sequential order. Consecutive sequences are shown as ranges (e.g., 85–119 means Scenarios 85 through 119 all contain this fractured pillar). Scenario 247 is Total Collapse — all pillars fractured simultaneously.

Note: All numbers in this table are scenario numbers (1–247), not page numbers. This table shows which scenarios involve each pillar — useful if you want to understand the full scope of a pillar's failure across the book. To navigate directly to your specific pillar combination and its page number, see Find Your Scenario at the front of this book.

Pillar	Full Name	Fractured in Scenarios
S	Spiritual Leader	1–7, 29–49, 85–119, 155–189, 211–231, 239–245, 247
H1	Husband Who Loves Sacrificially	1, 8–13, 29–34, 50–64, 85–99, 120–139, 155–174, 190–204, 211–225, 232–237, 239–244, 246–247

Pillar	Full Name	Fractured in Scenarios
E1	*Encourager & Nurturer*	2, 8, 14–18, 29, 35–39, 50–54, 65–74, 85–89, 100–109, 120–129, 140–149, 155–164, 175–184, 190–199, 205–209, 211–220, 226–230, 232–236, 238–243, 245–247
P	*Protector & Provider*	3, 9, 14, 19–22, 30, 35, 40–43, 50, 55–58, 65–68, 75–80, 85, 90–93, 100–103, 110–115, 120–123, 130–135, 140–145, 150–153, 155–158, 165–170, 175–180, 185–188, 190–195, 200–203, 205–208, 210–216, 221–224, 226–229, 231–235, 237–242, 244–247
H2	*Heart of Integrity*	4, 10, 15, 19, 23–25, 31, 36, 40, 44–46, 51, 55, 59–61, 65, 69–71, 75–77, 81–83, 86, 90, 94–96, 100, 104–106, 110–112, 116–118, 120, 124–126, 130–132, 136–138, 140–142, 146–148, 150–152, 154–155, 159–161, 165–167, 171–173, 175–177, 181–183, 185–187, 189–192, 196–198, 200–202, 204–207, 209–213, 217–219, 221–223, 225–228, 230–234, 236–241, 243–247
E2	*Example Who Inspires Potential*	5, 11, 16, 20, 23, 26–27, 32, 37, 41, 44, 47–48, 52, 56, 59, 62–63, 66, 69, 72–73, 75, 78–79, 81–82, 84, 87, 91, 94, 97–98, 101, 104, 107–108, 110, 113–114, 116–117, 119, 121, 124, 127–128, 130, 133–134, 136–137, 139–140, 143–144, 146–147, 149–151, 153–154, 156, 159, 162–163, 165, 168–169, 171–172, 174–175, 178–179, 181–182, 184–186, 188–190, 193–194, 196–197, 199–201, 203–206, 208–211, 214–215, 217–218, 220–222, 224–227, 229–233, 235–240, 242–247

Pillar	Full Name	Fractured in Scenarios
R	*Reprover & Wise Mentor*	6, 12, 17, 21, 24, 26, 28, 33, 38, 42, 45, 47, 49, 53, 57, 60, 62, 64, 67, 70, 72, 74, 76, 78, 80–81, 83–84, 88, 92, 95, 97, 99, 102, 105, 107, 109, 111, 113, 115–116, 118–119, 122, 125, 127, 129, 131, 133, 135–136, 138–139, 141, 143, 145–146, 148–150, 152–154, 157, 160, 162, 164, 166, 168, 170–171, 173–174, 176, 178, 180–181, 183–185, 187–189, 191, 193, 195–196, 198–200, 202–205, 207–210, 212, 214, 216–217, 219–221, 223–226, 228–232, 234–239, 241–247
D	*Discipliner*	7, 13, 18, 22, 25, 27–28, 34, 39, 43, 46, 48–49, 54, 58, 61, 63–64, 68, 71, 73–74, 77, 79–80, 82–84, 89, 93, 96, 98–99, 103, 106, 108–109, 112, 114–115, 117–119, 123, 126, 128–129, 132, 134–135, 137–139, 142, 144–145, 147–149, 151–154, 158, 161, 163–164, 167, 169–170, 172–174, 177, 179–180, 182–184, 186–189, 192, 194–195, 197–199, 201–204, 206–210, 213, 215–216, 218–220, 222–225, 227–231, 233–238, 240–247

How to Read Your Scenario

Every scenario in this book follows the same three-part format. This page is a reference for first-time readers.

Fractured Pillars	The pillars that have failed. These are the structural commitments this father is no longer keeping. Each represents a cost being absorbed somewhere in the home.
Solid Pillars	The pillars still functioning. Note: solid does not mean unaffected. Solid pillars carry additional load when others fail — and that load has a cost too.
What Happens to the Family	The specific cost to the wife, the children, and the generation that follows. This is not speculation. It is the documented outcome of this combination of failures, named plainly so it can be seen clearly.

Finding Your Scenario

Two ways in:

1. If you know which pillars are fractured — use Find Your Scenario at the front of this book. Each section is organized by the number of failing pillars. Within each

section, scenarios follow the SHEPHERD acronym order.

2. If you know what you are observing but not which pillars — use the Symptom Index at the back. It maps observable patterns (in yourself, your wife, your children, your home) to fractured pillars and scenario numbers.

If you are unsure — start with the Self-Diagnostic on page 3. Eight questions. Honest answers.

A Word on Reading These Pages

This book names what is happening — not to condemn, but to locate. A man who can read a scenario and say that is my home is not a man without hope. He is a man with a map. The framework that is failing can be rebuilt. But it cannot be rebuilt until it is named.

About the Author

Douglas Androsky is the founder and president of Fathering the Fatherless, a nonprofit organization built around a single conviction: that a father's legacy is not measured by what he achieves but by what he passes on.

Doug's work begins with a recognition that most men were never shown what fatherhood fully looks like — not because their fathers did not love them, but because their fathers were working from incomplete frameworks themselves. The SHEPHERD model emerged from years of study, counseling, and his own reckoning with what it means to be the kind of father a family is designed to need.

He is the author of *Built to Father*, the foundational volume in the *Built to Father* trilogy, and *When the Framework Fractures*, its diagnostic companion. Built to Father: The Study Guide is forthcoming.

Fathering the Fatherless operates on the conviction that intentional fatherhood — pursued honestly and rebuilt when it fractures — changes families across generations. The work is not theoretical. It is personal.

Fathering the Fatherless

fatheringthefatherless.org

Also in the Built to Father Trilogy

Book One

Built to Father

The SHEPHERD Framework for Fathers

The foundational volume. Introduces all eight pillars of the SHEPHERD framework and builds the complete architecture of intentional fatherhood — what each pillar means, why it matters, and what it costs a family when it is missing. Required reading before — or alongside — this companion volume.

Book Three

Built to Father: The Study Guide

The Companion Workbook to Built to Father

Thirteen structured sessions, pillar by pillar through the SHEPHERD framework. Built for three contexts: solo work, a husband and wife working through it together, or a small group with a 55-minute facilitator guide. Each session contains individual reflection questions, couples discussion prompts, and one non-negotiable accountability commitment — a specific action, not a vague intention, that every man names before he leaves the room.

Where *Built to Father* builds the framework and *When the Framework Fractures* names what is broken, the Study Guide is the instrument for doing something about it.